AUSTRALIA AND NEW ZEALAND
The Law Book Company Ltd.
Sydney : Melbourne : Perth

CANADA AND U.S.A.
The Carswell Company Ltd.
Agincourt, Ontario

INDIA
N. M. Tripathi Private Ltd.
Bombay
and
Eastern Law House Private Ltd.
Calcutta and Delhi
M.P.P. House
Bangalore

ISRAEL
Steimatzky's Agency Ltd.
Jerusalem : Tel Aviv : Haifa

MALAYSIA : SINGAPORE : BRUNEI
Malayan Law Journal (Pte.) Ltd.
Singapore

PAKISTAN
Pakistan Law House
Karachi

Sponsorship of Sport, Arts and Leisure:

Law, Tax and Business Relationships

Sponsorship of
Sport, Arts and Leisure:
Law, Tax and Business Relationships

by

Stephen Townley LL.M.
Solicitor

and

Edward Grayson M.A. (Oxon.)
of the Middle Temple and of the South-Eastern circuit,
Barrister

with forewords by

Lord Goodman, C.H.

Dick Jeeps, C.B.E.
Chairman of the Sports Council
and
Sir William Rees-Mogg
Chairman of the Arts Council of Great Britain

London
Sweet & Maxwell
1984

Published in 1984 by
Sweet & Maxwell Limited of
11, New Fetter Lane, London.
Computerset by Promenade Graphics Ltd., Cheltenham.
Printed in Great Britain by
Robert Hartnoll Ltd., Bodmin, Cornwall.

British Library Cataloguing in Publication Data

Townley, Stephen
    Sponsorship of sport, arts and leisure: law, tax and
    business relationships.
    1. Performing arts sponsorship—Law and
    legislation—England 2. Sports—Sponsorship—
    Law and legislation—England
    I. Title   II. Grayson, Edward
    344.203'82   KD2206

    ISBN 0-421-30410-3

Acknowledgments

Mr. Bruce Alexander
Lord Campbell of Alloway Q.C.
Professor W. R. Cornish
Mr. Martin A. Ellis
Mr. Gilbert Gray Q.C.
Mr. David Grice
Mr. George Hill
Mr. William R. Kallaway
Mr. Barry Kernon F.C.A.
Miss Claire Mainprice
Mr. Stuart Mayes
Mr. Rob Merkin
Mr. Patrick Nally
Mr. Charles Palmer O.B.E.
Mr. Luke Rittner
Mr. Geoffrey Rivlin Q.C.
Mr. R. A. G. Rogers
Dr. Werner Rumphorst
Miss Wendy Shockett
Mary Vitoria
Mr. Charles Woodhouse

The Amateur Athletics Association
The Association for Business Sponsorship of the Arts
The Arts Council of Great Britain
The Barbican Centre
The Board of Inland Revenue
The British Broadcasting Corporation
The Central Council of Physical Recreation
The European Broadcasting Union
The Football League Limited
The General Association of International Sports Federations
H.M. Customs and Excise
H.M. Treasury
The Home Office
The House of Commons, Education, Science and Arts
    Committee on the Public and Private Funding of the Arts
The Independent Broadcasting Authority
The International Amateur Athletics Federation
The International Tennis Federation

The London Festival Ballet
The London Philharmonic Orchestra
The Office of Arts and Libraries
Opera North
The Professional Footballers Association
The Royal Academy of Arts
The Royal Shakespeare Theatre
The Sports Council
West Nally Ltd.
The Librarians and the respective staff of the Institute of
  Advanced Legal Studies and the Honourable Society of the
  Middle Temple
The day and night library staff of the *Daily Telegraph* and
  the *Sunday Telegraph*

Foreword by Lord Goodman, C.H.

It is evidence of the importance now being attached to raising (*i.e.* non-governmental) monies for the Arts that the authors of this book have thought it worth their while to devote such care and attention, and in such detail, to the subject. It has become more and more evident with the years that money has to be winkled out of private or commercial purses if the Arts are to be sustained at a proper level for a civilised country. Government after government in this country have shown enlightenment and, by governmental standards, generosity in supporting the Arts. It has only recently been a bi-partisan matter. The willingness to support the Arts has not been affected or reduced by political considerations. If anything, governments have displayed a splendid want of self-interest in subsidising activities which do not earn universal electoral support. It was not without significance that at a time when she was the Minister of the Arts, Jennie Lee (before she became Lady Lee) lost her seat against the electoral trend because she was represented as devoting her efforts to precious and recondite considerations, such as the Arts, instead of devoting herself to more obvious political ends.

The need to subsidise the Arts arises therefore primarily because there will not be enough money from any government to sustain all the artistic causes worthy of support; and to the argument that artistic causes should earn sufficient support from the fee paying public, the answer is, alas, a rude noise. While public support may be readily forthcoming for established artistic objects such as a Shakespeare play or a Verdi opera, it is desperately difficult to generate it for any modern work that has no mass appeal. If modern music and modern painting and modern literature are to survive they must have enlightened support and to an extent beyond what the immediate public response can provide. But there is perhaps another reason, perhaps more important, why subsidy is crucial. No one can want all artistic support to stem from an Arts Council or any similar body, however virtuous and well-meaning. There must be a Court of Appeal. The artist rejected by the Arts Council may be the one artist, wholly worthwhile, whose message does not evoke a response from any public body. He may be the one artist whose work gives rise to a prejudice—and no human being is free from prejudice—

which prevents support, however otherwise deserving. The private purse can rectify this situation and it will be a sad day when it is not available to do so. Hence I commend this book not only because of the obvious skill and care with which it has been written but because it supports a cause which—as a modest servant of the Arts over many years—I regard as vital if they are to be sustained as they deserve to be sustained.

Goodman   May 10, 1983

Joint Foreword by the Chairmen of the Sports Council and of the Arts Council of Great Britain

The provision of financial assistance from commercial sources to Sport and the Arts has a long and honourable tradition in this country but it is only during the last decade or so that changes in attitude and regulation have furthered the development of this vital and welcome source of funds. The impact for sport has been considerable. It is estimated that between £50–60 million is given to Sport by British business and that the total expenditure, including marketing and promotional expectation of that investment, brings the figure to well over £100 million. The Arts, substantially supported by public finance, see business sponsorship as a unique supplement currently estimated to be running at over £12 million a year.

This unique book brings together for the first time aspects of the law governing relations between sponsors and recipients and their respective tax positions. Although its detail is primarily intended to guide legal/commercial advisers the book also contains a careful analysis of the range and variety of properties and rights which may be available for sponsorship. It will therefore be welcomed in particular by those organisations who have approached sponsorship comparatively recently and who will wish to explore these possibilities fully.

Both the Sports Council and the Arts Council of Great Britain welcome the opportunities which business sponsorship provides in the field of leisure and we are confident that this book will assist Arts and Sports organisations as well as their current and potential sponsors towards the realisation of the greatest possible mutual benefit from their association.

Dick Jeeps, C.B.E.
Chairman,
The Sports Council

Sir William Rees-Mogg
Chairman,
The Arts Council of Great Britain

Preface

This book is intended as a detailed practical guide for those involved in the business of sponsorship and their professional advisors. The idea of writing a book on sponsorship was first conceived during Stephen Townley's employment as the in-house solicitor to a company which had become a specialist in the sponsorship field. In general terms, the content of the book has been devised to answer the questions and deal with the problems that Stephen Townley experienced during that period. The book therefore relies upon English law, although some of those problems had an international flavour and occasional references have been made to Commonwealth and American cases. The Treaty of Rome has also been considered, particularly in relation to competition law and the exercise of intellectual property rights.

An invitation was extended to Edward Grayson by Stephen Townley and the publishers to join as co-author because of his pioneer work in writing *Sport and the Law* and also his experience as a practising barrister in domestic and international legal matters concerning sport.

After discussion and planning, we each undertook separate responsibilities for preparing different parts of the text. In consequence we jointly prepared the original draft of Chapter 1. Stephen Townley prepared the first drafts of Chapters 2 and 4 to 15 and Edward Grayson prepared the first drafts of Chapters 3 and 16. Each chapter was then subjected to separate and joint criticism by each of us. We then discussed the final draft with joint and several responsibility accepted for the whole.

The target readership for this book encompasses not only the lawyer but also the sports, Arts or leisure administrator, their agents and business advisors. Trying to communicate with a fragmented market has come down to a question of style and balance. The material, it is hoped, has been presented clearly with sufficient legal content and citations to satisfy the requirements of the legal practitioner; at the same time, the law has been applied to factual situations which, with assistance from the index, should make the book of value to the lay reader. It is also hoped that the precedents will prove useful. No pretence is made, however, that the book has been conceived for "armchair reading."

The first few chapters of the book have been devoted to introductory material which will be of interest to all those involved in sponsorship. Except for these introductory chapters, no attempt has been made to divide each chapter into separate sport, the Arts or leisure issues.

Galley proofs were returned to the publishers during the late summer of 1983 which was the final time at which it was possible to adjust the text to incorporate new developments. For this reason, the very important "Committee of Enquiry into Sports Sponsorship" of the Central Council of Physical Recreation (C.C.P.R.), *The Howell Report* which was published on November 17, 1983, has not been incorporated into this text although it was anticipated at p. 24. With the kind co-operation of the publishers we were able to incorporate changes in the law as at September 30, 1983.

We have each received much help from others who have supplied support, material, information, comment and criticism. Some of those who have been particularly helpful have also been identified on the next page and special gratitude is acknowledged to Lord Goodman, C.H., Sir William Rees-Mogg and Mr. Dick Jeeps, C.B.E., for their respective forewords, and to Mr. J. Gawade for undertaking the difficult task of preparing the index. The views expressed in the book, however, are solely our own. Finally we would like to thank our respective families for their patience and understanding during both the conception and execution of this work.

Stephen Townley　　　　　　　　　　　Edward Grayson
250 Bedford Chambers,　　　　　　*4 Paper Buildings,*
Covent Garden　　　　　　　　　　　　　　　*Temple*

December 1, 1983

Contents

Table of Cases

Table of Statutes

EEC LEGISLATION

Table of Statutory Instruments

Table of Abbreviations

1. Scope and Definition of Sponsorship

Historical Perspective

Few lawyers approaching uncharted legal territories can afford to ignore the advice tendered by a distinguished Scottish practitioner and writer, Sir Walter Scott. He caused Counsellor Pleydell to observe in *Guy Mannering*,

> "A lawyer without history or literature is a mechanic, a mere working mason; if he possesses some knowledge of these, he may venture to call himself an architect."

For sponsorship, as distinct from patronage, our problem is that the raw materials of the history in the form of legal literature are as sparse as the history of sponsorship itself. Because sponsorship is the business deal which separates it from patronage, it was not required as a funding concept in recreational society until fiscal legislation destroyed the base from which private patronage sprang.

Certainly the pioneers of modern British sporting sponsorship at national level, cricket, created precedents in the nineteenth century which are often overlooked or forgotten in identifying a modern, twentieth century phenomenon of the leisure world. In 1861, Felix Spiers and Christopher Pond, expatriate Englishmen, had established substantial catering contracts for their supply of refreshments to the Melbourne and Ballarate Railway. To publicise their enterprises they sent an agent to England. As a method of advertisement an invitation was given to Charles Dickens for a series of public readings. These readings failed to materialise. A substitute proposal was implemented, however, which was to arrange for the then finest and first ever English cricket team to tour Australia. This was assembled through the organisation of the Surrey County Cricket Club Secretary, William Burrup. The team was captained by H. H. Stephenson, also of Surrey, and it succeeded on and off the field. During the Australian winter

Messrs. Spiers and Pond returned to Britain to create a famous catering company until its ultimate absorption by the Express Dairy Group. About the same time other enterprising cricket sponsors, John Wisden and James Lillywhite, conceived the idea of advertising their sports goods, shops and equipment through annual publications. The name of one survives in print, the other in London's lights as a store; and dusty sporting book shelves confirm their pattern from Gamages, Spalding and other examples for our own times.

The years between the two World Wars witnessed more subtle forms of sponsorship. Employment offers were made to and accepted by famous university cricketers. These enabled the amateurs to play cricket nearly all the year round whilst in the paid service of their employing companies. One such company was controlled by arguably cricket's greatest benefactor, the late Sir Julian Cahn. In due course, when two modern England amateur cricket captains created private limited companies to exploit their reputations the M.C.C. bowed to the inevitable. Gentlemen and Players were abolished in 1962, and a year later the Gillette (currently the Nat. West) Cup was born. Sponsorship had arrived at Lord's, and sporting sponsorship exploded.

The Arts soon caught up with sport in awareness of the new dimension. 1976 saw the foundation of the Association for Business Sponsorship of the Arts (A.B.S.A.), whose secretary in 1983 became Secretary-General of the Arts Council. The Sports Council, in 1982, appointed its own sponsorship broker to work on a part-time consultancy basis. As recently identified by H.R.H. the Prince of Wales in an important newspaper interview,[1] increased leisure brought about by unemployment, early retirement (and, we would also submit, modern technology) needs a well organized and thoughtful approach. Such ideas point perhaps to the creation one day of a Leisure Council.

Without sponsorship it is now clear that sport, art and leisure could not survive economically at the public level. A proper understanding of sponsorship's place in a legal framework will hopefully encourage and expand its growth.

Definition

Sponsorship, according to the *Oxford English Dictionary*, is "the state of being a sponsor." Thus one might correctly

[1] *The Liverpool Echo*, June 17, 1983.

ask, what is a sponsor? Again the *Oxford English Dictionary* is of some help and offers a number of variants on a theme. The first is "one who answers for an infant at baptism; a godfather, or godmother"; the second is "one who enters into an engagement, makes a formal promise or pledge, on behalf of another; a surety"; the third is the application of either one or two to "objects" rather than people, "All the good days behind him are sponsors, who speak for him."[2] The fourth definition which appeared for the first time in the 1931 edition is "a business firm or person who pays for a broadcast programme which introduces advertisements of a commercial product." This latter definition is clearly influenced by American usage of the term.

Before returning the *Oxford English Dictionary* to the shelf there is one further historical quotation which is of interest.[3] "It knits them unto me, and me to them, That bond of sponsorship." Although some of the earlier definitions of sponsorship may seem of little relevance to sponsorship as it is understood today in the context of sponsored sport or arts events, the common thread is unquestionably that sponsorship is a bond. Indeed, the bond is the quintessence of sponsorship law.

In more recent times sponsorship has become important in both political and sociological terms. Subsidies and grants for the arts has fallen under the recessionary economic axe, and therefore arts organisations have looked for financial support from commerce in the form of sponsorship. Sociologically, sports and recreational facilities which are part financed by sponsorship may contribute to diffusing tensions and racial problems in overcrowded inner city areas. Again, financial support in the form of sponsorship, which can be channelled into inner city sports projects, is seen as being very important.

The relevance of sponsorship to the community as a whole has increased interest in finding an up-to-date definition. The Economist Intelligence Unit prepared a report[4] which analysed sponsorship as being in the nature of a "business deal." The Council of Europe, at the third Conference of European Ministers responsible for sport held in Palma, Majorca in 1981, defined sports sponsorship as follows:

[2] Emerson in 1870s in *Society and Solitude*, Works (Bohn) III, 134. The origin of the term appears to be Roman from *sponsio*. More up-to-date definitions have appeared in recently published dictionaries.

[3] Kingsley in *Saint's Tragedy* IIv.

[4] In 1977, which was updated in 1980.

> "By sport sponsorship is meant any agreement under which one of the parties (the sponsor) supplies materials, financial or other benefits to another (the sponsored) in exchange for its association with a sport or sportsman, and in particular permission to use this association with a sport or sportsman for advertising, especially television advertising purposes."

Without rejecting the definition offered to the European ministers, but bearing in mind that this book deals with wider aspects than sports sponsorship, the definition which will be used throughout this text is as follows:

> "Sponsorship is a mutually acceptable commercial relationship between two or more parties in which one party (called the sponsor) acting in the course of a business, trade, profession or calling seeks to promote or enhance an image, product or service in association with an individual, event, happening, property or object (called the sponsee)."

This definition comprises a number of elements which when understood, enable the scope of sponsorship law to be understood. These elements are analysed in detail during the remainder of the chapter; however, they may be summarised as follows:

(1) COMMERCIAL RELATIONSHIP BETWEEN TWO OR MORE PARTIES

Sponsorship, rather like marriage, is a relationship that one has with other people. It is equally inconceivable, for instance, that one could sponsor oneself as one could marry oneself. The relationship is commercially based insofar as the sponsor will provide either money or some other service or benefit of value to the sponsee.

(2) SPONSORS' OBJECT IS PROMOTION IN THE COURSE OF A BUSINESS, TRADE, PROFESSION OR CALLING

The sponsor must intend to gain promotional benefit from the sponsorship relationship. This is one basis upon which sponsorship may be distinguished from patronage. A patron makes a gift, whereas a sponsor makes an investment. Since the sponsor's motives in making the investment are commercial rather than altruistic it is necessary that he is engaged in some form of business activity for the benefits to accrue.

(3) THE PROMOTION MAY BE OF AN IMAGE, PRODUCT OR SERVICE

Some sponsorships are in the nature of corporate promotions in that they enhance or create awarenesss of a company rather than any particular product, *e.g.* "X Co. London Marathon" rather than "X Co. Razors London, Marathon."

(4) THE ASSOCIATION MAY BE WITH AN INDIVIDUAL, EVENT, HAPPENING, PROPERTY OR OBJECT

The association is the substance of the rights and licences that the sponsor will acquire from the sponsorship relationship, *e.g.* the right for the sponsor to describe its beer as the "Official Beer of the World Cup." The association can attach to anything that the sponsee has to offer, *e.g.* the Soccer World Cup, a pop group, an exhibition of art treasures or the propagation of a new variety of rose.

For the purpose of a more detailed analysis of these elements reference may be made in each case to the following example: X Co. sponsors an athletics meeting in which the world's fastest milers will be invited to compete against each other. X Co. may acquire its sponsorship rights and licences from the International Amateur Athletic Federation (I.A.A.F.) which is the body responsible for international athletics or subject to I.A.A.F. rules from its United Kingdom representative body, the British Amateur Athletics Board (B.A.A.B.). The I.A.A.F. or B.A.A.B. may appoint a commercial agent to represent its interests in the sponsorship transaction. The sponsorship rights and licences which X Co. acquires are an exclusive association of X Co.'s name with the event so that the event will become the "X Co. Mile " and also the exclusive right to use the event title on X Co.'s soft drink products.

Mutually acceptable commercial relationship between two or more parties.

In the above example there are at least five different parties who may be involved in the sponsorship relationship: X Co., the I.A.A.F., the B.A.A.B., the commercial agent and the athletes themselves.

The majority of sponsorship relationships are contractual. This is no co-incidence since the law of contract regulates modern day barter arrangements where one party supplies money, goods or services in return for something that he wants. Sponsorship might be achieved, through a trust or a "non-enforceable" relationship *i.e.* one that does not give rise to legal rights as between the parties. Both the sponsor and the recipient of the sponsorship, *i.e.* sponsee, should identify whether the relationship is intended to be enforceable or not.

(1) ENFORCEABLE SPONSORSHIP

(a) *Contracts*

A contract comprises an offer by one party and an acceptance of that offer by the other party. As between such parties there must be a "consideration" and they must have capacity to contract, *i.e.* minors and lunatics have limited capacity to make binding contracts. In the simplest and indeed most common terms, consideration will mean money. The American equivalent of consideration is "compensation" which is mentioned solely because it might convey more readily to the layman the impression of value in any contractual relationship.

X Co. in the example would offer to pay the I.A.A.F. £x "in consideration" of the I.A.A.F. calling the athletics meeting the "X Co. Mile." If the I.A.A.F. accepts that offer then prima facie a contract arises. What could also occur, however, (which is common in sponsorship) is that X Co. could have provided "consideration" partly in the form of money and partly in the form of benefits in kind. Suppose, for example, as part of its agreement with the I.A.A.F., X Co. offered to supply video cameras to ensure that the event was properly recorded. The offer would therefore be X Co. paying the I.A.A.F. £x and supplying video cameras free of charge, in consideration of which the I.A.A.F. will name the event the "X Co. Mile." If the I.A.A.F. accept this offer then prima facie a contract will exist.

There are some common misconceptions as to what constitutes a contract. No attempt is made here to deal with the law of contract in detail. Further discussion of the legal issues is dealt with later in the book. Some of the more common misunderstandings are as follows.

It is not an essential requirement in most circumstances that contracts be in writing. There are, of course, exceptions but such exceptions are unlikely to be experienced in the sponsorship relationship. X Co. in the example could have made its contract with the I.A.A.F. entirely verbally. As a general observation it is not wise to try and deal with sponsorship contracts of any size without a written contract or at least written evidence of its most important terms. Elementary as the advice may be, it is always a good idea to write a letter summarising at least the rights and licences to be acquired by the sponsor and how much he is paying for them. It is a question of degree. Thus a brewery company giving £50 a year to a rowing club to name a boat after it is different from a sponsor paying £5,000,000 for a series of complex sponsorship rights and licences for a theatrical production.

The Incorporated Society of British Advertisers (I.S.B.A.) has recently produced a *Guide to Sponsorship*. That guide states that "No company should commit itself to any form of sponsorship without a written contract which clearly lays down what is expected of sponsor and recipient and what is expected by each of them as well as what financial obligations are involved and what conditions apply concerning termination of the contract."

Another common misconception is that "silence" can amount to acceptance. For example, if X Co. wrote to the I.A.A.F. and said "We offer £x for the following sponsorship rights and unless we hear from you by June 1, we shall assume that our offer has been accepted," no contract would come into existence if the I.A.A.F. remained silent.

The idea that consideration needs to be fair according to an "objective" criterion is also incorrect. Consideration need only be "adequate" in the sense that it must have some value, but that value may be nominal. It makes no difference in the example whether X Co. paid £1.00 or £20,000 for their sponsorship rights. In either case a contract could arise. As already discussed, consideration could be provided in cash or in goods or services or any combination thereof. The consideration, however, must be contemporaneous with the particular transaction in hand. There would be no consideration if the I.A.A.F. gave X Co. sponsorship rights to the mile race because X Co. had previously contributed substantial funds to the I.A.A.F. on another project.

A contract is enforceable by the parties to it. An agreement between Y Co. and the Guildford Hockey Club would be enforceable between those parties but in the absence of very unusual circumstances, no one else. This concept is known as privity of contract. It has practical implications to the sponsorship relationship in a number of ways. It is often, for example, the practice of Japanese advertising agents to enter into contracts in their own name rather than that of the sponsorship client. Unless it is a true agency relationship (discussed below) the sponsoring company could not directly enforce the terms of the agreement against the sponsee. Similar difficulties could arise if a sponsor entered into a contract with the father of a sportsman in relation to the son's services, even where the son has capacity to contract (but for infancy purposes special considerations apply.)

It is occasionally the practice for contracts to be signed by agents rather than principals. Everyone will, for example, be familiar with the concept of a travel agent where one enters a shop to book a holiday. The travel agent acts as the middleman for the tour operators and when one signs an agreement with him, one is effectively signing with the tour operator.

Contracts are undoubtedly the most frequently used form for the creation of a sponsorship relationship, and it is worth noting that contracts usually arise from a series of offers and counter-offers rather than one. For example, X Co. may make an offer for sponsorship of the mile for £1,000 and the I.A.A.F. may decline saying that they would accept £2,000. This is a counter-offer. A contract comes into existence on acceptance of the terms on which the offer was made. Acceptance in writing may be a term of the offer and in all but a few cases acceptance must actually be communicated to the person making the offer.

(b) *Quasi-contract*

Where one party to a contract has paid a sum of money or rendered services to the other for some counter-performance, which is then not delivered, he is normally entitled to recover that money on a quasi-contractual basis. Thus if the sponsorship involved a promotion associated with the World Cup where, on entering a garage and purchasing petrol the consumer was entitled to a coin featuring the world cup logo, a separate enforceable claim or remedy would arise with respect to the coin[5] under one of the categories of quasi-contract.

[5] See p. 70, n. 66.

(c) *Trusts*

The concept of a trust developed within the law of equity. Cases or disputes heard before a Court of Chancery were dealt with on principles of "conscience". Initially there were no fixed rules upon which the court proceeded. Thus if someone had a grievance which did not fall within the law of contract as, for example, where there had been no express agreement, he might be able to bring an action in the Court of Chancery. The court, if it heard the case, would attempt to find an equitable solution within its own procedural framework.

There are several different types of trust. An example of a simple trust would be for X Co. to declare that it was holding a specific sum of money in favour of an Athletics Youth Project. In this case X Co. would be the trustee and the Youth Project the beneficiary. The main difference between trusts and contracts is that in the case of a trust there is no requirement that there should be any agreement. The declaration of a trust if proved would suffice. A trust may also, in normal circumstances, be enforced by its beneficiary without consideration. There are certain similarities between a beneficiary under a trust and a sponsee. A beneficiary, however, is the correct term to apply only in the case of a trust relationship.

Trusts are rarely used as the means of establishing the sponsorship relationship, but they are used (particularly in Arts sponsorship) to gain financial advantages for the sponsee through utilising the sponsorship funds for charitable objects. X Co. could, for example, enter into a sponsorship contract with the I.A.A.F. to receive recognition with an I.A.A.F. Youth Charity Trust. The trust could, for example, be called the "X Co. Youth Athletics Foundation." The sponsorship relationship will therefore be controlled by a contract and the charitable trust is only relevant in so far as the I.A.A.F. Youth Trust could reclaim part of the tax paid by X Co. on the sponsorship funds.

Trusts have featured increasingly in recent years as devices to enable amateur sportsmen to retain their status as amateurs and in the widest sense to make provision for their future. The 1982/83 rules of the Rugby Football Union state, for example, that "the game is an amateur game. No one is allowed to seek or to receive payment or other material reward for taking part in the game." It is certainly arguable that if a trust were created without the knowledge of a rugby player, under the terms of which the player was to receive funds after he had retired from the game, that this would not damage the amateur status of players. The 1981 I.A.A.F. congress in Rome caused something of a sensation at the time when it proposed to alter its traditional amateur rules allowing athletes to benefit from sponsorship funds negotiated through their representative federations. This was to be on the basis that money received by the federation would be held in trust for the athlete and payable on his retirement. The taxation advantages of charitable status are considered below in Chapter 16.

Certain commercial companies find it advantageous to set up charitable trusts in parallel with their normal business activities. The funds of such trusts must be expended on charitable objects and are often used for patronage rather than sponsorship.

(d) *Promises made under seal*

Contracts, as already mentioned, usually require consideration. There are, however, circumstances where consideration may not exist. Suppose, for example, that an arts organisation decides to name a theatre bar after a commercial company—Nightingale Music. Nightingale Music may have paid substantial funds to the arts organisation over previous years. No contract will exist with respect to the theatre bar, due to the absence of consideration, past consideration being no consideration.

What is Nightingale Music to do if it suddenly decides that it would like the bar named after it but does not wish to provide further funds? The answer is to obtain a written commitment from the arts organisation concerned, under seal. A seal is a signature on a document bearing the word "seal" or some other indication that it is to take effect as a deed under seal.

(2) NON-ENFORCEABLE RELATIONSHIPS

The circumstances in which one is likely to experience non-enforceable sponsorship relationships are few and far between. They do exist, however. The more conservative sponsor may well contribute funds to a sports or arts organisation with every expectation of receiving promotional value in return, although this will never be stated in a contract. It is the object of promotion in paying the funds that distinguishes this from patronage. However, it must be admitted in these circumstances that the distinction between sponsorship and patronage is somewhat blurred.

Non-enforceable sponsorships fall into two basic categories. The first is where, as discussed above, the sponsor and/or sponsee never intended to create an enforceable relationship. The second is where they intended to create an enforceable relationship but something went wrong and the sponsorship is unenforceable on a technicality. An example of this latter type could be where the sponsorship contract required the transfer of land. Contracts for the sale of land are the major exception to the general rule that contracts need not be in, or evidenced by, writing. Although the parties intended the contract to exist the absence of writing renders it unenforceable at law.[6]

Sponsor is acting in the course of business or trade, profession or calling and his objective is promotion

Consider the case where a friend is "sponsored" 10p for every mile he completes in the Gillette London Marathon. Although such an arrangement may be regarded as sponsorship in a popular sense it is not sponsorship within a commercial context discussed in this book. It is not commercial sponsorship because the sponsor is not acting in the course of a trade or business and his objective in providing the funds is not one of promotion.

There are examples of sponsorships where it is difficult to understand how a sponsor can expect to gain promotional value from a particular relationship. It would be difficult to see, for example, how a whisky distiller could gain any promotional benefit from sponsoring a schools competition. The objective of promotion is however a subjective test and the whisky example might be considered a bad business decision; nevertheless, it is sponsorship.

The promotion may be of a person, image, product or service

Sponsorship of the Arts tends to be biased towards promotion in a corporate sense rather than brand promo-

---

[6] s. 40(1) of the Law of Property Act 1925.

tions. It is the image of Mobil, for example, that is promoted by its sponsorship of the Treasures of Ancient Nigeria Exhibition rather than the oil, petrol or other products which it manufactures. Sports promotions in contrast often involve brands. An example of a service rather than a product would be British Airways. Arts sponsorship is often local in basis and can be directed towards improving good will within a community. This may also enhance the image of the company with its staff where, for example, they receive free tickets.

In association

The relationship between the sponsor and the sponsee has already been dealt with. The rights and licences arising from the association between the sponsor and sponsee can be distinguished from the legal basis of the relationship itself. Suppose Nightingale Music wished to sponsor a country music event. It would enter into a contract with the organisers. The legal basis of the relationship would be contractual. The contract would specify the particular rights and licences passing to Nightingale Music which Nightingale Music felt were required to achieve its marketing objectives; for example, the right for Nightingale Music to describe itself as "The Official Video Company of the Country Music Festival" or the right to call the event the "Nightingale Music Country Festival," or the licence to use the official symbol of the Country Music Festival on its products.

The association often involves the licensing of intellectual property to the sponsor. The licence for the sponsor to use the mascot of an event on its products involves a licence of intellectual property. This is discussed in greater depth later in this book.[7]

An individual event, happening, property, or object

In theory almost anything is sponsorable. The only limitation however, is a practical one as to whether the event, happening, etc., is capable of promotion. Promotion is invariably linked with the media. A sponsorable property is therefore one which is likely to attract media coverage. Examples are sports events, sports personalities, rock con-

[7] See Chap. 8.

certs, classical concerts, orchestras, sky diving, chess tournaments, exhibitions, the Papal visit, films, television programmes, juke boxes, litter bins, posters, raising the "Mary Rose," etc.

Distinctions

Having defined what sponsorship is, this section concludes by describing what it is not and why.

(1) PATRONAGE

Patronage is a gift in which the "object of promotion" is absent. This is evidenced by the fact that many patrons conceal their identity. The absence of promotional motivation on the part of the patron can only be judged on a subjective basis as their is clearly a difference between a bad investment in a particular sponsorship property and a pure gift. It is difficult to arrive at a working distinction between the two concepts since the test is one of motives. One can say that the majority of sponsorships will be contractual and therefore enforceable between the parties. In contrast most examples of patronage are pure gifts and do not give rise to an enforceable contract. Many patrons also make gifts outside the course of a business or trade. This is another practical basis for distinguishing patronage from sponsorship.

It is important that a company is able to distinguish between sponsorship and patronage in so far as the former is a legitimate business expense and the latter is not. The decisions of the Inland Revenue may be relevant here and one must not confuse deductability for the purposes of business expenditure from special tax concessions that may exist in connection with charitable donations. Where one is answerable to shareholders as in a United Kingdom corporate structure the distinction is also fundamental, sponsorship being business expenditure and patronage being a gift. Japanese companies, in contrast do not have quite the same corporate shareholder structure. This may explain why many are actively involved in sponsorship.

(2) ADVERTISING

A sponsor of an event may well acquire advertising as part of a package of sponsorship rights. Such advertising may be acquired where, for instance, a football federation offers stadium boards at a match or where a sponsor, through its sponsorship of the federation, acquires a stadium board as part of a package of sponsorship rights. It is probably correct to include sponsorship as a type of advertising in so far as advertising encompasses public relations, marketing and sales promotion.

If there is a practical distinction between sponsorship and advertising, it is that advertising is a direct form of communication and sponsorship relies more upon indirect communication or suggestion. The sponsor usually enhances his sales through playing on the association, credibility and goodwill attached to the sponsee. Sponsorship can also be self-liquidating and many sponsors recover their investment in the sponsorship from merchandising and similar activities. This is rarely the case in advertising, where the cost of the campaign will, assuming it is successful, be recovered from profit on sales.

Valuing sponsorship properties

The question of fixing a price as between the sponsor and sponsee is difficult. The price, like any other commodity, will depend upon market forces.

The anticipated media coverage of a sponsored event often has particular relevance to price. Events which will be seen on television and in which stadium advertising boards or other sponsor identification will be seen tend to be more expensive than events which do not receive such coverage. Specialist consultants such as "Sportscan" have grown up to evaluate which sports events receive the greatest amount of television coverage. Other agencies will count up the column inches that a sponsored event receives in the newspapers.

One advertising agency has devised a system called "Matchmarker" analysis. This involves recording a televised event and monitoring the exposure of each stadium advertising board in relation to the total television coverage of an event and the size of the audience. A survey amongst viewers is then conducted to measure recall.

A straight media comparison may also be made between the cost of, for example, a 30 second commercial at peak viewing time and a sponsored event.

In reality comparisons are difficult to make because in many circumstances one is not comparing like with like. The statement by Lord Leverhulme on advertising has much relevance in this context. He said "I know that half the money I spend on advertising is wasted but I have no means of knowing which half."

Sponsorship can offer great value for money when compared with conventional advertising. It also has many spin-offs and social benefits which are less easy to find in direct advertising. Attending a sponsored event can be extremely pleasurable even for the battle-weary chairman.

2. Setting the Scene

For the sponsor and his adviser, an understanding of the structure and hierarchy of Sport, Arts and Leisure is essential information. Substantial bad feeling, not to mention law suits, can arise through failure to appreciate, for example, that there can be an official mascot representing a governing body such as Federation Internationale de Football Association (F.I.F.A.) and also an official mascot representing a major F.I.F.A. competition such as the Soccer World Cup. Pepsi Cola could, in this example, acquire exclusive rights as part of a sponsorship package to one and Coca Cola could acquire exclusive rights to the other. Both could be promoted at the same time with considerable embarrassment to all concerned.

This chapter, as its title suggests, intends to provide an overview of the various organisations that the sponsor may deal with and explain how such organisations relate to the sponsor and to each other.

There are three broad groupings which are common to most sponsorships. The first is the rights owners, *i.e.* the organisations or individuals who actually own the sponsorship properties. The second consists of representative bodies which may get involved in negotiations or act as a catalyst between the sponsor and the sponsee. The third is the broadest group classified as "others." These are organisations or individuals who are neither rights owners nor representatives, but who nevertheless may have an important role to play in the success of the sponsorship relationship such as the media.

The sports scene

(1) AMATEURISM

Sponsorship is possible at most levels throughout the sports hierarchy. Amateurism may prevent an individual who has amateur status from being sponsored or permit him to be sponsored on condition that he does not receive the funds. The problems created by amateurism in sport are dealt with in more detail at page 100.

The majority of sports these days are "open" in the sense that their structure allows both amateurs and professionals to co-exist and compete within the same framework. Some sports, however, are totally amateur. The Olympic Games was restricted to amateurs in its modern format (circa 1896) although its origins allowed amateurs and professionals to compete alongside each other.

(2) RIGHTS OWNERS

Rights owners are divided into two categories: sanctioned and non-sanctioned. The sanctioned category are those rights owners who exist within the generally accepted structure of a particular sport. Conversely non-sanctioned categories exist outside it. The distinction may not always be obvious to the sponsor, however, he should be aware of it. A good example of the distinction occurs in tennis. The International Tennis Federation is universally accepted by all components of the game *i.e.* national federations, clubs, players, etc, as having the exclusive and ultimate authority for world tennis except for the major professional circuits for men and women (the Grand Prix and Women's Series). These are administered by two bodies on which the I.T.F. has representative but no controlling power. These are the Men's International Professional Tennis Council (M.I.P.T.C) and the Women's International Professional Tennis Council (W.I.P.T.C). Both the I.T.F., M.I.P.T.C. and W.I.P.T.C. operate within the generally accepted structure of the game and are therefore "sanctioned rights owners."

In contrast there are substantial tennis tournaments staged by private promotors who are in a position to control professional tennis players through management contracts. These promotors may not ask for the sanction of the I.T.F. and are therefore regarded as "non-sanctioned rights owners."

Why, one might ask, is it necessary to make the distinction? From the sponsor's viewpoint there are advantages and disadvantages in dealing with either type of rights owners. There is a degree of certainty, however, that if the sponsor deals with a sanctioned rights owner, the sponsorship funds will be used for the benefit of the game as a whole. This will not always be the case with some non-sanctioned rights owners who are in business solely to make a profit. Here there appears to be less incentive or control to ensure that a proportion of that money will filter down to the grass roots of the sport. This is perhaps an oversimplified view since many private promotors fully appreciate that it is sound marketing to ensure that a proportion of profits are re-invested in the sport.

(a) *Sanctioned*

(i) *International federations*—Rights owners in the sporting world exist within a hierarchy that is reasonably consistent throughout different sports. That hierarchy starts at the top with the international federation, such as F.I.F.A. and the I.A.A.F. These international bodies will have an overriding responsibility for all aspects of the sport. The I.T.F.'s objects in the 1983 rules and standing orders stated at clause five "The principles and objects of the federations shall be: (1) To make, amend, uphold and enforce the rules of tennis and (2) to promote and develop the game universally and at all levels".

The international federations will often hold competitions themselves such as the I.A.A.F. First World Championships in Athletics. They may undertake technical responsibilities on behalf of their members and affiliates in competitions organised by other people such as the Olympic Games. They may also sanction or delegate the sanction of competitions organised within their hierarchy. Most international federations will ask a sanction fee for this. International federations are at the top of the ladder in each sport jurisprudentially; therefore they are the source of all commercial rights and licences within their domain. Their relationship with associates and affiliates, *i.e.* national federations down to club level, is almost always contractual. The international federations may therefore permit ownership of sponsorship rights by other members within their hierarchy.

(ii) *Organising Committees / I.O.C*—Organising committees can arise at various stages throughout the hierarchy. As their name implies they are set up to organise a specific event or series of events. It is customary in most sports for the organising committee of an international event to be the national federation of the host country. Thus the organising committee for the I.A.A.F. First World Championships in Athletics was Suomen Urheiluliitto which is the I.A.A.F.'s affiliated national federation for Finland where the event was held.

Organising committees will normally receive a percentage of income raised from the competition. This will ensure that some funds are available to offset the local costs of staging the event. I.A.A.F. rules, for example, state that the host federation which acts as the organisation committee for the World Championships in Athletics shall receive 75 per cent. of television and marketing income from the event.

The International Olympic Committee (I.O.C.) is dealt with here as it is the supreme organising committee for the Olympic Games. It will however appoint separate organising committees for each Olympic Games. The organising committee for the 1984 Olympics in Los Angeles is, in fact, a purely private business consortium. The I.O.C. is a very powerful organisation in its own right and has become identified with an ill-defined "Olympism" movement. The Olympic Games are ostensibly amateur and sponsorship opportunities are therefore limited. The I.O.C. does engage in merchandising and the Los Angeles Committee has appointed official suppliers. The I.O.C. is represented in each country by a National Olympic Committee.

The definition of amateur status within a sport and in so far as it may be a criterion for competing in the Olympics, is determined by each international federation but must be approved by the Executive Board of the I.O.C. The National Olympic Committees may usually receive donations from commercial companies. The national teams themselves may also receive commercial support provided that it is within the definition of amateur status adopted by the applicable international federation. A number of international federations' regulations state that the general and fundamental principles of the Olympic Charter override the federations' own regulations in so far as participation in the Olympic Games is concerned. So this effectively passes the buck back to the I.O.C. to define amateurism for participation of that sport in the Olympics.

(iii) *Continental Associations*—Next in the hierarchy usually comes the continental association. The I.A.A.F. in common with many other International Federations has continental associations for Africa, Asia, Europe, North America, Oceana and South America. The European Federation which has jurisdiction over the United Kingdom is the European Athletic Association. Their 1982 president was based in England, the secretary in France and the treasurer in Switzerland.

The activities and visibility of continental associations varies from sport to sport. In football, for example, the Union des Associations Européennes de Football is very active and will own commercial rights (under the authority of F.I.F.A.) to events such as the European Cup and Cup Winners' Cup. It would also sanction the participation of say, a European soccer club such as Liverpool F.C. in an intercontinental tournament.

(iv) *National Federations*—The rules of the International Federations will often contain a statement along the following lines "The National Governing Body for [   ]in any country shall be eligible for membership. Only one member for each country or territory shall be recognised by the [   ] as the only National Governing Body for all amateur [   ] in such country or territory they represent."[1]

The national federation will usually be involved in the implementation of the International Federation's rules and policy within its territory. It will also organise tournaments or competitions and control the activities of its members. Examples of national federations are the English Basketball Association, the British Amateur Athletic Board, the Football Association and the Lawn Tennis Association. Recognition by the International Federation is usually by application. The application will need to establish the claim to supremacy within the domestic territory and if it succeeds, a fee is usually paid to the international federation.

The national federations may own rights to any sponsorship property which is permitted under the rules of the international federation. As previously discussed, where the national federation hosts an event on behalf of the international federation, the "cake" in terms of sponsorship rights and/or income will often be divided between the international federation and national federation. The national federation

---

[1] See the I.A.A.F. Handbook.

will normally own commercial rights to its national team.

(v) *Regional Associations*—In those sports where such organisations exist the regional association will usually undertake a co-ordinating role between the national federation and the clubs.

(vi) *Leagues*—Leagues are a form of organised competitions in which clubs or individuals participate. The sanction of the national federation is usually required where they are to operate at a national level. A fee or charge will normally be levied for that sanction. In a number of sports, of which football and basketball are good examples, the leagues are very important bodies. In economic terms large transactions can mean that the leagues are of more immediate importance to the potential sponsor than the national federations themselves.

League competitions may involve the acquisition of certain rights owned by the clubs or individuals which participate in the league. For example a league sponsor might require a stadium advertising board to be displayed at a club's ground. This would be achieved by an agreement with the participant club or individual, the terms of which could be incorporated as part of the League rules.

(viii) *Clubs*—Clubs are an association of individuals. Clubs are often affiliated to their national or regional associations. Such affiliation will usually involve the payment of a sanctioning fee or annual subscription. Some clubs are not affiliated or associated at all. Most clubs own rights to their teams and competitions which they host.

Club sponsors may only wish to associate themselves with specific teams or individuals within a club, for example the first team.

(viii) *Individuals and players' pools*—Individuals may belong to clubs or teams. If they do then any rights which they do not grant to the club team via a specific agreement or by virtue of the rules of membership will be retained by them. Occasionally individuals will "pool" such rights. Players' pools are common in football. In the Soccer World Cup, for example it has been reported that royalties from sales of the England squad's rights went into a "players' pool." It is correct to say that most individuals who achieve fame or success in professional sport these days will be represented by commercial agents or managers.

(b) *Non-sanctioned*

It is quite feasible to stage a sports event and to own rights to or in it outside the generally recognised hierarchy of a particular sport. In certain sports, top fee earners will have entered into professional management contracts under the terms of which the manager might well be in a position to instruct the player as to what competition in which he or she can participate.

Some competitions such as "Superstars" exist outside the recognised structure of sport because there is no existing structure into which they can fit.

Rights ownership in unsanctioned events tends to be concentrated in the hands of the organiser who is usually an entrepeneur. This contrasts with rights ownership in sanctioned events which may be divided between several different parties.

(c) *Assignees*

The third category of rights ownership is the assignee. Sponsorship is essentially a business deal and will attract the entrepreneur who is prepared to trade in sponsorship properties much as some people trade in commodities.

(3) REPRESENTATIVES

Each rights owner may be represented individually or as a group by other organisations. Such organisations may have an active or a passive part to play in the sponsorship relationship.

(a) *Agents*

Agents are frequently used by rights owners in sponsorship transactions. The agency relationship because of its frequent use is analysed in detail later in the book. An agent in this context is someone who has the authority of the rights owner to either negotiate or conclude a sponsorship agreement on their behalf.

Certain agents specialise in acting for and on behalf of

federations, whilst others specialise in representing individuals. Whatever an agent's speciality, the gap which he fills, will be to provide advice on topics such as marketing, merchandising, law, taxation, trade marks and event management. These skills are not normally available within the sport itself. Agents may also be able to offer advice on packaging an event in such a way as may have greater appeal to sponsors.

Agents tend to be appointed on the basis that they are entitled to an agreed percentage of income raised. The agent may on occasions, however, be required to put up a fixed sum guarantee against commissions earned. The level of commission required varies from agent to agent although 30 per cent. on sponsorship income raised is a rough average. The agent will normally be expected to meet costs out of this sum such as travel, staff, office presentations, etc.

In certain circumstances an apparent agent will not be an agent at all when he "buys out" all commercial rights to an event. In such a case he will be acting like a commodity broker or trader buying at one price and selling at another. He would then be categorized as an assignee under (c) above.

(b) *Unions*

Trade unions do exist in a number of sports. Tennis, for example, has its Association of Tennis Professionals with their headquarters at Garland, Texas, for professional men players, and the Womens Tennis Association based in San Francisco for women professionals. English football has its Professional Footballers Association (P.F.A.)

The co-operation of players, who may be represented by their associations can be extremely important for the sponsor. Unions tend not to get involved in sponsorship negotiation directly. They may become involved, however, in ensuring that their members' interests are protected by sharing in any sponsorship income which is achieved by their clubs or competitions. One of their more spectacular feats was the complete ban imposed by baseball players in the United States in the summer of 1980. This action had a direct effect on sponsors. In 1982 a similar situation occurred in American football where the players went on strike in order to secure a percentage of television income. In Europe the Formula One drivers sued their controlling federation F.I.S.A. in the summer of 1982 following threats by F.I.S.A. to withdraw the licences of the drivers who had boycotted the South African

Grand Prix. Withdrawal of licences could obviously have affected the whole of sponsored motor racing.

Unions may become involved with sponsors through representation in negotiating committees. Football has a professional negotiating committee, for example, made up of four representatives of the P.F.A., nine members of the Football League and an independent chairman.

(c) *Federations forums*

Such forums exist at both national and international level. At international level there is, for example, the General Association of International Sports Federations (G.A.I.S.F.). This body is open to membership by all international federations—whether their sport is involved with the Olympics or not and also international federations with sports related activities, *e.g.* the International Federation for Sports Medicine.

G.A.I.S.F's objects are sufficiently wide to enable it to become involved in various policy aspects of sponsorship. Indeed sponsors are invited to attend G.A.I.S.F. sessions in Monte Carlo. G.A.I.S.F.'s main functions, according to its President, are "information, co-ordination and co-operation." It undoubtedly has the potential to perform a highly constructive role in guiding its membership on sponsorship and other commercial matters.

A further organisation was formed in 1981 called the International Assembly of National Confederations of Sport. Its main purpose is to act as the international representative body of the independent national sports federations. It provides a forum and means of co-ordination of problems for the national sports federations.

At a national level the Central Council of Physical Recreation is the representative body of sport and recreation in the United Kingdom. It has in membership all the governing bodies of sport and recreation who elect its executive committee. Its members may look to it for independent guidance on questions of sponsorship. The C.C.P.R. publishes a document entitled "Sports Notes," listing potential sponsorship opportunities offered by its membership. It has also operated a "Sponsors of Sport" scheme for a number of years. In 1981 it set up a committee of enquiry into sports sponsorship under the chairmanship of the Right Honourable Denis Howell M.P.

(4) OTHERS

(a) *Media*

The price of any particular sponsorship property will usually bear a close relationship to the media coverage which the sponsorship is likely to receive. What point would there be in a sponsor acquiring advertising boards at the soccer World Cup as part of a sponsorship package, if there was no reasonable certainty that media coverage would result.

Television companies or the press are rarely directly involved with the sponsorship contract. The sponsor might require the rights owner to use its best endeavours to ensure that proper credit is given to the sponsors by the media or procure television coverage of the event.

In certain situations events may be sponsored or co-sponsored by a media organisation such as a newspaper. The advantage in such circumstances is that other sponsors are certain to receive media coverage. Where a media sponsor is involved in an event such as the Daily Mail Ideal Home Exhibition, then there is believed to be a practice between such newspapers to refer to the event by its full sponsored title. It is a headache for many sponsors who must rely upon their goodwill with the media to ensure they receive proper credit.

Not all sponsorships rely upon the media for their success. One can also foresee the growth of sponsorships in which the media itself is the sponsee, such as cable television and satellite broadcasting.

(b) *Venue owners*

The owner of a venue where a sponsored event is to take place may be the same person as the rights owner *e.g.* the R.F.U. owns Twickenham Stadium. Where this is not the case, problems can arise as the venue may be subject to prior commitments which conflict with those granted to the sponsor.

(c) *Governments*

The Minister who has responsibility for sports is a Joint Under Secretary at the Department of the Environment. The Minister and several government departments may become involved in sponsorship in a variety of ways. With government expenditure cuts it is clearly desirable for the Minister to encourage contributions via sponsorship from commerce and industry. The Minister has also been involved in the voluntary agreement between tobacco producers on controlling sponsorship of sport by tobacco companies.

Within the general heading of government falls the Sports Council as the body charged by the government with overall responsibility for the welfare of sport in this country. Its budget allocation for 1983/4 was £27.03 million which it dispersed on various schemes and projects throughout the United Kingdom. The Sports Council acts through various regional offices.

The Sports Council has an interest in encouraging sponsorship of sport. It is, however, concerned to see generally that sponsorship funds are used for the benefit of the sport as a whole and not just the top level. It was instrumental in establishing the Sports Sponsorship Advisory Service which acts rather like a marriage broker in introducing sponsors to sports organisations which are looking for sponsorship. A similar service has just been set up by the Scottish Sports Council.

Political interference by governments is not unknown in the world of sports sponsorship both directly and indirectly.

(d) *Sponsors*

There is, at present, no organisation which officially represents the interests of the sponsors themselves, but the Incorporated Society of British Advertisers (I.S.B.A.) is the industry association which represents all its client companies on advertising which would include sponsorship.

(e) *Advertising and public relations specialists*

These organisations (advertising and P.R. agencies or consultancies) have an involvement with sponsorship in a variety of ways. The sponsors' advertising agency may, for example, be responsible for the creative execution of the sponsorship. Thus, it could suggest ways in which the rights and licences acquired by the sponsor could be incorporated as part of the sponsors' overall advertising campaign.

The I.S.B.A. has produced a useful booklet on sponsorship and was associated with the organisation of the First World Congress on Sponsorship in 1982.

The Arts scene

The component elements of the Arts world are different from those of sport. The overall structure does not, in contrast to sport, exist at numerous different levels like a multi-tiered wedding cake. In so far as the Arts may be said to have a structure, it falls into two broad categories of being subsidised and non-subsidised. The subsidised sector receives support from the government either directly or through the offices of the Arts Council of Great Britain and the non-subsidised sector is self-supporting. At a national level most Arts organisations interested in sponsorship have a professional administrator with responsibility for seeking sponsorship. Such responsibilities are often combined with others which fall under the broad heading of fund raising. This approach characterises one difference in approach between Sport and Arts sponsorship. Arts bodies tend to look to sponsorship as a means of supplementing their income, whereas certain sports bodies see sponsorship income as financing their total requirements for an event.

It is difficult to define the scope of the Arts. The Arts certainly encompass dance, drama, literature, and music and visual arts such as painting, sculpture, photography, film and crafts. It would be unusual for traditionalists to include pop groups within the term Arts. Another basis for definition might be that anything supported with funds from the Arts Council must be Art. This would ignore the non-subsidised sector, however, such as much of the West End Theatre. Some guidance might also be sought from the approach adopted by the Inland Revenue where Art may be relevant to charitable status, and also by the National Heritage Act 1983 and the tax and VAT concessions of 1983 legislation.

The entrepreneur is less evident in Arts sponsorship than in the sphere of sports. For the purpose of analysis the usual rights owners in the Arts world have been divided between rights held by venues, rights held in relation to plays, productions etc. and rights held by individuals and groupings. Copyright and the Performers Protection Acts 1958, 1963 and 1972[2] are particularly relevant to rights ownership in the Arts world.

---

[2] See Performers Protection Acts 1958, 1963 and 1972 discussed below, p. 146.

(1) RIGHTS OWNERS

(a) *Venues*

There are a number of established venues which will host Arts events or exhibitions on a regular basis, for example, the South Bank Complex, the Barbican Centre and Queens Hall, Glasgow. Some of these venues may be able to offer sponsorship rights not only to the venue itself or to events or exhibitions which take place there, but also occasionally rights to the performers themselves. Sponsorship rights to the venue itself are unusual. Examples of sponsorship rights in relation to the venue have included the Mobil Oil Company's sponsorship which provided funds for the production of guides to the 12 primary galleries of the Victoria and Albert Museum; also Amoco's sponsorship of the appropriately named Torch Theatre and Plessey's sponsorship of the Museum of Moving Images.

At a local level the town hall library or village school may host a rural crafts, painting or amateur theatrical production. The town hall or village school in such circumstances is likely to seek sponsorship funds to enable the exhibition or production to take place.

Identifying the owner of commercial rights, as between the venue owner and the production or exhibition which takes place there and the performers, will depend upon which rights the sponsor wishes to acquire and the terms of the contract between the venue owner and the theatrical or other company and the performers.

In many cases the venue will be owned by the company which performs or exhibits in it. The venue owner will usually be in a position to offer all permanent rights to the venue such as naming an auditorium or bar after the sponsor. Sponsorship of the venue itself is unlikely to be of interest to the potential Arts sponsor unless he can be sure that events will be regularly staged there.

(b) *Plays, productions, concerts, exhibitions, competitions, compositions, festivals*

The largest volume of sponsorship income to the Arts goes in the direction of sponsored productions, concerts, exhibitions, competitions or similar events or works. As already discussed, there can be an overlap between rights owned by the venue and those owned in relation to individual performers or to the whole company whilst performing a play. There may be a sympathetic overlap where for example the Royal Shakespeare Company has control over its theatre at Stratford-Upon-Avon and puts on a sponsored production of, for example, *Henry IV, Part II*. Since the venue, performers and company are owned or controlled by common interests, conflicts are unlikely to arise. However, where the venue owners are different from the performers and company, conflicts can and do arise.

Where a large event is staged such as a "Festival of Music, Arts and Dance" the organisers of the festival will usually own most commercial rights to the festival. Such rights again may conflict with the orchestras, dancers or other companies or individuals who participate in the festival. A sponsor who wishes to acquire rights to use recordings or videos of artists performing at the festival, needs to unravel the question of rights ownership. In each case the sponsor will need to identify which specific rights he requires and if he feels any doubt about the ability of the other party to deliver should ask for evidence or guarantees regarding such ability. The Performers Protection Acts 1958, 1963 and 1972 and copyright generally which are discussed below[3] are important to consider in such circumstances as well as the contract between the festival organisers and the performers or company.

It is usual for a theatrical company to own commercial rights to its own productions or performances as a company. Therefore, the Royal Shakespeare Theatre would, in the authors' view, own the majority of commercial rights to its production, of, for example, *Henry IV, Part II*, notwithstanding that the production took place at the Barbican Theatre. If the sponsor seeks to use the image or likeness of individuals comprised within the company in a sponsored video, the sponsor should confirm that the individuals have consented in writing to the use of their performances.[4]

Productions, concerts, exhibitions, festivals and similar events may be one-offs. They may also form part of a series of events such as the Philharmonia performing Haydn's "The Creation" as part of the Du Maurier concert series. They may be organised on a regional basis or on a national or

---

[3] *Ibid.* Chap. 9.
[4] *Ibid.* p. 146.

international basis such as Leeds International Pianoforte Competition.

(c) *Individuals and groupings*

The usual owner of commercial rights to an orchestra such as the Philharmonia will be the entity which employs the musicians. In many cases the entity will have obtained an assignment or release from the members or performers which will permit the use of their performances.[5] Such assignments or releases between the individuals and entities are usually limited to the individuals whilst they are performing a particular production. Similarly the Royal Shakespeare Theatre which is a corporation incorporated by Royal Charter and registered as a charity is likely to own commercial rights to the Royal Shakespeare Company and individuals therein, certainly whilst performing a production. An individual such as a mime artist will own sponsorship rights to himself. Again the special statutory rights of the individuals to control commercial exploitation of their performances must be considered here.[6] An artist, sculptor or composer will own commercial rights to their paintings, sculptures or compositions respectively; for example, T.D.K. commissioned a series of modern paintings as part of their 1981/82 advertising campaign. Clearly the artist was in a position to negotiate commercial terms with the sponsor.[7] A photographer will own commercial rights to photographs which he may take except where they are commissioned.

Sponsorship of individuals or groupings is less common than sponsorship of a concert or theatrical production, in which the individual or grouping participates. Sponsorship of individuals can exist at a purely local level where, for example, a land reclamation company covenanted an annual fund to provide a permanent town artist to be resident in Rochdale.

(d) *Entrepreneurs and assignees*

In the world of Arts there is probably less room and more limited returns for entrepreneurs. There seems no reason,

---

[5] Certain industry agreements may exist with bodies such as Equity.

[6] See Performers Protection Acts 1958, 1963 and 1972 discussed below, p. 146.

[7] For further reading, see "Arts Review" (January 1982) – the issue dealing with sponsorship.

however, why "Mr. Fix It" could not purchase and trade in commercial rights with, for example, the involvement of an orchestra in a national festival or exhibition.

(2) REPRESENTATIVE BODIES

(a) *Agents*

Sponsorship agents exist and fulfill a useful role in the Arts world. They have a creative role to play as true specialists and supplement the role of the "in house fund raiser." Arts agents are engaged to perform similar functions to sports agents, *i.e.* they offer consultancy services in relation to packaging an Arts event or series of events in a manner more likely to appeal to sponsors. Some Arts agents are also able to offer professional services such as trade mark and tax advice.

(b) *Unions*

The Musicians Union and Equity have, to date, had little direct involvement in sponsorship matters. Equity, the Theatre Managers Association and other groups have influenced or attempted to influence contractual agreements which could have involved sponsored events. The B.B.C., for example, went to the Court of Appeal to prevent the unions pulling out the plugs on satellite relay due to political issues.[8] One can, however, sense a mood of concern over the increasing reliance placed upon non-Arts Council finance for the continued support of the Arts in Great Britain. It may be easier for a sponsor motivated by business interests to turn off the financial tap than the Arts Council.

(c) *A.B.S.A.*

The Association for Business Sponsorship of the Arts is a company limited by guarantee and also a registered charity. It is difficult to decide under which heading it can best be mentioned; however it has made a significant contribution to sponsorship of the Arts. A.B.S.A. was formed in 1976 by a group of business executives. It has two objectives: (1) to

---

[8] See *British Broadcasting Corporation* v. *Hearn* [1977] 1 W.L.R. 1004.

encourage business support for the Arts, and (2) to look after the interests of companies who support the Arts.

A.B.S.A. is not a fund raising body or a sponsorship broker in the sense that it will actively seek sponsors for Arts events or organisations. Upon request, however, it will seek Arts events for sponsors. It also organises seminars for Arts administrators to help them present their case to potential sponsors. To that extent it is probably best regarded as a business members' forum.

(3) OTHERS

(a) *Governments*

The Office of Arts and Libraries created within the Department of Education and Science was the department which, under the Minister for the Arts, had chief responsibility for the Arts in Great Britain until 1983. It produced comprehensive evidence for the House of Commons' Education, Science and Arts Committee's Eighth Report on *Public and Private Funding of the Arts* which is much commented upon in Chapter 16. After the 1983 General Election, responsibility was transferred to the Privy Council Office with the Minister in the House of Lords and the spokesman in the House of Commons, such as the Minister responsible for Sport, as an Under Secretary in the Department of Environment. Nevertheless political interference by government is virtually unknown in British Arts sponsorship.

(b) *The Arts Council of Great Britain*

The Arts Council is an independent organisation incorporated by Royal Charter and having charitable status. It received an annual grant of approximately £93.5 million for the year 1983/84 from the government which enables it to carry out its work as the principal channel for government aid to the Arts. The Scottish and Welsh Arts Councils are sub-committees of the council and receive their funds from it.

A large number of Arts organisations which the Council supports with funds, particularly at national level, also receive sponsorship funds, for example The Royal Shakespeare Company. Certain prominent Arts organisations such as the Royal Academy of Arts exist without financial support from the Arts Council.

The Arts Council also supports the independent regional arts associations which have responsibility for promoting the Arts within their area. The Arts Council has an interest in encouraging sponsorship but is also clearly concerned with maintaining the independence and integrity of Arts organisations which it supports. The Sports Council is, no doubt, similarly concerned.

The British Council has responsibility for promoting British culture overseas and has a full-time sponsorship officer. The British Film Institute and Craft Council each have a separate responsibility for supporting their own disciplines.

(c) *Media*

The media is as vital to the overall success of the sponsorship relationship in the Arts as it is in sports and leisure. The emphasis, however, is probably less on television since advertising boards at Arts events are unusual. The press and radio are therefore important.

(d) *The sponsors and advertising and public relations specialists.*

These have been discussed above under the heading "Sports Scene."[9]

Leisure

Leisure is an immense topic ranging from pop concerts to videos and chess. Therefore it is impossible to examine each structure separately, as a definitive list of leisure activities can never be compiled. Representative examples of some of the more popular categories are as follows:

(1) SPONSORED MUSICAL EVENTS

The Rolling Stones 1982 European Tour was sponsored by a number of commercial companies. Sponsorship rights were purchased in the first place by a firm of marketing consultants from a management company which held certain rights from the Rolling Stones. Marketing consultants then sold the

[9] See p. 26 above.

sponsorship rights to the sponsoring clients. Sponsored records may arise out of such events.

Rights ownership starts with the musicians themselves. Managers and agents, however, proliferate throughout the pop music industry. The contractual position of the musicians with record companies should also be considered, regarding the use of recordings and the image and likeness of the musicians. The musicians' union has not played a direct part in sponsorship negotiations to date. The media is, of course, important to the success of the sponsorship.

(2) SPONSORED BOOKS

Sponsored books are an established marketing tool in the United States. Gradually they are beginning to gain a foothold in the United Kingdom. There are a number of ways in which they may work. A simple example might be a brewery company sponsoring the production of a book on the history of real ale. The identity of the rights owner will depend upon whether or not the author has an agreement with the publishing house. It would be usual for the prospective sponsor to open discussions with a publishing house before the author is signed. The sponsor would need to come to some satisfactory financial arrangement with the publisher. This could mean sharing the risk of publication and therefore the project costs. Alternatively a rights fee could be paid by the sponsor.

Certain publishing houses have developed specialist departments for sponsored books. Sponsored books have also been produced in conjunction with a number of national newspapers. Forums and agents have not as yet developed solely in relation to this type of sponsorship. The media is less important to the success of sponsored books than, for example, sponsored sports events since the book itself, carrying the sponsored title or message, goes directly to the consumer.

(3) SPONSORED VIDEOS

There are obvious conceptual similarities between sponsored videos and sponsored books but greater complexities can arise from sponsored videos in view of the number of parties who may have legal interests in the material. The

Victor Company of Japan (J.V.C.) acquired the right to sell, as part of a package of sponsorship rights, videogrammes of the Soccer World Cup carrying its company name and logo together with the advertising slogan "Official Video Company of the World Cup," within defined territories. Delivery of these rights to J.V.C. involved securing a recording from a company which televised the event (unless J.V.C. had installed its own cameras). Prima facie that television company will own the copyright in its recording. F.I.F.A., as the fountain of all commercial rights to the World Cup, would need to limit television rights acquired by such companies to broadcasting to ensure that no rights conflicted with those granted to J.V.C. Other examples of sponsored videos include Courvoisier on teaching golf and Pedigree Petfoods on dog care.

Rights ownership of sponsored videos of musical or theatrical but not sports, events will also require a consideration of the Performers' Protection Acts 1958, 1963 and 1972. The simplest form of sponsored video will give rise to a contract between the sponsor and a video production company.

Some companies now exist which specialise exclusively in the production of sponsored videos and it is undoubtedly an area offering much scope for further development. Unions which represent the interests of those individuals who have an interest either under the Copyright Act 1956 or the Performers' Protection Acts, such as Equity, have naturally shown an interest on behalf of their members in the development of the video market. Industry agreements currently exist between the B.B.C. and I.B.A. regarding the exploitation on B.B.C. and I.B.A. programmes on video format. Such agreements affect videos generally rather than sponsored videos in particular.

(4) SPONSORED BROADCASTS

Sponsored broadcasts involving television and radio, are discussed later. The Government White Paper on Cable Television has accepted the recommendations of the Hunt Committee[10] favouring the production of sponsored programming for cable television distribution. Clearly this is an

---

[10] Cmnd. 8679.

area to be watched and it is anticipated that a Bill will shortly be enacted.

In the United States it is quite common for radio and television programmes to be sponsored by commercial companies. The opening credit to such programmes may contain an announcement to the effect that "This programme is brought to you by X Co."

Advertisements by X Co. may also be included during the broadcast. The further development of local radio in the United Kingdom might, if current broadcast regulations are relaxed, offer scope for development in this area. Satellite television, where the broadcast footprint extends over the United Kingdom, will inevitably create difficulties with different television standards, since some countries permit broadcast sponsorship and others do not.

(5) SPONSORED RECORDS AND SOUND RECORDINGS

Sponsored records and sound recordings generally arise from sponsored musical events. As with videos and broadcasts, records usually involve difficult questions of rights ownership some of which are discussed later.[11] Certain airlines offer "in flight" audio entertainment, the content of which is sponsored.

(6) SPONSORED CONSERVATION PROJECTS

A number of sponsored conservation projects have been organised. Gulf Oil for example sponsored the production of the Gulf Oil Motorway Nature Trail. The Department of the Environment has recently sought to promote the benefits of conservation sponsorship through publication of a booklet on conservation and business sponsorship. The Nature Conservancy Council is also much involved in this area.

(7) SPONSORED EDUCATION PROJECTS

Sponsors such as General Accident have contributed funds to produce posters and the like in relation to schools. Rights owners are likely to be local authorities or particular schools on a local basis.

[11] See p. 131.

(8) SPONSORED TOURISM AND TRAVEL

Apart from sponsored education tours and travel, the English Tourist Board,[12] the British Tourist Authority and British Rail are actively concerned in developing these valuable industries and have recognised the benefits of sponsorship in this regard.

[12] See, for example, *The give and take of Sponsorship* (1982) published by the English Tourist Board.

3. Legal Framework

This chapter examines the potential legal identities or personalities of the sponsor and sponsee and highlights some of the more important features which result from the different legal identities. An appreciation of the consequences arising from the legal identities of the sponsor and sponsee is important. The term "legal identity" is the name tag or legal classification of the different types of organisations whose existence is recognised by the law. A company incorporated with limited liability is one type of legal identity. A chartered corporation is another. The selection of a particular legal identity will depend upon a diverse range of factors. These might include tax advantages, control of decision-making or limiting the financial liability of members to initial capital subscribed. It is often desirable to take professional advice as to the most suitable legal identity from a solicitor or accountant. Sponsorship exists at every level of commerce, from multi-million pound transactions in soccer to a few pounds contributed to a local brass band. Such a variety of levels of trade produces many different legal identities particularly in relation to sponsees. Sponsors are usually established trading concerns which will exist as limited liability companies.

The most usual legal identities found in sponsorship are:

(a) individuals;
(b) unincorporated associations;
(c) corporations limited by shares;
(d) corporations limited by guarantee;
(e) chartered corporations; and
(f) charities.

The following case illustrates the particular risks to individual committee members of an unincorporated members club who enter into agreements. During the 1890s, a grandstand collapsed at Blackburn Rovers Football Club ground. Blackburn Rovers was not incorporated as a company but organised as an unincorporated members club run by a committee. The committee had employed an incompetent builder to repair the stand, which resulted in the accident. The victim originally sued the club committee as representing the whole club. After an amendment to the claim the county court judge held that the members of the committee and not the club itself were personally liable and gave judgment in favour of the plaintiff. An appeal against the decision was dismissed on June 5, 1896 by the High Court which confirmed that the persons to blame were the committee.[1] A year later in 1897, the then Blackburn Rovers Football Club was converted into the present Blackburn Rovers Football and Athletic Company Limited, thus preventing similar problems arising from unincorporated status.

It is difficult to provide a comprehensive list of the specific problems which may arise as a consequence of dealing with a particular legal identity. Some of the more important are as follows:

Capacity

Until such time as an individual attains majority, which is currently 18, he or she has limited ability to enter into enforceable contracts, depending on what may or may not be construed by the courts to be necessary.[2] In one case legal incapacity as an infant could not be used by a young boxer to avoid forfeiting a purse withheld because of a breach of the governing body's rules.[3] In another case legal incapacity as an infant was again rejected when pleaded to avoid liability for a world tour contract for exhibition billiard matches to prepare and train for a professional billiard playing career.[4] Conversely it could be argued that a Rolls Royce ordered for a minor by an extravagant agent for image-building purposes could be avoided. Legislation and court cases have similarly created disabilities for mental patients.

Agency

Broadly speaking, an agent is only able to bind his principal to a contract to the extent of his authority. Agency has

---

[1] *Brown* v. *Lewis* (1896) 12 T.L.R. 455.
[2] See the Infants Relief Act 1874 and also p. 54.
[3] *Doyle* v. *White City Stadium* [1935] 1 K.B. 110; see also p. 54.
[4] *Roberts* v. *Gray* [1913] 1 K.B. 520.

particular relevance to contracts made on behalf of members of an unincorporated association. Agency may be established on the basis of actual, implied or ostensible authority. Ostensible authority arises where no actual or implied authority exists but the agent is nevertheless held out by those who have actual authority, *e.g.* directors or owners of a business.[5]

Ultra vires

The doctrine of *ultra vires* has particular relevance to limited liability companies. Such companies are obliged to state in their incorporation documents, *i.e.* Memorandum and Articles of Association, the general area of business in which the company is to engage. This is contained in the objects clause. It is conceivable that contracts beyond the scope of such objects will not be binding upon the company. The effect of this doctrine has been considerably reduced in recent years, by drafting the object clauses widely and by statutory protection[6] given to outsiders dealing with the company in good faith. Before such protection, a member of the public dealing with a company was deemed to have constructive knowledge of limitations to enter into contracts imposed by the company's public documents *i.e.* a company's Memorandum and Articles of Association.

Form

In certain limited circumstances it may be a requirement that a contract is executed under a corporate seal.

The most likely risks arising from a failure to identify the legal status of the contracting parties are as follows:

(a) exposure of personal assets, *i.e.* house, car, etc., where none was intended;

(b) the inability of the sponsor and or sponsee to enforce the terms of the sponsorship agreement; and

(c) the inability of the sponsor to enforce a judgment against the assets of the sponsee. This risk may be reduced by seeking indemnities and guarantees in appropriate circumstances. Assets may be subject to prior claims and charges; and for enforcement pur-

---

[5] See also Chap. 5.
[6] European Communities Act 1972, s.9(1).

poses, the geographical location of the legal indentity controls a court's jurisdiction over assets.

Individuals

Where the sponsee is an individual and enters into a contract with the sponsor in that capacity, then few immediate legal complications are likely to arise. An individual, provided he has capacity, *i.e.* is not a minor or lunatic, can agree to anything which is legal. An individual's assets would normally be available to meet his liabilities.

Individual sponsees are often represented by agents. They will be bound by contracts negotiated by an agent within the agent's authority.

Some individuals will arrange for a management company to be incorporated. The management company will enter into an agreement with the individual for his exclusive services. The management company will then sell those services to the sponsor. If something were to go wrong, the sponsors remedy in contract is likely to be against the management company and not the individual. This situation should be distinguished from one of agency. An agent enters into a contract on behalf of the principal. In the above circumstances a management company is the principal.

Unincorporated associations

Except for certain fiscal purposes, an unincorporated association has no separate legal existence apart from its membership.[7]

The United Kingdom recreational explosion in the nineteenth century produced an extension of earlier patronage alongside club formations to benefit from it, and also the growth of former school associations. They created common interests without the commercial or trading intentions which caused Parliament to codify existing common law and equity rules into the Partnership Act 1890. Nearly 30 years earlier, the first Companies Act 1862 consolidated earlier company legislation.

No legislative rules were considered necessary for non-commercial or non-trading or non-industrial activities in

---

[7] See *Carlisle & Silloth Golf Club* v. *Smith* [1913] K.B. 75, where the club was liable to income tax assessment with respect to visitors' green fees.

recreational fields. Untaxed income funded private patronage and competitive or private sport did not require safety legislation or industrial action. Without legislation, therefore, the legal relations between a club, its members and the outside world were based upon rules of common law (contract) and equity (trustees and beneficiaries). From the sponsorship standpoint they require examining from both an internal and an external viewpoint.

(1) INTERNAL

The relationship between the members of a club and the club itself, will be contractual. The terms of the contract will usually be found in the membership rules.[8]

Overlapping with the members' contractual relationship is their entitlement to share in the membership assets in the event of dissolution; such assets are usually vested in trustees.[9]

Individual members will not normally make their personal assets available for the satisfaction of liabilities arising under contracts entered into on behalf of all the members.[10] Members will be personally liable and place their own assets at risk only where they give such authority expressly or by implication to an individual or committee.

(2) EXTERNAL

In the absence of any corporate legal personality outsiders can only deal with the club members in an individual and/or representative capacity, in the latter case on behalf of the other members.[10] Thus the Blackburn Rovers Club Committee in 1896 was held to have contracted personally with an incompetent grandstand repairer and thereby to be personally liable in negligence to the innocent injured victim. The general body of membership was not liable since it had not authorised the committee to enter into the original contract.

Ultimately the sponsor will wish to know whether he can gain access to the membership assets if something goes wrong. The sponsor's ability to do so will depend on establishing that the person or committee who agreed to the

---

[8] *Clarke* v. *Dunraven (Earl), The Satanita* [1897] A.C. 59.
[9] See "The Dissolution of Unincorporated Non-Profit Association" [1980] M.L.R. 629–649.
[10] *Wise* v. *Perpetual Trustees Co.* [1903] A.C. 139.

contract did so with the authority of the membership. Such authority will often be delegated to officers within the club *via* the club constitution so that specific authority will not be required in each case. Delegation may be subject to limitations, *e.g.* to enter into contracts up to £1,000. If the officer or committee were to exceed his or their authority then he or they may be personally liable.[11] From the individual or committee's viewpoint, he or they should feel some reassurance if the club rules or constitution provides them with an indemnity against liability arising in such circumstances.

Where large sums of money are at stake, it is recommended that in dealings with an unincorporated association, the sponsor should always satisfy himself that the agreement has been negotiated and signed in accordance with the association's constitution. Depending upon what the constitution says, it may be prudent to insist that a copy of a resolution approving the contract is produced. The contract should also contain a warranty that the signatory had full authority to sign.

In addition to the members club discussed above, certain unincorporated associations exist as proprietory clubs. A proprietory club's relationship with its members depends upon the contract between the proprietor, which is often a limited liability company, and the members. In contrast, the relationships in a members club depend upon the contract between the members themselves. A proprietory club will deal with outsiders as principal and not as agent for the members.

A limited liability company is occasionally established by an unincorporated association to hold trade mark applications. This is discussed later.

Membership of unincorporated associations is not limited to individuals, and many international sporting federations are formed as uincorporated associations. Their membership comprises national federations and other constituent bodies. Under English law the same legal principles apply as with individuals.[12] No particular form of contract is required merely because of unincorporated status.

---

[11] See the Blackburn Rovers case, *supra*. However, liability may only be for the excess.

[12] See *Reel* v. *Holder* [1981] 1 W.L.R. 1226, and also [1979] 1 W.L.R. 1252 for a valuable explanation of how such organisations exist. In that case, because the head office of the defendant unincorporated association (I.A.A.F.) and the representatives were all located in London, the English courts had jurisdiction to hear the claim.

Companies limited by shares

An incorporated company has a separate legal personality or identity from those who own it.[13] This shifts the legal responsibility from individual members and committee members to the legal *persona* of the company, and avoids the personal liabilities found occasionally in unincorporated associations.[14] This also shifts control to share power. Articles of association can restrict transfers of shares and therefore control of the company.[15] If, however, such restriction is waived the control could be lost.

A shareholder in a company limited by shares is only liable for the company's debts to the extent of any unpaid sums due on his shares, *i.e.* if he is issued with five £1.00 shares and 50p per share remains unpaid, then the maximum liability he has for the company's debts is £2.50.

The responsibility for managing the affairs of a company is usually delegated to a board of directors.[16] There is no special form that a contract with a limited liability should take except where this is required by special enactments, *i.e.* the Company Seal need not be affixed.[17]

Companies limited by guarantee

Prior to December 22, 1980 companies limited by guarantee were required to have a share capital. Since that date a share capital in a guarantee company is no longer possible.[18]

The basic legal difference between the ordinary share and the guarantee company is that the member's liability to the extent of the guarantee does not have to be called on until after commencement of any winding-up. One very important practical difference between the two is that the accountancy and disclosure of corporate information requirements tend to be less stringent in a guarantee company than a share company. The guarantee company is traditionally funded

---

[13] *Salmon* v. *Salmon & Co.* (1897) A.C. 22.
[14] Except for extreme circumstances concerning directors.
[15] See *Berry and Stewart* v. *Tottenham Hotspur Football and Athletic Co. Ltd.* (1935) Ch. 718.
[16] See Table A, art. 80.
[17] See Companies Act 1948, s.32(1).
[18] s.1(2) of the Companies Act 1980, and as now regulated by the Companies Act (Commencement No.2) Order 1980 (S.I. 1980 No. 1785).

from group sources, subscriptions or fees and is progressively used for and by professional, trade research, and other similar bodies. It is also progressively used by governing sports bodies. In addition, it qualifies for exemption under section 25 of the Companies Act 1981 from use of the word "limited" if its objects are "the promotion of commerce, art, science, education, religion, charity or any profession and anything incidental or conducive to any of those objects." Sport is conspicuous by its absence from this statutory list.

The guarantee structure comes close and conveniently to the framework within which a charity is capable of being structured to meet the applicable statutory and case law formalities.

Companies limited by shares, or by guarantee and the doctrine of ultra vires

In both circumstances the *intra* or *ultra vires* principle concerns construction and knowledge of the company's objects clause in its Memorandum of Association.

The case of *Re Jon Beauforte (London) Ltd.*[19] illustrates the difficulties that can arise. The manufacturing company concerned with women's clothing objects switched to wooden veneer panels, which were *ultra vires* the objects clause of the company. In a liquidation, the Chancery judge rejected a coke merchant's claim after the liquidation for payment for supplies. The merchant had actual and clear notice that the coke was to be used in the veneer factory and by constructive notice of the Memorandum, therefore, he was aware that the transaction was *ultra vires* the company.

The European Communities Act 1972, s.9(1)(g) has now modified this strictness by shifting in effect the burden of proof to two basic requirements. If these are satisfied, the agreement will be enforceable against the company. The requirements are;
  (a) the stranger must have acted in good faith, and
  (b) the transaction must have been decided upon by the directors.[19a]

---

[19] [1959] Ch. 131.
[19a] See also *International Sales and Agencies Ltd.* v. *Marcus* [1982] 3 All E.R. 551, where Lawson J. was concerned primarily with constructive trust moneys rather than *ultra vires*.

These last requirements themselves contain built-in factual issues requiring ultimate decisions from the courts because;

    (i) good faith is arguably destroyed by actual although not by constructive notice so that the *Re Jon Beauforte* claim would in all probability be allowable and not *ultra vires*, if heard today and

  (ii) "directors" would arguably apply to all situations including single company directors. A possible exception could be the defaulting director of a multi-national company board exceeding his authority to contract or never having obtained it: to be personally but not representatively liable. Here, too, as in unincorporated circumstances, a specific representative term could be incorporated into the sponsorship contract regarding authority to contract especially where the parties are strangers.

The European Communities Act 1972 only applies to transactions decided upon by the directors. It would not effect the situation where, for example, the Company Secretary outside his authority placed an order for motor cars.[20] Agency and authority in these circumstances are still relevant. Where suspicions are aroused it may be prudent to ask for a copy of the board resolution approving the agreement or confirming that the officer, if not a director, has authority to bind the company.[21]

Charities

The legal framework for charities is either a trust deed or a company structured to covenant its profits to the parent charity at the end of each financial year. Whichever is preferred the key element must be to satisfy the qualifying requirements as established under the traditional four heads of charitable status in the United Kingdom, *i.e.*:

  (a) for the relief of poverty;

  (b) for the advancement of education;

  (c) for the advancement of religion; and

  (d) for other purposes beneficial to the community.[22]

---

[20] *Panorama Developments (Guildford) Ltd.* v. *Fidelis Furnishing Fabrics Ltd.* (1971) 2 Q.B. 711.

[21] See H. Bond, "Ultra Vires – a re-assessment" [1983] N.L.J. 561.

[22] *Income Tax Special Purposes Commissioners* v. *Pemsel* [1891] A.C. 531.

The fiscal advantages of securing charitable status are considerable and are dealt with in a later Chapter. The fiscal authorities recognise this, and the Inland Revenue's guidelines, albeit prepared with the Arts in mind for a House of Commons Select Committee, state specifically, "Many of the bodies which promote activities in the Arts are established charities." Sport was not specified, partly because it was not within the House of Commons or Revenue's immediate terms of reference, and also because it got off to a false start four years after the *Pemsel* directive in 1891.[23] Now the House of Lords has given the green light in qualified terms with these words of the Lord Chancellor, the Right Hon. the Lord Hailsham of St. Marylebone from the unanimous decision in the F.A. Youth Trust Deed case[24]:

> "I do not think that the courts have as yet explored the extent to which elements of organisation, instruction, or the disciplined inculcation of information, instruction or skill may limit the whole concept of education. I believe that in some ways it will prove more extensive, in others more restrictive than has been thought hitherto. But it is clear at least to me that the decision *In re Mariette*[24a] is not to be read in a sense which confines its application for ever to gifts to a particular institution."

In this context and against this background the world of sport has not yet recognised or become fully aware of the potential developments which are before it for this particular legal identity. One problem is that many sporting units contain sections or subdivisions eligible for charitable status within a larger legal framework which would not qualify. Any youth section within the age levels indicated by Lord Hailsham at a badminton, cricket, football, golf, tennis or yachting club, could be "hived off" administratively and physically, *e.g.* part of the accommodation allocated for charitable levels or limits *after consultation* with the Charity Commissioners and the Inland Revenue. The Revenue objection to the F.A. Youth Trust Deed accepted by the Charity Commissioners resulted in litigation to the House of Lords. Even if this "hived off" conception created initial

---

[23] See *Re Nottage* [1895] 2 Ch. 649, a yacht racing prize issue which could conceivably be decided differently today.
[24] *I.R.C.* v. *McMullen* [1981] A.C. 1 at 17.
[24a] [1915] 2 Ch. 284.

teething problems within an organisation, the fiscal advantages would probably be worthwhile in the end.

In addition to the general and traditional charity area, there is unlimited scope within the unexplored territories of the Recreational Charities Act 1958. It was initially considered in the F.A. Youth Trust Deed case, but not pursued in the House of Lords. Here, too, the Charity Commissioners and the Inland Revenue should be approached for guidance.

No particular form of contract is required merely because of charitable status. This will depend upon what legal identity the charity takes, *e.g.* a company limited by guarantee. The particular legal identity will also determine whether questions of capacity and agency apply.

One curious imbalance between charitable and corporate requirements has been noted in an article by Professor Bird[24b]: "... it is surprising that the accounting and auditing requirements of the Charities Act 1960 are so much less onerous than those in legislation governing most other types of organisation." This may not affect many who would contemplate to what extent their legal framework would or could be adjusted to charitable status. It is the kind of issue which in the end is conditioned by the learned author's conclusion: "Most charities have standards of morality and effectiveness in their actual operations much higher than that shown in their accounts." It can be an appropriate starting point for reflecting upon what legal framework to adopt.

Corporations incorporated by royal charter

Many Arts bodies such as the Royal Shakespeare Theatre, the Royal Academy of Arts, the Royal Opera House, are incorporated by Royal Charter. The power to create a chartered corporation rests with the Crown.

This royal prerogative is founded in common law. The members of a chartered corporation created by the prerogative are under no liability for the debts of the corporation, the Crown having no power at Common Law to attach liability to the individual members of the corporation. The Court of Appeal affirmed this in a case in the same year as *Pemsel's* case which laid down the guidelines on charities in 1891.[25]

The corporate autonomy is complete.[26] The royal chartered

[24b] "Charities Called to Account," (1980) *The Accountant*, p. 963.
[25] *Elve* v. *Boyton* (1981) 1 Ch. 501 at 507.
[26] *Sutton's Hospital Case* (1612) 10 Co. Rep. 1(a), 23(a), 30(b).

corporation can deal with its property, bind itself by contracts, and do all such acts as an ordinary person can do. Only the Crown can annul the charter, but the life expectancy of a chartered corporation may be set out in the document which creates it. Thus the present British Broadcasting Corporation royal charter came into operation on August 1, 1981, and runs for 15 years. The word royal is not necessary for the title; and it does not appear in many corporations structured in this way, exemplified not only by the British Broadcasting Corporation, but also by the Arts Council of Great Britain, the Sports Council and the Jockey Club. The qualifying standards for consideration as a chartered corporation must be self-evident from the standpoint of the public interest: they are constitutionally distinguishable from corporations incorporated by the Act of Parliament.

The doctrine of *ultra vires* does not apply to chartered corporations. Their charters create complete autonomy. The Crown does have the power through complex technical procedures for annulment. At common law a corporation's contracts had generally to be made in writing under its common seal. As already mentioned this does not apply to limited liability companies.[27] Since the Corporate Bodies Contracts Act 1960, a chartered corporation's contracts need not be in writing or under seal.

[27] See p. 45.

4. Particular Aspects of the Sponsor/Beneficiary Relationship Examined

The contract

Standard form agreements under the headings long and short form are set out in Appendix 1 of this book.[1] Reference will be made to these standard form documents throughout this chapter. In sponsorship situations of even the most basic type, it is recommended that a written record is desirable.

(1) ESSENTIAL ELEMENTS

(a) *Offer*

The long form agreement reflects an offer made by the sponsor to acquire the various promises and licences detailed in paragraph 1 in return for the consideration stated in paragraph 5. Thus the offer comprises four stadium advertising boards at the sponsored event and other rights including the use of the mascot and symbol in return for the consideration.[2]

The contract will usually be prepared following verbal negotiations after agreement has been reached on the main terms.

Where pre-contract negotiations take place it may be important to establish at what point a contract is made. This is a matter which will be determined by the intention of the parties at any particular stage in the discussions. In one case, for example, an individual was offered a council house on the basis that if he signed and returned the agreement for sale then it would be countersigned by the council. The individual did as requested but the agreement was never countersigned or returned by the council. It was nevertheless held that a contract existed.[3] This occurred because the action of the

---

[1] See p. 292.
[2] See p. 294.
[3] *Storer* v. *Manchester City Council* [1974] 1 W.L.R. 1403.

individual in signing and returning the agreement for sale, was all that was required of him to accept the council's offer.

(b) *Acceptance*

No contract will exist until an unconditional acceptance has been communicated to the person making the offer, *i.e.* the offeror. Where it has been stated orally or in previous correspondence that this must be in writing and signed by both parties before the contract will become binding then, notwithstanding communication of verbal acceptance to the offeror, the contract will become enforceable at law only when a written contract has been executed[4] by both parties. Where writing and signature by both parties is not required as a formality but a written agreement has been sent out by the sponsor or sponsee unsigned, then the date when the contract is made will depend upon the intention of the parties. If it is stated, for example, in an accompanying letter that "if you will sign and return the contract, we will countersign it," the contract is made the moment it is signed by the sponsor and put into the post. Post is an exception to the normal rule that acceptance only takes place when it is actually received by the offeror. Where instantaneous communications are used such as telex then acceptance occurs when it is received. Thus in a recent case where a telex was sent from London to Vienna the contract was not made until the telex was received in Vienna.[5]

The importance in deciding whether and when acceptance has taken place, is that an offer may be withdrawn at any time before it is accepted.[6]

(c) *Consideration*

The common law requires a contract to be supported by consideration unless it is made under seal.[7] Equity, however, acting on principles of conscience has intervened progressively in recent years to give limited legal effect to promises made without consideration.[8] Consideration in the standard

---

[4] This is a common practice in conveyancing. See *Tiverton Estates* v. *Wearwell Ltd.* [1975] Ch. 146.

[5] *Brinkibon Ltd.* v. *Stahag Stahl und Stahlwarenhandelsgessellschaft mbH* [1982] 2 W.L.R. 264.

[6] *Payne* v. *Cave* (1789) 3 Term Rep. 148.

[7] See p. 10.

[8] See, for example, *Dillwyn* v. *Llewelyn* (1862) 4 De G.F. & J. 517; *Inwards* v. *Baker* [1965] 2 Q.B. 29.

form agreements means money and or goods and or services which the sponsor pays or provides or is obliged to pay or provide to the sponsee.

(d) *Intention to create legal relations*

There must be a genuine intention on the part of both parties to make a contract. If two parties sign a written document such as the standard form agreement, then the natural assumption is that the parties intended to make a contract. If the document, however, was expressed to be a "gentleman's agreement" or "binding in honour only," then it would be assumed that the sponsor and sponsee did not intend to make a contract but merely a non-binding agreement. Social or domestic arrangements are not usually intended to have any legal effect.[9] Within this category the courts have placed competition prizes at a golf club and a jalopy race for charity.[10]

(e) *Mistake*

Mistake when applied in the law of contract has a special meaning which is unlikely to be familiar to the layman. Where both parties are mistaken as to the existence of the subject-matter of the contract then the contract will be void. If, for example, a sponsorship contract is made in relation to a tennis star and unbeknown to either party before the contract had been entered into the tennis star had died, then the contract would be void.[11] Another example might be where the sponsee and sponsor enter into a contract to sponsor an event which, unknown to either party, has already been cancelled.[12] If the sponsee knew the tennis star was dead or the event was cancelled, then this would amount to fraudulent misrepresentation. If the star died or the event was cancelled after the contract came into existence then the contract might be "frustrated."

Where only one party makes a mistake or both parties make a different mistake so that the parties are at cross purposes the contract is only void in limited circumstances. If, for example, the sponsee entered into a contract with a

[9] See generally *Balfour* v. *Balfour* [1919] 2 K.B. 571.
[10] See Treitel, *The Law of Contract* (6th ed., 1983), pp. 125–126.
[11] *Strickland* v. *Turner* (1852) 7 Exch. 208.
[12] *Griffith* v. *Brymer* (1903) 19 T.L.R. 434.

sponsor believing that he was dealing with a highly prestigious company whose name he knew and in fact the sponsor was a small company with a similar name but a bad reputation, then it is likely the contract would be valid.[13] If the sponsor had known that the sponsee was making the mistake and the mistake was fundamental in the sense that the sponsee only wanted to deal with that particular large company then the mistake would probably render the contract void.[14] If an ice cream company believed it was sponsoring a marathon taking place in May and it turned out that it was mistaken and the marathon takes place in December, then such a mistake by one party might make the contract void.[15]

A void contract is one under which no property can pass. It is as if the contract was never made in the first place and therefore the parties will be restored, insofar as is possible to their original bargaining positions.

(f) Duress, undue influence and equitable fraud

Consent given under duress is no consent at all. A contract made in these circumstances may therefore be rescinded at common law. Duress usually involves a threat of violence to person or property which coerces a party into making a contract. It should be distinguished from the situation in which one party uses a dominant bargaining position to extract the best terms.[15a] Where duress cannot be established but some undue pressure has been applied then equity may intervene to set aside the transaction.

A presumption of undue influence exists between certain parties who are in an especially close relationship which could be open to abuse, such as solicitor and client or parent and child. In other circumstances positive evidence is required. Undue influence is a form of equitable fraud. This contrasts with the more familiar form of fraud at common law, which enables the innocent party to avoid the contract and may give rise to criminal liability.

---

[13] See *Kings Norton Metal Co. Ltd.* v. *Edridge, Merrett & Co.Ltd.* (1897) 14 T.L.R. 98, C.A.

[14] See *Cundy* v. *Lindsay* (1878) 3 App. Cas. 459.

[15] See *Raffles* v. *Wichelhaus* (1864) 2 H. & C. 906.

[15a] See *Pao On* v. *Lau Yin Long* [1980] A.C. 614 and contrast with economic duress as applied in *Universe Tankships Inc. of Monrovia* v. *International Transport Workers' Federation* [1982] 2 W.L.R. 803.

(g) *Capacity*

The parties must have the capacity to contract. The most common groups which have limited capacity are minors, *i.e.* persons below the age of 18; mental patients; drunken or drugged persons and companies or corporations acting beyond the powers set out in their documents of incorporation. Where a person deals in good faith with such a company then the contract will be enforceable against the company even if it went beyond the company's statutes provided that it was decided upon by the directors.[16]

Minors are perhaps the group most likely to be affected by limited capacity to enter into sponsorship agreements. There are two types of contract with a minor which are legally binding upon him or her. These are first, contracts for necessaries which are linked to a minor's "station" in life and include such items as food and education. Thus, in one case, an infant was held liable for repudiating a contract, whilst it remained partly unperformed, under which he was to receive instruction in playing professional billiards.[17] The second type of contract binding on minors are contracts of employment.[18] Such contracts and those reasonably similar are binding provided that taken as a whole, they are for the minor's benefit. Thus, a minor who was a boxer was bound by a term in a contract under which he had agreed to box. The term, which was consistent with "fair play" and therefore in the public interest, enabled the "purse" to be withdrawn in the event of his disqualification.[19] In another case a contract in which a minor granted exclusive publishing rights to his memoirs was held to be enforceable against the minor.[20]

(h) *Form*

Certain statutes require contracts to be in writing or some other formality to be complied with. This is quite apart from those particular requirements related to different legal identities already discussed in Chapter 3. These statutes are

---

[16] See p. 45.
[17] *Roberts* v. *Gray* [1913] 1 K.B. 520.
[18] These are also affected by various statutory provisions such as the Employment of Children Act 1973.
[19] *Doyle* v. *White City Stadium Ltd.* [1935] 1 K.B. 110.
[20] *Chaplin* v. *Leslie Frewin (Publishers)* [1966] Ch. 71.

unlikely to apply to the normal sponsorship contract and may therefore be ignored in that context. They might, however, have relevance where an agent or other contractor is engaged by the sponsee to sell sponsorship on his behalf. In such cases it is often the practice for the sponsee to receive a percentage of total income generated from the sale of sponsorship properties. In certain cases, however, the agent or contractor may be asked to guarantee that the sponsee will receive a minimum sum. In the very rare case that the agent guarantees to pay where the sponsor defaults such a contract would need to be evidenced in writing.[21] If the agent is merely issuing a guarantee in relation to his own performance, then that would not need to be evidenced in writing.

The other circumstance where writing could be potentially relevant involves contracts for the "sale or other disposition of land or any interest in land."[22] The right to erect advertising boards at a venue will be a contractual licence and in the absence of adjoining land owned by the agent will not amount to an easement. It is most unlikely, therefore, that any "interest in land" will be dealt with in the normal sponsorship situation.

(2) CONTRACTUAL TERMS

(a) Express or implied

The terms of a contract will be those expressly agreed by the parties, together with those which have not been expressly agreed but are implied. The express terms, in the standard long form contract are contained in paragraphs 1–14.[23] The more common terms which are implied into contracts relate to the quality of goods or services and are intended to protect the consumer. Examples of such terms may be found in the Supply of Goods and Services Act 1982. Such terms will be of limited relevance to a sponsorship contract. In certain circumstances terms may be implied where not expressly stated in the contract where it can be shown they were clearly within the contemplation of the parties at the time of reaching agreement.[23a] Terms implied through custom or trade usage operate in a similar way.

[21] See Statute of Frauds 1677, s.4.
[22] Law of Property Act 1925, s.40(1).
[23] See App.I, p. 293.
[23a] See *Waite Hill Holdings Ltd.* v. *Marshall* (1983) 133 New L.J. 745.

(b) *Express terms excluding or restricting liability*

The courts will interfere with the terms agreed by the parties in the contract on two main grounds. First, where, as a matter of construction, the court believes that a clause in the contract excluding liability was never intended to apply.[23b] This has only occurred in a handful of cases. Since the House of Lords decision in *Photo Production Ltd.* v. *Securicor Transport Ltd.*[23c] It is clear that an unambiguous clause may be relied upon to exclude or limit liability even by a party who committed a fundamental breach of the contract. As a matter of construction, exclusion and indemnity clauses will always be construed very strictly.[23d] Where the court however is dealing with a clause limiting rather than excluding liability the same strictness need not be shown. Thus the fact that Dutch cabbage seed was ordered but another variety was supplied which failed to grow did not prevent the supplier relying upon a clause limiting his liability.[24]

The second is under Statute, illustrated by the Unfair Contract Terms Act 1977. Under section 2(1) of the Act it is not possible for the parties to exclude responsibility for death or personal injury resulting from their negligence. It is possible to exclude or restrict liability in the case of other loss or damage (*i.e.* not death or personal injury) arising from negligence but only when the term excluding or restricting liability satisfies the test of reasonableness.[25]

Since sponsorship often involves events attended by large numbers of the public, such as a football match, these provisions are important. The sponsee could not, for example, include a clause in the contract which would enable him to escape liability for his negligence where some injury befell the sponsor whilst attending the event. Where, however, the injury was caused as a result of the sponsee assigning intellectual property rights to the sponsors such as a logo for use on

---

[23b] *Canada Steamship Lines Ltd.* v. *R.* [1952] A.C. 192.

[23c] [1980] A.C. 827.

[23d] See the judgment of Lord Fraser in *Ailsa Craig Fishing Co.* v. *Malvern Fishing Co.* [1983] 1 All E.R. 101.

[24] *Mitchell (George) (Chesterhall) Ltd.* v. *Finney Lock Seeds Ltd.* [1983] 2 All E.R. 737. The appellants who had supplied the seeds were unable to rely on the limitation clause, however, since s.55 of the Sale of Goods Act 1979 applied. In the circumstances it was held that it would not be fair or reasonable to permit the appellants to limit their liability.

[25] Unfair Contract Terms Act 1977, s.2(2).

T-shirts then by means of an exception in the Act[26] it may be possible to exclude liability for negligence causing death or personal injury. The dye used in the logo included on the T-shirt might for example produce a skin disease.

Where it is attempted to exclude liability for breach of contract rather than negligence, then again the Act has potential relevance but only where the sponsee or sponsor contracts on written standard terms of business. In these circumstances a term excluding or restricting liability for breach of contract cannot be relied upon as a defence to that breach, unless the term satisfies the requirement of "reasonableness."[27] Further, the sponsee cannot rely on any clause in the contract which enables him to render a "substantially different" performance than that contemplated or no performance at all unless that clause satisfies the test of reasonableness.[28]

The Act only applies when standard written terms of business are involved. Most sponsor contracts will be adapted or altered in negotiations with the potential sponsor.[29] It is difficult to fix standard terms when each contract may need to be tailored to suit different marketing requirements.

Where it is necessary to show that the clause is reasonable in order to rely upon the exclusion then reasonableness in this context means "that the term shall have been a fair and reasonable one to be included having regard to the circumstances which were, or ought reasonably to have been, known to or in the contemplation of the parties when the contract was made."[30] There are a number of factors which are relevant in determining "reasonableness" which are set out in the Act.[31] Where the contract is negotiated point by point as

---

[26] *Ibid.* Sched. 1, para. 1(*c*). It is doubtful that the exception will apply to a licence rather than an assignment.

[27] *Ibid.* s.3(2)(*a*).

[28] *Ibid.* s.3(2)(*b*); this section has been much criticised and the last sentence is perhaps an oversimplification of its effect. See David Yates, *Exclusion Clauses in Contracts* (2nd ed., 1982), pp. 93, 94. Also see *Doyle* v. *White City Stadium, supra,* where the purse was withheld for breach of the rules.

[29] For the effect of which, see Lord Dunpark in *McCrone* v. *Boots Farm Sales* 1981 S.L.T. 103 at 105.

[30] Unfair Contract Terms Act 1977, s.11(1).

[31] *Ibid.* Sched. 2.

it will be in most sponsorship transactions then it is suggested that it would be difficult to prove that any term was unreasonable.[32] The fact that one party may be covered by insurance and that his underwriters would meet his liability seems to be relevant.[32a]

The Unfair Contract Terms Act 1977 does not preclude the possibility of including an indemnity or "hold harmless" clause in the contract between the sponsor and sponsee. It does impose the reasonableness requirement where the indemnity appears in a consumer contract.[33]

The Act will also apply to *force majeure* clauses which exclude responsibility for performance.[34] *Force majeure* clauses are common in sponsorship contracts. *Force majeure* should be distinguished from frustration discussed below.[35] *Force majeure* clauses attempt to set out what is to happen where events beyond the control of either party intervene. The usual scope of such clauses involves strikes, lockouts, mechanical breakdown, etc. Many such clauses provide that the contract will continue where a *force majeure* event intervenes, but delay in performance as a result of *force majeure* will be excused. Events which frustrate the contract must not be foreseen by the parties and essentially render performance impossible. The standard contract contains such a clause.

(c) *Variation of terms*

Where the contract is not in writing then in the event of a dispute the court would seek whatever evidence was available to prove what the parties had agreed. This might include letters, sales proposal documents, oral evidence and the like.

Where, however, the contract is in writing, then the courts will not normally look at any other evidence except the written contract to establish the terms.[36]

---

[32] See *R.W. Green* v. *Cade Bros. Farms* [1978] 1 Lloyd's Rep. 602.
[32a] See *Mitchell (George) (Chesterhall) Ltd.* v. *Finney Lock Seeds Ltd.* [1983] 2 All E.R. 737 where a similar provision now incorporated within the Unfair Contract Terms Act was considered.
[33] Unfair Contract Terms Act 1977, s.4, and see also *Smith* v. *South Wales Switchgear* [1978] 1 W.L.R.165.
[34] Unfair Contract Terms Act 1977, s.3(2)(*b*).
[35] p. 63.
[36] *Jacobs* v. *Batavia & General Plantations Trust* [1924] 2 Ch. 329.

It is possible to vary the terms of a contract at any time by mutual agreement. It is preferable that any variation should be in writing since that will avoid confusion in deciding what the changes are. It is nevertheless possible to vary a written agreement orally, unless it concerns land where amendments must be in writing under section 40 of the Law of Property Act 1925. It is often the practice to include an express term in a contract which states that the contract may only be varied by a written document signed by both parties. No variation except in this form will be valid. Such a term is included in the standard form agreement.

(d) *Representations as terms*

During the course of sponsorship negotiations various statements will be made by or on behalf of the sponsee. For example, that an event has received 10 hours of television coverage per week or that previous exhibitions have been attended by one million people. Such statements may induce the sponsor to enter into the agreement. Where they are particularly material to the sponsor's commitment, then the sponsor may insist that they are incorporated as specific terms of the contract. The courts are occasionally willing, particularly where one of the parties has some special knowledge, to construe such statements as being included in the contract even where they have not been expressly incorporated.[37] Where the statements are or become specific terms then the contract itself may specify the remedy, if these terms are broken.

The remedies which are available for representations which are not included in the agreement but which turn out to be false, are set out in the Misrepresentation Act 1967 and are also supplemented by those available at common law and the law of tort. Remedies available for false representations which have been included in the contract will depend upon the intention of the parties and will be ascertained from the construction of the contract as a whole. Although the Misrepresentation Act is capable of applying to false representations included in the contract, it is more likely that the remedy will be an action for breach of contract. Where the representation is not incorporated into the contract the courts

[37] See *Dick Bentley Productions* v. *Harold Smith (Motors)* [1965] 1 W.L.R. 623.

have occasionally found a collateral contract existing in parallel to the original. The representation has been incorporated within the collateral contract and if false, has given rise to breach of the collateral contract.[38]

In order to be actionable under the Misrepresentation Act 1967, the misrepresentation must be a false statement of fact. A mere expression of opinion such as "in our opinion this event will receive two hours of television coverage each week" will not amount to a false representation if it does not receive two hours' coverage.[39] In contrast a statement that an event *has* received two hours' television coverage in previous years will amount to a misrepresentation, if false. A mere sales puff will not be treated as a statement of fact and thus phrases like "the best in the world" cannot amount to a misrepresentation. A statement of future intention is not a fact and will not therefore be actionable.

The misrepresentation must also be material to be actionable. That is, it must have been at least one of the factors which induced the person to whom the misrepresentation was made to enter into the contract. In one case therefore where a company prospectus contained a false statement that a certain important person was on the board of directors. The plaintiff could not prove misrepresentation since he acknowledged in cross examination that he was not influenced by this fact in subscribing for shares in the company.[40]

The remedies for misrepresentation are as follows:

(a) fraudulent misrepresentation: (i) damages in tort for deceit and (ii) rescission;

(b) negligent misrepresentation: (i) damages under section 2(1) of the Misrepresentation Act 1967 and (ii) rescission (or where court decides rescission should not be allowed, damages in lieu of rescission under section 2(2) of the Misrepresentation Act 1967); and

(c) innocent misrepresentation: (i) rescission (those misrepresentations made without fault) and (ii) rescission and damages (those misrepresentations made through negligence), or where the court decides rescission should not be allowed damages in lieu thereof under section 2(2) of the Misrepresentation Act 1967.

---

[38] See *Andrews* v. *Hopkinson* [1957] 1 Q.B. 229.
[39] Unless whoever makes the statement knows it to be false, in which case he will be misrepresenting his belief: *Jendwine* v. *Slade* (1797) 2 Esp. 572.
[40] *Smith* v. *Chadwick* (1884) 9 A.C. 187 at 194.

An example of a fraudulent misrepresentation in the context of sponsorship would be the sponsee representing that he had obtained a contract with a television company to cover a sponsored event when, in fact, the television company had declined the broadcast. The sponsor, however, must have acted on the representation and suffered loss.[41] A negligent misrepresentation might occur on the same facts when the sponsee had not yet heard from the television company but believed that, in all probability, they would broadcast the event. An innocent misrepresentation on the same facts would arise where the sponsee believed that the television company had committed itself to broadcast the event, but the company had, in fact, merely reserved the discretion to do so.

Rescission attempts to restore the parties to their former positions, *i.e.* as if the contract had never been made. Money paid by the sponsor will therefore need to be returned and the sponsor will no longer be in a position to exercise the licences arising under the sponsorship contract. Damages arising under the law of tort, *e.g.* fraudulent misrepresentation, are directed to restoring the injured party to the position he occupied before the tort was committed. In contract, the object of damages is to put the injured party in the position he would have been in, had the contract actually been performed. It may require some thought, therefore, in deciding how the action is framed.

(3) PRIVITY OF CONTRACT

Privity of contract is an important concept to appreciate within the context of the sponsorship contract. Privity in essence means that only the parties to a contract are allowed to enjoy its benefits or enforce its terms. Common law does not recognise third party rights under contracts, but equity may operate to enforce beneficiaries' rights through trustees. As will be discussed later some sponsorship situations involve layers of interlinked contracts. A sponsored sports event, for example, may involve the sponsee appointing an agent, which is one contract. The agent may contract on behalf of the sponsee, which is a second contract. The sponsee may need to contract with the owners of the venue where the event is staged, which is a third contract. The athletes who will take

---

[41] But note *Junior Books* v. *The Veitchi Co.* [1982] 3 W.L.R. 477.

part in the event may need to contract with the sponsee, which is a fourth contract.

The concept of privity is perhaps best explained by an example. In one case a company which manufactured tobacco wished to prevent retailers from selling tobacco below a particular price. The manufacturers sold some packets of tobacco to the wholesaler and attached to each packet a notice stating that the tobacco was sold "upon the express condition that retail dealers do not sell the packet tobaccos or cigarettes below the prices above set forth." There was thus a contract between the manufacturer and the wholesaler. The wholesalers then sold the tobacco to a firm of retailers. No contract existed between the manufacturers and retailers. The manufacturers were unable to enforce the condition on resale price directly against the retailers.[42]

(4) PERFORMANCE AND BREACH

(a) *Performance*

The general rule is that performance must precisely match the respective obligations of the parties contained in the contract.[43] If the sponsee were to provide the sponsor with two tickets instead of five as expressed in the contract or three advertising boards rather than six then the sponsee has failed to discharge his contractual obligation. He is not therefore entitled to payment. This situation can lead to apparently unjust results. Thus where C. agreed to serve as mate on a voyage between Jamaica and Liverpool but died two thirds of the way through the voyage it was held that he was due no wages at all.[44]

The strict rule, however, is softened by a number of exceptions. The first is severance of the terms of a contract. Whether the obligations arising under the terms of the contract are severable depends upon the intention of the parties. The standard form agreement (long form) expressly makes the terms arising under that contract severable. A sponsor is unlikely, therefore, to be entitled to withhold payment on the basis that one of several promises and/or licences have not been fulfilled.

---

[42] *Taddy & Co.* v. *Sterious & Co.* [1903] 1 Ch. 354.
[43] *Paradine* v. *Jane* (1647) Aleyn 26.
[44] *Cutter* v. *Powell* (1795) 6 Term Rep. 320.

The second exception is where one party is prevented by the other from fulfilling his contractual obligations. In such circumstances the innocent party could bring an action for damages arising from breach of contract or sue for *quantum meruit* to obtain reasonable remuneration for the work done.

The third exception is that of substantial performance. This doctrine means that "so long as there is substantial performance the contractor is entitled to the stipulated price, subject only to a counterclaim for the omissions or defects in execution."[45]

The fourth exception is where the party who is entitled to strict performance of the contract agrees to accept partial performance. In these circumstances a new contract on the basis of the partial performance is substituted for the original.

The fifth exception arises under the doctrine of frustration. Frustration occurs where some major and unforeseen event intervenes after the contract has been entered into. For example, a government expropriates a company's interests in an oil field.[46] In such circumstances the contract effectively freezes at the point of the unforeseen event and the parties' obligations to each other are discharged as of that moment. The original application of the doctrine was in cases where, for example, a contract existed for the hire of "The Surrey Gardens and Music Hall" and the music hall was subsequently destroyed by fire,[47] or where "Cheerful Charlie Chester," a music hall artiste was called up for war service in 1940 and it was held that his contract with his agent was frustrated,[48] or where an artiste or performer dies.

The doctrine has, however, been applied to cover cases which may have a particular relevance to sponsorship, particularly insofar as cancellation of sponsored events are concerned. In one case, a room in the Pall Mall was hired for the day that a coronation procession was scheduled to take place. The contract of hire made no reference to the procession but it was understood to be in the minds of both parties. The procession was subsequently cancelled due to the King's illness and it was held that the contract was frustrated.[49] Where, however, there is more than one event

---

[45] Smith's Leading Cases (13th ed.) 19.
[46] *B.P. Exploration Co.(Libya) Ltd.* v. *Hunt (No. 2)* [1982] 2 W.L.R. 253, H.L.
[47] *Taylor* v. *Caldwell* (1863) 3 B. & S. 826.
[48] *Morgan* v. *Manser* [1948] 1 K.B. 184.
[49] *Krell* v. *Henry* [1903] 2 K.B. 740.

contemplated by the contract, then the situation may be different. Thus in another case a contract was entered into on the express terms that a boat was to take passengers "for the purpose of viewing the naval review and for a day's cruise round the fleet." The review was cancelled but the fleet was still there. It was held that the contract was not frustrated since the cancellation of the review had not affected the performance of the whole contract.[50]

Frustration will not apply, however, where one party is aware that an event is likely to occur. Thus where X gave a company the right to display an advertisement at X's hotel for seven years with the knowledge that the hotel was likely to be the subject of a compulsory purchase order, which it was, no frustration arose.[51] Where both parties are aware of the probability of an event intervening then there is argument as to whether the frustration can or cannot arise.[52]

Where the parties expressly provide what is to occur when an unforeseen event arises,[53] then that will exclude the operation of the cases outlined above. It is a matter of construction in each case to determine whether the clause setting out what is to happen covers the event which occurs.

The Law Reform (Frustrated Contracts) Act 1943 sets out the position of the parties in the event of frustration occurring, assuming, of course, that they have not provided for this in the contract. The effect of this Act is briefly as follows: money paid before the frustrating event can be recovered; money due before the frustrating event which has not been paid, ceases to become payable. Where money is either paid or due before the frustrating event then the expenses of either party may be awarded. A party who receives a valuable benefit under the contract before the frustrating event may be required to pay a just sum for it.

The long form contract also provides at paragraph 7 that no automatic right to terminate or withhold payment arises where either party fails to perform. Such a right only arises after notice has been served and the failure to perform has not been remedied within a certain number of days.

---

[50] *Herne Bay Steamboat Co.* v. *Hutton* [1903] 2 K.B. 683.
[51] *Walton Harvey Ltd.* v. *Walker & Homfrays Ltd.* [1931] 1 Ch. 145.
[52] See Treitel, *The Law of Contract* (6th ed., 1983).
[53] See the Long Form Contract, para. 9.

(b) *Breach*

Breach and performance are reverse sides of the same coin. Where a party fails to perform in accordance with the exact terms of a contract then he is said to be in breach. Where breach arises before the time due for the performance then it is said to be anticipatory. Thus if a company sponsored an individual who was to sing in a musical concert and before the concert took place the singer withdrew, then that is anticipatory breach. Anticipatory breach gives the innocent party the right to treat the contract as discharged[54] and to sue immediately for non-performance even before performance is actually due. He must be certain, however, that the other party is not going to perform.[55] Alternatively the innocent party may insist on performance. Thus where an order was received to place advertising plates on litter bins and before the plates could be made the order was cancelled, the innocent party nevertheless had the plates made, displayed them on the litter bins and recovered the price agreed for the full three year term of the contract. The only performance required in this case by the advertiser was payment.[56]

(5) REMEDIES FOR BREACH OF CONTRACT

There are a number of possible legal remedies which are available to the innocent party where a breach of contract occurs. The following example illustrates some of these: X sponsors a show jumping event and acquires four stadium advertising boards, the right to use the slogan "Official Sponsor" and use of the event logo on products. In return for this X is to pay a fee to Y of £10,000, half of which is due before the event and the balance afterwards. X receives the other rights but no stadium advertising boards at the event. X may sue Y for damages which will include the proportion of the total contract price represented by the advertising boards and perhaps promotional and advertising expenses which Y

---

[54] But note *Decro-Wall International S.A.* v. *Practitioners in Marketing* [1971] 1 W.L.R. 361, which involved slightly late payments of money due under a contract. Rescission was not available since damages were an adequate remedy.

[55] *Woodar Investment Development* v. *Wimpey Construction U.K.* [1980] 1 W.L.R. 277.

[56] *White and Carter (Councils)* v. *McGregor* [1962] A.C. 413.

knew X was to undertake on the basis that his boards were to be displayed. X may, if the advertising boards are a sufficiently important element of the contract, treat himself as discharged from further performance, *i.e.* paying the balance of the £5,000. Furthermore, and subject to the court's discretion, X could obtain an order for specific performance which would compel Y to erect the advertising boards or an injunction to prevent their removal by Y after they had been erected.

(a) *Damages*

The object of the court in awarding damages for breach of contract is to place the injured party in the same position as if the contract had actually been performed.

There are two matters to consider in any claim for damages. The first is whether the particular loss is recoverable and the second is how such loss is to be quantified. For a contractual loss to be recoverable it must be the result of the breach either in the sense that it is a natural consequence of it (*i.e.* it is presumed to be within the contemplation of the parties) or it is an unusual consequence which in the special circumstances of the case is foreseeable as a probable consequence of the breach.[57]

Quantifying a loss where a breach of a sponsorship contract has occurred is difficult where the sponsee is at fault since the sponsor's loss will consist of a number of different elements. It will be up to the sponsor to prove each of these elements. If his advertising boards were not displayed, for example, then the sponsor's loss may comprise: (i) the money already paid to the sponsee; (ii) an element representing the loss of profit which would have accrued on sales had the boards been displayed; and (iii) promotional and similar expenses thrown away on the basis that the boards were to be displayed, such as booking advertisements on television and contemporaneous advertising in the local press. If the sponsor is denied the opportunity of renewing the contract in accordance with the terms of an option, damages may be very difficult to assess.[57a] The fact that the potential damage may

---

[57] *Hadley* v. *Baxendale* (1854) 9 Exch. 341, 351 and *Koufos* v. *Czarnikow (C.)* [1969] 1 A.C. 350.

[57a] See, however, *Fraser* v. *Thames Television Ltd.* [1983] 2 W.L.R. 917 for a recent example of damages resulting from failure to honour an option.

seem somewhat speculative is no reason why, if the loss is proved, damages should not be awarded. In one case, heard in 1911, for example, an actress was offered the opportunity to attend an interview for a part in a play along with 49 other actresses. Subsequently and in breach of a contract the opportunity was denied to her. It was held that she was entitled to £100 damages.[58]

Where a breach of contract occurs and the injured party accepts the breach as discharging the contract he must take reasonable steps to mitigate his loss.[59] In a sponsorship situation this might involve cancelling promotional or other activities if this is possible.

(b) *Action in debt*

An action for an agreed sum is an action for a debt. If a sponsee erected stadium advertising boards, notwithstanding that the sponsor had failed to make any payment in accordance with the agreement, then the sponsee could sue for the sum due in debt. Neither remoteness nor mitigation would arise.[60]

(c) *Discharge through breach*

Where a term of a contract is broken then the right of the innocent party to treat the contract as if it had ended as from the date of such breach depends upon the relative importance of the term to the parties. It is common to define the most important terms of a contract as conditions and the less important terms as warranties. This distinction is not perfect but will suffice for purposes here. Broadly speaking, where the breach relates to a condition, the innocent party can treat the contract as discharged from that moment and sue for damages.[61] In other words the innocent party is not required to render further performance. Where the term which is breached is a warranty, the innocent party must continue to perform the contract but may bring an action for damages. Although it has become somewhat unfashionable to classify terms of a contract as conditions or warranties, the rationale

[58] *Chaplin* v. *Hicks* [1911] 2 K.B. 786, C.A.
[59] *Pilkington* v. *Wood* [1953] Ch. 770.
[60] *White and Carter (Councils)* v. *McGregor* [1962] A.C. 413.
[61] See *Bunge Corp.* v. *Tradex Export S.A.* [1981] 1 W.L.R. 711.

of such a distinction is still valid. The court must decide whether the innocent party to a breach of contract can be adequately compensated by damages or whether additionally he should be relied on to terminate the contract. The relative importance of the terms to the parties must obviously have some bearing upon this. Discharge through breach should be distinguished from rescission which arises in the case of mistake, misrepresentation and similar matters. Rescission is occasionally used to describe the innocent parties' right to terminate in the contract in the widest possible sense. The reader should therefore not be surprised to see rescission used in this wider sense.

(d) *Rescission*

Rescission in the narrow sense is only available in the case of misrepresentation, mistake, duress and incapacity. Where it applies, the parties are restored insofar as possible to their original positions as if no contract had ever existed.[62]

(e) *Specific performance*

Specific performance is a discretionary court order compelling someone to do something, *i.e.* perform an obligation contained in the contract. Damages may be awarded as well as, or instead of, specific performance. Specific performance is not available in a contract for personal services. Thus a sponsorship contract with a theatrical company for a particular performance could not be enforced by the sponsor against the theatrical company if that had the effect of compelling an individual to engage in the performance. Specific performance would also not be available to enforce a promise under seal without consideration. Where the sponsor wishes to enforce obligations which do not directly concern individuals these legal problems will not arise.

The application of specific performance to restrain athletes under contracts with particular clubs from moving has received considerable judicial examination in the United States.[63] The remedy has been applied there where the athlete is of unique ability, inadequate remedies are available at law and irreparable harm to the plaintiff will result from the

---

[62] See *Johnson* v. *Agnew* [1980] A.C. 367.
[63] See, for example (1981) 35 *Southwestern Law Journal* 803.

move. The solution in the United States seems a fair compromise although it is doubted that the same attitude would be taken by the English courts.

The message to the sponsor on the application of specific performance in the English courts is that it may not be used directly or indirectly to compel a particular performance involving an individual to take place.

(f) *Injunction*

An injunction is the reverse of specific performance, being an order from the court to restrain a party from breaking the contract. As a remedy this may have particular importance wherever exclusive rights are granted to the sponsor. Where exclusive rights are granted then the sponsor may be in a position to obtain an injunction restraining the sponsee from granting those rights elsewhere. The courts will not issue an injunction where its effect is indirectly to compel the performance of a personal service contract. Thus where a manager had an exclusive management contract with a rock band, the court refused to issue an injunction preventing the band from engaging another manager since that would mean they would have to employ the original manager.[64] In contrast, where there is no compulsion to employ a particular individual then an injunction may be issued. Where an actress had agreed only to work for a particular studio the court issued an injunction which restrained her from acting for third parties, the logic there being that she could engage in work other than as an actress, and that the injunction did not actually compel her to work for any particular studio. This seems a somewhat false distinction from the previous case.[65] Damages may be awarded in lieu of an injunction and the court will be reluctant to issue an injunction where damages are an adequate remedy.

(g) *Quasi contract*

The most likely application of a claim in quasi contract is where a total failure of consideration occurs. Thus one party may fail to perform any of his obligations under the contract.

---

[64] *Page One Records v. Britton* [1968] 1 W.L.R. 157.
[65] *Warner Brothers Pictures Inc. v. Nelson* [1937] 1 K.B. 209, and see also *Lumley v. Wagner* (1852) 1 De G.M. & G. 604.

In such circumstances, money paid may be recovered and money due may be retained without any obligation to pay.[66]

Another category of quasi contract is *quantum meruit*, which arises where the contract does not deal expressly with remuneration. In such circumstances, a claim for *quantum meruit* is a claim for reasonable remuneration.

(h) *Estoppel and acquiescence*

Estoppel arises where one party leads the other to suppose that the strict rights under the contract will not be enforced.[67] In these circumstances the party may be estopped from exercising his contractual rights.[68] Similarly where one party through acts of encouragement or acquiescence causes another to act to his or her detriment then the courts may protect the innocent party by preventing the other party from enforcing the strict terms of the contract. Estoppel and acquiescence are not remedies in the conventional sense since they are more akin to defences. However, they are important and can perhaps be regarded as remedies in a wide context.

(i) *Declaratory judgment*

A declaratory judgment is a statement given by the court in relation to the facts of a particular issue. The courts will not however act upon hypothetical questions.

(6) PROPER LAW AND SETTLING DISPUTES

It often falls to be determined in international contracts both where, how and under what law, disputes arising under the contract are to be resolved. Where these matters are not dealt with in the contract as they have been in the long form standard agreement, then it will be up to the court in a country where a claim is brought to determine whether it has jurisdiction to hear the matter. Situations can arise when English courts will have to apply foreign laws since that is the clear intention of the parties expressed in the contract.

Where the parties agree to settle their disputes by arbitra-

---

[66] *Esso Petroleum Co.* v. *Customs and Excise Commissioners* [1976] 1 W.L.R. 1, which involved a free World Cup coin.

[67] See *Hughes* v. *Metropolitan Railway Co.* (1877) 2 App. Cas. 439.

[68] See *Reel* v. *Holder* [1981] 1 W.L.R. 1226.

tion or in the courts or arbitration procedures of a foreign country, then any proceedings brought to resolve the dispute by other means may be stayed. Since many examples have arisen where the stay of proceedings on the basis of an arbitration or foreign jurisdiction clause has been employed as a tactic to avoid or delay proceedings, the language of such clauses tends to be construed restrictively by the courts. For example, a clause in which the parties agree to resolve all "disputes" by arbitration will only apply when a genuine dispute exists and not where there has been an admission of liability.

The secondary relationships

(1) LICENSOR AND LICENSEE

The sponsorship contract usually gives rise to a secondary relationship between the sponsee and sponsor which is one of licensor and licensee. A distinction has already been made between those rights which a sponsor may acquire such as stadium advertising boards at a venue, and those which exist as property in their own right and are licensed to the sponsor. The latter rights include mascots, logos, music, etc.

The relationship between the licensor and licensee, *i.e.* sponsee and sponsor respectively, will be governed by the express or implied terms of the contract.[69] There are a number of important aspects to watch insofar as licensing between the sponsee and sponsor is concerned, of which two are of particular importance. The first is defining the extent of the licence. The second is ensuring that the sponsor protects the ownership and goodwill attaching to the copyright, trade marks, etc., with which he has been licensed. The latter point may also apply the other way around when the sponsee is required to use the sponsor's company name which is also a registered trade mark.

(a) *Extent of licence*

This will be a matter of construction depending upon the terms of the contract. The long form standard agreement is

---

[69] Where no contract exists, the concept of resulting or express trust and fiduciary duties might be relevant since intellectual property can exist as trust property (*Ward, Lock & Co. Ltd.* v. *Long* [1906] 2 Ch. 550).

clear in that the licence only extends to using, for example, the mascots and symbols on or in connection with the promotion of company products or services. It would be beyond the terms of the licence to promote some third party's products. The importance of defining the extent of a licence has been shown in a recent case. An architect prepared plans for the purpose of obtaining planning permission on a building. He received a nominal fee for his work. The plans were used without the architect's consent to actually construct the building. It was held that since this went beyond the scope of the licence, the architect's copyright had been infringed and he was entitled to claim damages from the licensee.[70] Similarly a licence to produce a work in "moving picture film" has been held only to authorise a silent film.[71]

Where the sponsorship contract is entirely silent on the extent of the licence, the court would have to do its best to ascertain its limits from the intention of the parties.[72] The amount of money to be paid for the licence could be important in determining the intention of the parties. Since the identity of a sponsor is usually important to the sponsee, it is unlikely that the court would construe a license as conferring a right on the sponsor to sublicense.[73]

One of the dangers in failing to deal with the sponsor's licence by way of a written contract is that the sponsee may find that he has granted the sponsor an irrevocable licence.[74-76] Where the court finds the licence to be revocable, then in the absence of any express term, it will be revocable on reasonable notice[77] Where the sponsor gives no consideration for the grant of the licence by the sponsee then it will be a bare licence and revocable at will, reasonable notice not being required.

Occasionally the Copyright Act itself will assist in clarifying the extent of a licence. For example, where the B.B.C. is granted a licence to broadcast an event by television, the extent of the licence will automatically include transmission of the signal by cable. Since a secondary market has now

---

[70] *Stovin-Bradford* v. *Volpoint Properties* [1971] Ch. 1007, but contrast *Blair* v. *Osborne & Tomkins* [1971] 2 Q.B. 78.

[71] *Pathé Pictures* v. *Bancroft* Macg. Cop. Cas. (1928–35) 403.

[72] See *Redwood Music* v. *Francis Day & Hunter* [1980] 2 All E.R. 817, *supra*, where a licence was implied.

[73] See *Dorling* v. *Honner Marine* [1965] Ch. 1.

[74-76] See *Blair* v. *Osborne & Tomkins* [1971] 2 Q.B. 78.

[77] *Dorling* v. *Honner Marine* [1964] Ch. 560 at 567.

opened up, which offers the possibility for the B.B.C. or others to raise income from sales to cable networks, this may be important.[78]

(b) *Protecting property and goodwill*

The positions of licensee and licensor are not currently recognised as imposing any fiduciary or other especially onerous duties on the licensee at law. The duties will be those stated or implied in the licence agreement, *i.e.* the sponsorship contract.

Since the property of the sponsee, *i.e.* mascots, logos, titles, etc., is being licensed to the sponsor, it is important to ensure that the sponsor does nothing to prejudice the sponsee's title and rights in those properties. The sponsee might reasonably insist, for example, that his logo is only associated with a particular quality of goods. If it were used on inferior goods this might result in consumers shunning other goods bearing the sponsee's logo. Establishing quality control may also be fundamental to the success of a sponsee in a passing-off situation where merchandising rights are concerned.[79] It may also be important for the sponsor to use a particular form of copyright or trade mark notice to ensure that the sponsee's rights are maintained.

For these reasons it is suggested that the sponsor's licence should be subject to express terms which ensure that he is obliged to protect the sponsee's property.

(2) JOINT VENTURERS

The nature of the sponsorship relationship is one of barter. The sponsor provides money, goods or services in return for which he will receive various promises and licences. Each party retains their independence although a certain symbiosis exists between them. It seems most improbable therefore that any form of common or joint venture will exist in a normal sponsorship transaction.

In certain rare cases, however, the sponsor and sponsee may create, deliberately or unintentionally, a legally recognised relationship of joint venturers. Where this occurs intentionally a limited liability company might be incorporated, each party owning shares. An alternative to this is a

[78] See p. 241.
[79] See p. 185.

partnership. The existence of a partnership may be implied by law even though the partners, *i.e.* sponsor and sponsee deny that they ever intended to create such a relationship. There is no requirement that a partnership should be in or evidenced by writing although it usually is. In contrast the existence of a corporation through which the joint venture operates can never be implied since a corporation requires legal formalities to be undertaken before it can be brought into existence. If the joint venturers decide to associate themselves through a jointly owned company, a deliberate act will be required, *i.e.* incorporation. Management control, ownership and profit-sharing will be important matters to resolve between the sponsor and sponsee in any joint venture.

(a) *Partnership*

The definition of a partnership is contained in the Partnership Act 1890. This states that a partnership is "the relationship which subsists between persons carrying on a business in common with a view of profit."[80] Carrying on business with a view of profit is the key element to the definition, and business includes "every trade, occupation or profession."[81] An arrangement between the television personality David Frost and a shell company in Bermuda which procured engagements for Frost and exploited his services was found to be a partnership. The arrangement involved a division of the profits of the venture in the proportions of 95 per cent. to Frost and 5 per cent. to the company.[82]

The partnership in the *Frost* case was deliberately created. Its facts could well apply to a sponsorship situation. If, for example, a sponsee agreed with a sponsor that they would combine their resources to maximise income for a sponsored event and then share profits, a partnership may well exist. This situation should be distinguished, however, from that where the parties divide income but do not share the profits. Most personalities have managers who take a percentage of the artiste's income in return for rendering management services. This will not create a partnership since there is no sharing of profits. Where the sponsee appoints an agent to produce income for a sponsored event and the agent takes a

---

[80] Partnership Act 1890, s.1(1).
[81] *Ibid.* s.45.
[82] *Newstead* v. *Frost* [1980] 1 W.L.R. 135; [1980] S.T.C. 123 and see also p. 271 below, for tax implications.

percentage of income raised as a fee, that is not sharing profits so no partnership will normally exist.

A sponsee which is an incorporated entity is a "person" and is capable of being a partner within the terms of the Act.[83]

As already indicated, a partnership may exist where the definition of the Partnership Act 1890 is satisfied notwithstanding the intention of the parties. If the court decides that such a relationship exists *de facto* then even a written statement by the parties that no partnership exists may be ignored.[84]

(b) *Consequences of joint venture*

Where the parties are co-venturers in a particular project, potential fiscal and third party liabilities in contract, tort or breach of trust may result. Whilst it is beyond the scope of this book to explore such consequences in any depth, certain important features are worthy of brief comment.

If a partnership exists then each partner is an agent of the firm and essentially may enter into commitments or do certain acts without the knowledge of the other partners but which will nevertheless, render the other partners liable.[85] Thus one partner might order goods or make a fraudulent statement and the other partners may find themselves responsible. Liability of a partner is a personal liability for all debts and obligations properly incurred (except in the small exception for limited partnership). In the case of an individual or group of individuals such as a club who are deemed partners, this might even result in exposure of their personal assets such as cars or houses to meet partnership debts. If the co-venture is conducted through a limited liability company no personal liability will arise although directors may bind the company in much the same way as partners. The fiscal consequences may involve exposure to capital, income or corporation taxes which were not intended and also have an effect on the deductibility of expenses.

(3) AGENCY

The sponsor may act as agent for the sponsee and in certain cases, the sponsor. Where such a relationship exists and the

[83] Interpretation Act 1978.
[84] *Fenston* v. *Johnstone* (1940) 84 S.J. 305.
[85] See Partnership Act 1890, s.5.

agent acts within his authority then the principal will be bound by the agent's contracts.

An agency situation might arise as between the sponsor and sponsee where the sponsee allows the sponsor to call an event or object owned by the sponsee after the sponsor. A motor race called the Marlborough Grand Prix, for example, might mean that Marlborough could enter into an agreement with a third party in relation to the event which would bind the sponsee. In contrast where an event is said to be "brought to you by our sponsors" then no agency situation is likely to arise.

Agency is discussed separately in the next chapter.

(4) SELLER/TORTFEASOR

(a) *The sponsee and the sponsor's defective products*

Sponsorship is a marketing device used to promote products or services or enhance a corporate image. This is achieved through the association between the sponsor and sponsee, the intention being to create the link in the eyes of the public between the one and the other. Where there is a direct association, such as the sponsee's logo being used on the sponsor's products, then it might be asked whether, and to what extent, a dissatisfied consumer of the sponsors products or services may look to the sponsee for redress. It is not every consumer remedy which is examined here. It is only those that it is thought might be relevant in some way to the peculiarities of the sponsorship relationship. An example to illustrate the scope of this section might be the use of a logo of a football federation on a particular brand of soft drinks. If, for example, a decomposing snail were found in the can, could the consumer bring an action against the Football Federation?

To a certain extent the answers to such questions may seem academic since the consumer's primary remedy for defective products or services will lie against the manufacturer or other parties engaged in the design, distribution or sale of the products or services. As a legal theory, however, the potential liability of a sponsee may be important since there is always the possibility that the sponsor could become bankrupt.

(b) *Products liability: principles*

The law of defective products is an amalgam of the law of

contract and the law of tort.[86] The law of contract has already been discussed at length. The factors which are additionally relevant to contract here in connection with defective products are that certain terms are implied in contracts for the sale or transfer of goods or supply of services which give the consumer rights against their immediate contracting party, *e.g.* retailers. Defective products under the law of tort involves developments in negligence and a move towards making manufacturers and others who have control over the quality of their product or service liable to the consumer without proof of fault.[87]

(c) *Contract*

Since the contract for the sale to the public of any goods or services connected or promoted in conjunction with the sponsorship is likely to be between the sponsor or his retailer and the consumer, no liability will arise for the sponsee. He is not a party to the contract between the sponsor/retailer and the consumer. Thus even where the sponsor sells his products using a slogan such as "recommended by John McEnroe" no liability can be attached to McEnroe under contract for defective tennis racquets since he is not a party to the agreement.[88] In the exceptional case, however, where a sponsee agrees to sell the sponsor's goods or services at the site of, say, a sponsored tennis event, then he could be liable to the consumer. This liability has nothing to do with the sponsorship relationship as such but depends upon the sponsee undertaking the position of seller between himself and the consumer. In these rather unique circumstances the sponsee will be responsible to the consumer for a number of matters (ignoring any express terms) which will be implied into the contract of sale by the Supply of Goods (Implied Terms) Act 1973, Sale of Goods Act 1979 and the Supply of Goods and Services Act 1982. These matters include the implied condition that such goods are of "merchantable quality."[89]

---

[86] The dividing line between them has been blurred by the House of Lords' decision in *Junior Books Ltd.* v. *Veitchi* [1982] 3 W.L.R. 477.
[87] See also the Consumer Safety Act 1978.
[88] A collateral contract might exist in limited circumstances.
[89] Sale of Goods Act 1979, s.14(2).

(d) *Tort*

Negligence imposes a legal duty to "take care" in relation to products or the supply of services. In the case of *Donaghue* v. *Stevenson* the decomposing remains of a snail were discovered in a bottle of ginger beer after some of it had been consumed. The ginger beer had been purchased by a friend of the person who consumed it. No contract existed between the person who consumed the ginger beer and the person who supplied it. It was nevertheless held that she could sue the manufacturer.[90] Establishing negligence involves proving the existence of a duty of care owed to the plaintiff, which is broken with the result that injury to person or property is sustained.

Liability in negligence for defective goods extends not only to manufacturers who are directly concerned with production, but others in the chain of distribution. Indeed, liability may go behind the manufacturer to designers. The question in sponsorship situations is the extent of the sponsee's liability in negligence to the ultimate consumer where he is seen to be associated with or to endorse the sponsor's products. Liability for defective products exists only on proof of fault in the sense of a breach of a duty of care. Where a sportsman endorses a tennis racquet or permits his photograph to be used in its promotion, the law is unlikely to expect him to check the quality of every tennis racquet which is manufactured. That is the province of the manufacturer. It is suggested, however, that if he endorses a product without inspecting or testing it and fails to impose an obligation on the manufacturer to sell tennis racquets which are the same quality as the tested sample, then he might have been shown to be negligent.

In recent years the law has also developed liability for negligent statements. The extent of such liability is not easy to extract from the relevant cases. It might arise, however, where someone negligently gives a misleading credit reference,[91] or where a company specialising in investment advice negligently gives advice to a client which results in a financial loss,[92] or

[90] *Donoghue* v. *Stevenson* [1932] A.C. 562.
[91] See the facts of *Hedley Byrne & Co. Ltd.* v. *Heller & Partners Ltd.* [1964] A.C. 465.
[92] See the facts of *Mutual Life and Citizens' Assurance Co.* v. *Evatt* (*Clive Raleigh*) [1971] A.C. 793.

incorrectly estimates the throughput of a petrol station to a prospective tenant.[93] In these cases the parties have either been in a direct contractual relationship or otherwise in close proximity to each other. It would be a considerable extension to find a sponsee liable to an unknown consumer where he endorses a sponsor's products. An alternative remedy could be a claim for misrepresentation under the 1967 Act. Since the *Junior Books* v. *Vetchi* case[94] which held that physical damage was not a pre-requisite to a claim for economic loss, the scope of liability for negligent statements may have been extended.

One can only speculate, therefore, as to how the law might develop. Each case would have to be considered on its facts. It is submitted that if the following facts were present, liability might be established: an express and unequivocal statement or endorsement or guarantee or the use of any registered trade mark[95] in circumstances where the sponsee had made no attempt to examine the quality of the product or to ensure that the sponsor was obliged to maintain a reasonable standard of quality. Conversely, mere use of photographs, signatures, logos, etc., are unlikely to give rise to any liability on the part of the sponsee.

There is American authority on a broadly similar point but, it is submitted, this goes beyond the likely result under English law. In the American case the plaintiff slipped on a vinyl floor whilst wearing shoes marketed under the defendant's "Good Housekeeper Consumers' Guarantee Seal." In the judgment it was stated that "one who endorses a product for his own economic gain, and for the purpose of encouraging and inducing the public to buy it, may be liable to a purchaser who, relying on the endorsement, buys the product and is injured because it is defective and not as represented in the endorsement."[96]

Where the sponsee is not solely responsible for the commission of a tort then he might be regarded as a joint tortfeasor with the sponsor.

There are developments afoot in the EEC with its Draft Directive on Products Liability and the Strasbourg Convention to impose strict liability, *i.e.* liability without proof of

---

[93] See *Esso Petroleum Co.* v. *Mardon* [1976] Q.B. 801, and also *Howard Marine and Dredging Co.* v. *Ogden (A) & Sons (Excavations)* [1978] Q.B. 574.

[94] [1982] 3 W.L.R. 477.

[95] As a trade mark, see p. 151 *et seq.*

[96] *Hanberry* v. *Hearst Corp.* 81 Cal. Rptr. 519 at 521.

fault on the manufacturer of products. This approach is in line with the American "deep pocket" philosophy.

(5) VICARIOUS LIABILITY

The relationship between the sponsor and sponsee is not vicarious in the sense that the sponsee will be responsible for the sponsor's acts or vice versa. If, for example, a spectator were injured whilst attending a sponsored event, he could not bring an action or claim against the sponsor if the sponsee had been negligent. If the sponsor had himself been negligent then a direct action could be maintained. If both the sponsor and sponsee were negligent then they might be joint tortfeasors.[97]

(6) OCCUPIERS LIABILITY

In most circumstances the sponsee will remain responsible for organising a sponsored event and therefore will be the occupier for the purposes of the Occupiers Liability Act 1957.[98]

---

[97] Compare with the facts of *Payne & Payne* v. *Maple Leaf Gardens Ltd.* (1949) 1 D.L.R. 569 (Canada).

[98] But note that Lord Hailsham of St. Marylebone, the Lord Chancellor introduced in the House of Lords on June 23, 1983 the Occupiers' Liability Bill for amending the law relating to liability for leisure activity injuries.

5. The Agent

The practical roles of both the sport and arts agent have already been briefly discussed. Most sponsorship agents will be expressly appointed under the terms of a contract. An agency relationship may be found to exist in certain circumstances without any express appointment. For example, the principal may "hold" someone out as his agent and in such circumstances may be estopped from denying the agent's authority. In contracting with an agent, the sponsor is contracting with the principal, *i.e.* the sponsee. The agent's authority should be confirmed where any doubts exist. If the agent were to go bankrupt then the sponsor's rights against the principal would not be affected. Money paid to the agent under a sponsorship contract, provided the agent has or is held out as having authority to collect money, will be equivalent to payment to the principal, *i.e.* the sponsee. Thus if the agent were to become bankrupt after receipt from the sponsor but before passing money to the sponsee, then the sponsor would still have performed his part of the contract, even though the money was never received by the sponsee.

In most sponsorship relationships the agent will be appointed by the sponsee to seek potential sponsors and undertake specific responsibilities. The text of this chapter looks to such a situation although it is conceivable that the agent might be appointed by the sponsor to seek suitable projects for sponsorship. Disputes between sponsees and agents are likely to arise in two areas: first, where the sponsee claims that the agent has not performed under the contract,[1] and secondly, an action by the agent claiming commission. These two circumstances are followed through the text.

---

[1] In this case, an alternative agent is often ready to take over. Such alternative agents should always be aware of the dangers of interfering with contracts.

Performance by the agent

(1) PERFORMANCE ACCORDING TO THE TERMS OF THE CONTRACT

An agency contract, like other contracts, must be performed strictly in accordance with its terms. If, for example, the contract obliges the agent to sell shares when they reach 85, then that is what the agent must do. He cannot wait to see if they go higher.[2]

In each case the contractual terms provide the starting point of reference. Terms requiring performance by a sponsorship agent often include: preparation and negotiation of contracts by sponsors[2a]; giving advice on event management, television and trade marks; undertaking a merchandising programme; collecting monies; maintaining proper books of account. In each case the precise terms of the clause must be understood.

An agent is unlikely to commit himself to an unqualified obligation to procure sponsors. If he did and failed to achieve any, he would be in breach of contract. What is more likely is that he will undertake to use "his best endeavours to locate sponsors." The effect of "best endeavours" clauses has recently received judicial comment in the Court of Appeal.[3] Its meaning is that the covenantor should take all steps which a "prudent, determined and reasonable owner, acting in his own interests and desiring to achieve that result, would take."[4]

An agent who undertook to use his "best endeavours" and did nothing would be in breach of contract. An agent who prepared sales documents, fixed meetings and undertook presentations would not be in breach of contract even if his efforts failed to produce any sales. Between these two possibilities is a "no man's land." An agent who is appointed on a sole and exclusive basis will almost certainly be required to put greater effort into his activities than a non-exclusive agent. An exclusive agent may represent the only possibility of the sponsee raising income. Where no time limit is fixed in the contract for the performance of the agent's responsibility,

---

[2] *Bertram, Armstrong & Co.* v. *Godfray* (1830) 1 Knapp 381.
[2a] See, for example, *O'Sullivan* v. *Management Agency and Music Ltd.*, unreported.
[3] *I.B.M. United Kingdom* v. *Rockware Glass Ltd.* [1980] F.S.R. 335 at 343.
[4] *Per* Buckley L.J. at 343.

a term that he will carry out his services within a reasonable time will be implied.[5]

In limited circumstances the agent may be prepared to guarantee his performance financially. This is only likely to occur where the sponsorship project is particularly attractive. The usual form of guarantee is an undertaking to make up any shortfall between the minimum guaranteed income and the income raised. A commissioned agent, the most common type of agent in sponsorship contracts, already has an incentive to perform since he will earn his commission on income raised.

An agent acting under a financial guarantee will be a true agent. Occasionally the agent may "buy out" the sponsorship assets from the sponsee. The agent in such circumstances will not be an agent at all but a principal trading in sponsorship assets. He will act in a similar capacity to a broker or investor dealing with other forms of investment such as commodities. The specialist agent will have a good idea of the market and a "buy out" suits many sponsees since the risk capital has been put up by someone else. Where the agent takes on this trading role he is likely to insist upon a very specific contract with the sponsee.

Proving breach of contract through non-performance by the agent will, it is submitted, be an uphill struggle. The uphill struggle is made easier where the agent's responsibilities are clearly set out. Cases do exist in sole agency where the courts have found an unconscionable bargain where the agent has no express responsibilities at all.[6] In other cases it is the language of the contract which is important. The specific responsibilities undertaken by agents will be determined by commercial factors, the size of the project and the sophistication of the agency itself.

(2) STANDARD OF CARE IN PERFORMING DUTIES

The degree of skill to be exhibited by an agent will rarely be defined in the contract. The law has its own yardstick. The yardstick can be used to measure both the standard to be exercised by an agent who receives a fee or commission and one who offers his services without charge. Where the agent offers his services for reward he will be required to exercise

[5] Supply of Goods and Services Act 1982, s.14.
[6] *Davis (Clifford) Management* v. *W.E.A. Records* [1975] 1 W.L.R. 61.

sufficient skill, care and diligence as may be reasonably necessary for the performance of the duties undertaken.[7] The standard laid down in the Supply of Goods and Services Act 1982 is to carry out services with reasonable care and skill.[8] It is submitted that the duties of an agent imposed by common law may be stricter than under statute. The sufficiency of skill will be judged by the standard displayed by sports, arts or leisure agents respectively.

A less onerous duty is owed by agents who (presumably as a favour to someone) offer their services without charge. The duty owed by a paid agent is in contract. The duty owed by a gratuitous agent is in tort.[9] The effect of the Unfair Contract Terms Act 1977 may be important here, as gratuitous services would not, it is submitted, be caught by the Supply of Goods and Services Act 1982.

In identifying the scope of an agent's duty in a sponsorship situation a number of specific responsibilities emerge. Assuming price to be the only criterion for the appointment of a sponsor, the agent will be under a duty to sell the sponsorship assets at the best price obtainable.[10] The agent must use proper care to ensure that the contract is binding in law.[11] The agent will be under a duty to keep the sponsee informed about important developments such as entering into new contracts.[12] An agent might be under a duty to use reasonable care to make general enquiries as to the solvency of the sponsors.[13] Where the agent offers advice, in particular areas such as television, contracting and trade marks, then the agent must take reasonable care to ensure that such advice is accurate. If the agent does not have the expertise "in house" to answer such matters, then he must obtain professional advice in order to discharge his duties.[14]

It is important to understand that an agent may give bad advice or fail to produce sponsors but provided he has discharged his duties in accordance with the agreement no breach of contract will arise.

[7] See *Bowstead on Agency* (14th ed.), p. 115.
[8] Supply of Goods and Services Act 1982, s.13.
[9] *Bagot* v. *Stevens Scanlon & Co.* [1966] 1 Q.B. 197.
[10] See *Solomon* v. *Barker* (1862) 2 F. & F. 726, a brokers case.
[11] See *Grant* v. *Fletcher* (1826) 5 B. & C. 436.
[12] See *Johnson* v. *Kearly* [1908] 2 K.B. 514.
[13] See *Heys* v. *Tindall* (1861) 1 B. & S. 296.
[14] See *Sarginson Bros.* v. *Keith Moulton & Co.* (1942) 73 Ll.L.Rep. 104. See also liability for negligent statements, p. 78, *supra*.

(3) FIDUCIARY DUTIES

The proximity of the relationship between the principal, *i.e.* sponsee and the agent is such as to impose certain duties of loyalty and good faith on the agent. The common thread of these duties is that an agent should not profit out of any special knowledge acquired by virtue of his position or from property that belongs to the principal, *i.e.* the sponsee. Similar principles will be discussed later in relation to trustees. The duties of an agent and trustee are distinguishable. An agent may in certain circumstances, however, be a trustee.[14a] These circumstances usually concern dealings with principals' property. If the agent does owe duties as a trustee rather than as an agent, then certain advantages may exist for the principal since proprietary remedies such as "tracing" trust property will be available. Trust property would also be unavailable in normal circumstances to the agent's creditors on his bankruptcy.

The fiduciary duties of agents may be dealt with in a number of ways. They are illustrated through examples of cases decided on different facts. It is submitted, however, that the basic principle upheld in each case is that the agent should not be able to gain an advantage from special knowledge, or property belonging to the principal. The following are examples of specific instances of the general rule.

(a) *Bribes*

An agent must not accept any bribe.[15] Thus an agent who received 600 fully paid up shares in a company which was awarded a contract by the principal was in breach of his fiduciary duty.[16]

In the case of a bribe the principal may also have an action against the person offering the bribe. Thus an agent employed by Salford Corporation received a commission from the contractor on any orders received. It was held that the Council could recover the amount of the bribe from the contractor.[17] An agent who accepts a bribe will not be entitled

---

[14a] *Harmer* v. *Armstrong* (1934) 1 Ch. 65.
[15] Accepting a bribe will also be a criminal offence. (Prevention of Corruption Act 1906, s.1(1).
[16] *McKays Case* (1875) 2 Ch. D. 1.
[17] *Salford Corp.* v. *Lever* [1891] 1 Q.B. 168.

to any commission or remuneration that he would otherwise have been entitled to from the principal.[18] The principal may dismiss an agent who accepts a bribe subject to any special provisions of the agency contract.[19] The dividing line between a bribe and a gift can be a narrow one.

(b) *Secret profits*

An agent must not use his position to make a secret profit for himself. A sports agent could not, for example, declare to the sponsee that he had sold a sponsorship opportunity for £100 if he had sold it for £250.[20] Nor could he retain the interest from investing funds which he held on behalf of clients.[21] The secret profit must accrue from the agency relationship with the particular principal. The principal could not expect the agent to account for profits made by the agent applying a particular sponsorship concept developed for the principal to other situations.[22] If the concept were protectable as a category of intellectual property then the situation would be different.[23] In one case an order was made after an agent had ceased to occupy that position, that he should deliver up customer lists which he had prepared during his employment as agent.[24]

(c) *Conflict of interest*

An agent will be in breach of his fiduciary duty if he acts in circumstances where a conflict of interests arises. Thus an agent employed to sell sponsorship assets cannot buy them himself.[25] In one case an agent bought the principal's ship for £90,000 and resold it almost immediately for £160,000. The agent was obliged to account for the profit.[26] Similarly an

---

[18] *Andrews* v. *Ramsay & Co.* [1903] 2 K.B. 635. See also *Mahesan S/O Thambiah* v. *Malaysia Government Officers' Co-operative Housing Society* [1979] A.C. 374.

[19] *Boston Deep Sea Fishing and Ice Co.* v. *Ansell* (1888) 39 Ch. D. 339.

[20] *The Converse of Fewtress* v. *Austin* (1816) 2 Marsh 217.

[21] See *Brown* v. *I.R.C.* [1965] A.C. 244.

[22] See *Lister & Co.* v. *Stubbs* (1890) 45 Ch.D.1.

[23] *Peter Pan Manufacturing Corporation* v. *Corsets Silhouette* [1964] 1 W.L.R. 96.

[24] *Measures Bros.* v. *Measures* [1910] 2 Ch. 248.

[25] See *Lowther* v. *Lowther* (1806) 13 Ves 95.

[26] *De Bussche* v. *Alt* (1878) 8 Ch.D. 286.

agent may not sell his own property to the principal.[27] Where, however, the agent makes a full disclosure of his interest then he will not be in breach of his duty. Thus an agent cannot act and receive a commission from both parties to a transaction unless this has been fully disclosed to both of them.[28]

(d) *Duty to keep accounts*

An agent is under a general duty to keep proper books of account, recording dealings with the client's property. Such accounts should distinguish the principal's money from that of the agent and third parties.[29] Such accounts should be available to the principal or his agent on reasonable notice.

(e) *Disclosure to principal*

Where the agent makes full disclosure to the principal of any secret profit, bribes, etc., and the principal confirms that the agent may retain them, this will amount to a waiver of the breach of a fiduciary duty.[30]

(4) REMEDIES AVAILABLE TO THE PRINCIPAL

Potential claims may be available to the principal for: breach of contract, tort, deceit and an action of account. The later remedy, as its name suggests, is an action based upon the production of an account regarding a particular transaction or series of transactions. All relevant information must be included such as deductions for disbursements, etc. The action will reveal the unauthorised profit made by the agent which will belong to the principal. It is important to know whether the agent's expenses may be deducted in calculating profit.

The majority of sponsorship agents will operate on the commission basis, that is, they will earn their fee on income accruing to the sponsee from sponsors introduced. If the agent fails to introduce a sponsor who concludes a contract, then the agent earns no commission. Thus he will not be able to recover his expenses or to claim the time and effort which

---

[27] *Re Cape Breton Co.* (1885) 29 Ch.D. 795.
[28] *Fallwood* v. *Horley* [1928] 1 K. B. 498.
[29] *Gray* v. *Haig* (1855) Beav 219.
[30] *Cane* v. *Allen* (1814) 2 Dow. 289.

the agent has put into the project. This understanding of the commission structure is reflected in the decisions of the court. The same principles, it is submitted, will apply to commissioned sponsorship agents as to estate agents and brokers, etc. In each case the starting point is, what are the express or implied terms of the contract. Where an agent operates on a fee rather than commission basis then he will be entitled to his fee unless it is conditional upon actual performance, *i.e.* introducing a sponsor.

(5) COMMISSIONED AGENTS

(a) *At what stage is the agent entitled to commission?*

This will depend upon the precise language of the contract but very clear and unambiguous words must be used if commission is to be payable without a sale.[31] Thus if the agency contract were to say "The agent is entitled to 30 per cent. commission on contracts signed by the sponsee with sponsors who have been introduced by the agent," commission will only become due once the contract is signed. If after signature the sponsor was unable to make payment then the agent should still be entitled to his commission on the full contractual sum. He has performed all that is required of him under the contract.[32] Conversely, if the agent were entitled to "30 per cent. commission on all income received by X" then commission would only be earned on income received. If the sponsor could not pay, the agent would be entitled to nothing. The clear intention of most parties to a sponsorship contract will be "commission on income," thus care should be taken to ensure that this is accurately expressed.

As has already been seen,[33] additional services may be provided by the sponsorship agent such as advice on television or merchandising trade marks, etc. In the absence of any clear provision in the contract dealing with payment, an agent is unlikely to be entitled to remuneration for these services either on the basis of an implied term or *quantum meruit*.[34] The likely construction which the court will place

---

[31] See *Luxor (Eastbourne)* v. *Cooper* [1941] A.C. 108 at 129.
[32] See *Bowstead on Agency* (14th ed.), p. 173 and *Midgley Estates* v. *Hand* [1952] 2 Q. B. 432.
[33] See p. 23.
[34] See p. 91 and note the Supply of Goods and Services Act 1982.

on such services is that they are to be included in the commission fee. It is sensible to incorporate within the agent's contract a professional services "charging" clause. Under such a clause, fees incurred by agents who engage the services of specialists such as trade mark attorneys and solicitors will be recoverable from the sponsee, *i.e.* principal.[35]

(i) *Is the agent the effective cause of the sponsorship contract?* Again, it will be a matter of construction to determine whether the agent is entitled to commission on any sponsorship income that materialises or only on that proximately caused by his effort. A clause in the agent's agreement stating that "the agent shall be entitled to 30 per cent. of all sponsorship income from the Festival of Arts, Music and Dance" means that the agent is entitled to 30 per cent. of all income and not just income that he produces. In contrast, if the contract stated that the "agent shall be entitled to 30 per cent. of income received by X from sponsors which the agent introduces" then commission will only be earned on sponsors introduced.

No general test of causation is relevant since all will depend upon the language. Clear language must be used, however, if the parties intend the agent to benefit where he is not the effective cause of the transaction. Effective cause in this context does not mean that the agent has to complete or even take part in the negotiations, or arrange any meetings or persuade either party to enter into the contract.[36] In one case the owner of a shop P, employed an agent A, to locate a tenant. A telephoned a prospective tenant, and X, having overheard the telephone conversation with the prospective tenant, inquired as to the address. The prospective tenant said it was "in Victoria." This was an incomplete address but eventually X found the premises. It was held that A was not entitled to commission from P when X became a tenant since X had located the premises himself.[37]

(ii) *What happens if the principal prevents the agent from earning his commission?* If the agency contract contains an express term that the "principal undertakes not to conduct or unreasonably arrange his affairs so as to deprive the agent of

---

[35] *Boots* v. *Elylane Ltd.* (1959) E. G. D. 212.
[36] See *Bowstead on Agency* (14th ed.), p. 185.
[37] *Coles* v. *Enock* [1939] 3 All E.R. 327.

commission" then the agent may have a claim against the sponsee, *i.e.* principal, for breach of contract should the principal interfere with the agent's task. The claim might arise where the principal declines to enter into the agreement after encouraging the agent to pursue it. It is important to ensure that the sponsee and agent have a clear understanding of the criteria for acceptance. Can the sponsee turn a sponsor down arbitrarily or only in particular circumstances? If so, these circumstances should be spelt out. The use of the term "sole" or "exclusive" will prevent the principal instructing another agent but will not of itself prevent the principal dealing directly.[38] If another agent is instructed then both the principal and second agent may be responsible to the first agent, the former for breach of contract and the latter for inducing breach of contract.[39]

Where no express term exists then the ability of the agent to succeed in a claim against the principal for preventing him earning commission will depend upon the court finding an implied term to that effect. A term is likely to be implied in very limited circumstances indeed. Where it is implied it will be on the basis of the presumed intention of the parties.[40] or to make the agreement commercially operative. On this basis a term may be implied that the principal will co-operate with the agent where such co-operation is essential to the performance of the agent's duties.

Termination may deprive the agent of commission. If the termination is not in accordance with the terms of the contract then the agent may claim breach of contract. If a sponsorship agent were appointed purely on a non-exclusive basis and he was rewarded by commission and he was not obliged to perform any services then the agreement would, it is submitted, be terminated without notice.[41] Certain agent's contracts provide for the payment of commissions after termination.

(6) NON-COMMISSIONED AGENTS

An agent may undertake to locate sponsors for a specific fee, *i.e.* at an hourly rate. His fee, unless it is conditional upon

[38] *Milson* v. *Beckstein* (1898) 14 T. L. R. 159.
[39] See *Keegan* v. *Private Eye Enterprises Ltd.*, unreported. Referred to in *The Times* and the *Yorkshire Post*, October 28, 1982.
[40] See *Luxor (Eastbourne)* v. *Cooper* [1941] A.C. 108.
[41] *Nelson (E. P.) & Co.* v. *Rolfe* [1950] K. B. 139, an estate agent's case.

securing sponsors, will be recoverable irrespective of his success in locating sponsors.

Expenses and indemnity

Most sponsorship agents recoup their expenses from their commission. Where this is not stated or implied from the language of the contract then the agent is nevertheless entitled to be reimbursed (including set off) for all legitimate expenses and to be indemnified against all losses and liabilities incurred by him in the execution of his duty.[42] This presumes that the agent is acting within his authority and has not contributed to the loss through some act or default on his part or engaged in an illegal transaction. It might apply to the situation where the agent incurs expenses on the authority of the principal in the defence of the principal's trade marks or copyright.[43]

The language of most sponsorship agents contracts will make it clear that expenses merge with commission. Where this is not the case it would be sensible to include a specific clause in the contract.

[42] See *Bowstead on Agency* (14th ed.), p. 201 and contrast p. 88, *supra, re* commission.
[43] See *Pettman* v. *Keble* (1830) 9. C.B. 701.

6. The Vesting and Delivery of Sponsorship Rights

Sponsorship frequently involves a series of interwoven contracts. An international sports federation for example will often delegate responsibility for holding a sponsored event to its domestic federation.[1] In return for this the domestic federation will receive a share of sponsorship income. The relationship between the international federation and the domestic federation will be contractual. The terms of the contract will either be included in a specific agreement in relation to the event or in the membership or competition rules. The membership rules are themselves a contract between each constituent member and the federation. The rules of the competition may also give rise to a contract between each of the members themselves.[2]

The sponsee in any sponsorship relationship must have authority to sell the sponsorship rights *i.e.* be the rights owner and ensure that the sponsor receives what has been contracted. For example, the International Tennis Federation is responsible for holding the Davis Cup tennis competition. The competition takes place at various locations around the world. Each domestic tennis federation will be responsible for hosting a Davis Cup tie. Where the I.T.F. contracts with the sponsor, certain rights included in that contract will involve use of facilities and display of advertising boards at the venue which may be owned by its domestic federation or others. The I.T.F will need to acquire these rights from its domestic federation to place itself in the position of being the rights owner. The I.T.F. will also need to impose an obligation on the domestic federation once rights are sold to display the particular sponsor's boards. Both aspects should be covered

[1] See p. 20.
[2] See *Clarke* v. *Dunraven* (1897) A.C.59.

by a contract and the terms of that contract may either be contained in a specific agreement between the I.T.F. and the domestic federation in the rules of the Davis Cup tennis competition, or in the general rules of membership of the I.T.F.

A similar situation might arise in the case of a sponsored theatrical production. The theatrical company which negotiates the agreement might need to acquire rights from the venue owner, such as the right to display sponsor banners. It will then need to ensure that the venue owner actually displays the banners in question. In contrast, with sports, such matters will usually be covered by a separate contract rather than incorporated within the competition or membership rules.

The I.A.A.F. has dealt with delivery required by athletes in Rule 17(c)(*iii*) of its 1983/4 handbook. This rule requires that a domestic federation enters into a contract with an athlete who is to benefit from a sponsorship contract setting out the athlete's obligations to the domestic federation which, in turn, have been promised to the sponsor.

There are a number of important matters for the sponsee to consider when it is necessary to contract with other parties for the delivery of rights to the sponsor. Certain of these matters may also be relevant to the contract between the sponsor and sponsee.

Incorporating obligations in rules of a sponsored competition

Rules made by any unincorporated association must be in accordance with its constitution. If power has been delegated to a committee to make rules then rules which are not made in accordance with this procedure will be invalid.[3] Careful drafting is necessary when drawing up rules for a sponsored competition which impose obligations on others. This is particularly true when it is attempted to incorporate the rules of the competition with the contract for membership of the association. The rights and duties of members insofar as the normal operation of the association is concerned should be kept separate from obligations imposed on such members by the rules of a sponsored competition. It would be inappropriate, and is undoubtedly a sensitive issue, for the sponsee to

---

[3] *Young* v. *Ladies Imperial Club Ltd.* [1920] 2 K.B. 523.

concede control of matters of administration, discipline and general policy or rules of a game to the sponsor, either through the sponsorship contract, or the rules of any sponsored competition. The consequences of failure to comply with the rules should be clearly thought out, *i.e.* is some form of liquidated financial penalty to apply? Is expulsion from the sponsored competition possible for breach of the rules? The obligation of the sponsee to refund money to the sponsor if rights are not delivered will need to be taken into account insofar as the sponsee might need some form of indemnity. Such indemnity might arise where, for example, a sponsee such as the I.T.F. needs to reserve rights which it acquires from its domestic federation, which will receive some or all of the sponsorship funds. There are a number of occasions in which the courts have assisted with the interpretation of rules. In one case rules of a club were made to be enforceable as contracts not only between the members and the club but also between the individual members themselves.[4] Lord Herschell stated "I cannot entertain any doubt that there was a contractual relation between the parties. . . . The effect of their entering for the race, and undertaking to be bound by these rules to the knowledge of each other, is sufficient, I think, . . . to create a contractual obligation. . . . "

It is impossible to exclude review by the courts of such rules insofar as matters of law are concerned. Interpretation of a particular term is always a question of law and therefore any of the rules, *i.e.* terms of the contract, may be reviewed by the courts. Any term purporting to exclude such review will be void on the grounds of public policy.[5]

Where the sponsee is concerned that a particular clause should have a very specific meaning then it should be defined precisely. In matters of interpretation of rules, the United Kingdom courts will not concern themselves with political issues which may be the background to someone trying to renege on a contract. Where the United Kingdom courts do become involved they will confine themselves strictly to the meaning of the words in English.[6] Rules which involve

---

[4] *Clarke* v. *Dunraven* (1897) A.C. 59 at 63.

[5] *Scott* v. *Avery* (1856) 5 H.L.Cas 811 and *Baker* v. *Jones* [1954] 1 W.L.R. 1005. See also *Law* v. *National Greyhound Racing Club Ltd.*, [1983] 3 All E.R. (No judicial review of decision of domestic tribunals.)

[6] See Lord Denning's comments on *Sten Fu Chang* v. *Stellan Mohlin* at 1230, referred to in the case of *Reel* v. *Holder* [1981] 1 W.L.R. 1226.

disciplinary procedures will be interpreted as, implying the right of legal representation at a hearing.[7] An example might be where an athlete could be fined or expelled if he fails to wear kit supplied by the sponsor. Where the rules specifically exclude legal representation, however, then such language may prevail.[8]

Where a contract of employment exists for a professional sportsman then the terms of the Employment Protection Act 1975 (as amended) will apply. Disciplinary procedures relating to employment issues should be dealt with in accordance with the provisions of the Act.

Contracts which may be against public policy

Contracts which are contrary to public policy are those which the courts refuse to enforce on the basis that they are against the public interest. Thus a contract to commit a crime is illegal. Certain other contracts which are contrary to public policy are not illegal but void. Three have particular relevance to sponsorship and the relationship between the sponsee and its associated bodies.

(1) CONTRACTS PURPORTING TO OUST THE COURTS' JURISDICTION

These contracts have already been discussed.[9] It is not possible to exclude the court from deciding questions of law although it is possible to exclude courts from reviewing questions of fact by agreement. Before the case of *Eastham* v. *Newcastle United Football Club*,[10] the Football Association (F.A) rules purported to inhibit players from seeking redress in the courts unless they had obtained the prior approval of the F.A. The point was never taken in the *Eastham* case. If it had been argued, this "ouster" provision would, in the authors' view, have been rejected.

(2) CONTRACTS IN RESTRAINT OF TRADE

A contract in restraint of trade is one in which the courts consider a party is unreasonably restricted from earning his

---

[7] *Pett* v. *Greyhound Racing Association (No. 1)* [1969] 1 Q.B. 125.
[8] *Enderby Town Football Club Ltd.* v. *Football Association* [1971] Ch.591.
[9] See p. 94.
[10] [1964] Ch.413.

future living. Examples include a retrospective ban by the Test and County Cricket Board (T.C.C.B.) on players who had joined the "Packer Circus" from playing English county cricket,[11] or a football transfer system preventing an individual from seeking employment elsewhere after his contract expires.[12]

For a particular term in a contract to be in restraint of trade the term must be excessively restrictive. If it is found to be so then it will be void unless its inclusion can be justified on the grounds of reasonableness.[13] In the Packer case it was argued that the restraint was reasonable because if it were not imposed, there would be a serious threat to the continued existence of cricket organised by the International Cricket Conference (I.C.C.), *i.e.* the recognised governing body of first class cricket at international level. Since, however, the ban had been retrospective, *i.e.* introduced after the players had already signed their contract with Packer's World Series Cricket, it was found not to be reasonable and restraint of trade was established.

It was indicated in the judgment of the Packer case that the interests of the I.C.C. and T.C.C.B. which they were entitled to protect through a "reasonable restraint" were not confined to financial interests. The sanctioned body, *i.e.* the I.C.C. was the "custodian of the public interest" which requires that the game should be properly organised and administered.[14] It should therefore make no difference whether a sport is amateur or professional in imposing reasonable restraints relating to how it is to be organised. It was assumed in a New Zealand case that this is a correct statement.[15] The T.C.C.B. subsequently used Slade J.'s argument, in what were arguably debatable circumstances, to justify a three year test match ban on leading players, who did not break national laws or rules governing cricket administration when they toured South Africa.[15a]

In alleging restraint of trade it is not necessary that those affected by the ban are in a direct contractual relationship

[11] *Greig* v. *Insole* [1978] 1 W.L.R. 302.
[12] *Eastham* v. *Newcastle United Football Club* [1964] Ch. 413, applied by the Australian High Court in *Buckley* v. *Tuthy* 125 C.L.R. 383.
[13] *Esso Petroleum Co.* v. *Harper's Garage (Stourport)* [1968] A.C. 269.
[14] *Greig* v. *Insole* [1978] 1 W.L.R. 302, Slade J. at 345.
[15] *North P. Blacker* v. *New Zealand Rugby Football League (Incorporated)* [1968] N.R.L.R. 547 at 566.
[15a] Referred to in the *Daily Telegraph*, March 19, 1982.

with the sponsee. It was sufficient for the purposes of the Packer case that the players' livelihood was potentially affected by the T.C.C.B. decision, even though they did not have a contract at that time, with the T.C.C.B. Where there is no livelihood to protect then sufficient trading interest will not exist for the courts intervention.[16] The question of whether Packer himself, through his company World Series Cricket rather than the players, could allege restraint of trade was not taken, but it must be doubted whether it could.[17]

It has been suggested[18] that anyone who has "some proprietary or other legitimate interest"[19] to protect should be in a position to bring an action. This is in line with the principle underlying the development of the English High Court procedural applications for judicial review. These require "a sufficient interest in the matter to which the application relates."[20]

Certain restraints in contracts between sponsees and its members or other parties may be in restraint of trade. To speculate on possible examples is difficult. A new rule introduced by the I.C.C. or T.C.C.B. in the Packer case restricting players from engaging in sponsored competitions might not be restrictive. The I.C.C. and the T.C.C.B. would need to be satisfied and prove to the court, if necessary, that such a restriction was not unreasonable. For sponsorship parties an important part of the decision in the Packer case was that the I.C.C. and T.C.C.B. rule was introduced retrospectively. Furthermore, Slade J.[21] also emphasised and may therefore have been influenced by the broad principle of public policy when he cited the "right to work" established by the court of appeal in the case of *Nagle* v. *Feilden*.[22]

A rule of a competition which required a professional tennis player to play in kit provided by the sponsor would probably not be in restraint of trade. The player's livelihood is hardly likely to be affected by such a condition. He can

[16] *R.* v. *The British Basketball Association*; *ex p. Mickan and Cheesman*, March 17, 1981. (C.A.T. No. 0116.)

[17] See *Boulting* v. *Association of Cinematograph, Television and Allied Technicians* [1963] 2 Q.B. 606 for the scope of declaration.

[18] Cheshire and Fifoot, *Law of Contract* (10th ed.) p. 359.

[19] But note *R.C.A. Corporation and R.C.A. Ltd.* v. *Pollard* (1983) 9 F.S.R. 9.

[20] Supreme Court Act 1981, s.31.

[21] Per Slade J. in *Greig* v. *Insole* [1978] 1 W.L.R. 302 at 362. See also *Law* v. *National Greyhound Racing Club Ltd.*, *The Times*, August 17, 1983.

[22] [1966] 2 Q.B. 633.

always play in other tournaments. A condition imposed between a league and a club which prevented the club entering into sponsorship agreements itself in view of potential league sponsors might be an unreasonable restraint.

(3) THE RIGHT TO WORK

It may be against public policy to apply rules of eligibility or status in an arbitrary way so as to deprive a person of the right to work. In one case, a female trainer was continually refused a trainers licence from the Jockey Club. The court established that the reason for the refusal was that she was a woman. The rules of the Jockey Club gave the stewards an unfettered monopoly and discretion to grant or refuse licences for trainers. The court held that it would be against public policy to administer the rule in such a way as to deprive women from obtaining a trainer's licence.[23] Lord Denning M.R. carefully distinguished this type of case where the exercise of the discretion could affect someone's livelihood from the case of normal membership of a club or society.[24] The Jockey Club ruling was based upon the monopoly which it had established regarding the grant of licences to work. It is important to note that no contractual relationship existed between the Jockey Club and Mrs Florence Nagle, and it was not a case of restricting Mrs Nagle from earning a living through the application of a contractual term. The case was fought and reported on the procedural preliminaries to a civil action. As a result of the Court of Appeal's ruling the Jockey Club surrendered to Mrs Nagle's attack. Today, not only do ladies train and ride under Jockey Club licences to work, they have also been elected with full contractual rights to membership of the Jockey Club.

Unlawful interference with contract/trade

Since sponsorship often involves a chain of interlinking contracts, the application of the tort of unlawful interference with contract or trade may be relevant. An action may exist here against a party who deliberately interferes with the performance of a contract. In *Lumley* v. *Gye*,[25] for example, a singer was under contract to perform at one theatre. With

---

[23] *Nagle* v. *Feilden* [1966] 2 Q.B. 633.
[24] *Ibid.* at 644.
[25] (1853) 2 E. & B.216.

knowledge of this contract the owner of another theatre induced the singer to perform at his theatre instead. Where an agent is employed and the sponsee signs direct with sponsor A in contravention of an undertaking given to a previous sponsor B the sponsor A and the sponsee may be liable under this tort.[26]

A declaration was made against the I.C.C. and T.C.C.B. in the Packer case. The basis of the declaration was that the I.C.C. and T.C.C.B. had induced Greig and the others to break their contracts with Packer, *i.e.* the World Series Cricket. The judgment contains an admirably clear statement of the law on such matters.[27] The elements required to establish the existence of the tort are as follows.

(1) INTERFERENCE

Interference in the Packer case was evident. The T.C.C.B. ban against players who had signed with World Series Cricket was clearly an inducement for the players concerned to break their contracts. The position of the I.C.C. was much the same since its purported change of rules would have given it the discretion to exclude certain players from its competitions. It is obvious which players would have been excluded. If the ban had been introduced before the players signed their contracts with World Series Cricket then the action could not have been established. The interference need not result in actual breach of contract to be actionable.[28]

It is suggested that indirect interference will only be actionable where the interference is accomplished by some underhand or unlawful means.[28] The law is still developing in this area. A year after the Packer case, the B.B.C. persuaded the Court of Appeal to overrule the decision of a lower court and thereby prevent industrial action interfering with the overseas television transmissions of the F.A. Cup Final.[29]

---

[26] See *Keegan* v. *Private Eye Enterprises Ltd.*, unreported, but see *The Times* and the *Yorkshire Post*, October 28, 1982.

[27] See Slade J. in *Greig* v. *Insole* [1978] 1 W.L.R. 302 at 332.

[28] *Per* Lord Denning M.R. in *Torquay Hotel Co. Ltd.* v. *Cousins* [1969] 2 Ch. 106 at 138. See also *Merkur Island Shipping Corp.* v. *Laughton* [1983] 2 W.L.R. 778 where even though a breach occurred, no damages became payable since the parties' non performance was excused by a *force majeure* clause.

[29] *B.B.C.* v. *Hearn* [1977] 1 W.L.R. 1004. See also the judgment of Slade J. in the Packer case, for the abortive attempt of the T.C.C.B. to justify their interference by relying upon the Employment Protection Act 1975.

(2) MOTIVES/KNOWLEDGE

Except perhaps in the case of indirect interference mentioned above motives are not relevant to the commissioning of this tort. It is important, however, that the interference takes place with knowledge of the existence of a contract between the parties.[30]

(3) DAMAGE

The party alleging the interference with the contract must normally show that he is likely to suffer more than nominal damage. In the Packer case, had the I.C.C. and the T.C.C.B. successfully prevented the players from performing their contracts with World Series Cricket, the financial loss could have been considerable. Similarly in a recent House of Lords' case[30a] the actions of tug-men and lock-keepers which resulted in a ship being unable to commence its voyage could have resulted in considerable financial loss for the owner.

Interference with contract may apply to sponsorship in a number of ways. In one advertising case, for example, a manufacturer of tyres entered into an agreement with the manufacturer of motor cars. The agreement involved an undertaking by the car manufacturer to only use "Bal-lon-ette" tyres on his cars at exhibitions. With knowledge of this contract, Dunlop removed "Bal-lon-ette" tyres from a car causing the car manufacturer to be in breach of his contract with the tyre manufacturer. This was held to be interference with the contractual rights. The action was brought by both the tyre manufacturer and car maker.[31]

The sponsee, sponsor, venue owner, athlete and performer are applied by its members to the "Athletes' fund," as set out knowingly induce a breach of contract.

Amateur sportspersons

Amateur status is determined by the rules of each controlling federation or similar body and will not necessarily affect sponsorship. Usually amateur status will be lost where the athlete is proved to have directly received sponsorship

---

[30] *British Industrial Plastics Ltd.* v. *Ferguson* [1940] 1 All E.R. 479.
[30a] *Merkur Island Shipping Corp.* v. *Laughton* [1983] 2 W.L.R. 778.
[31] *G.W.K. Ltd.* v. *Dunlop Rubber Co. Ltd.* (1926) 42 T.L.R. 376.

funds. The rules for each sport will require careful reading to determine exactly what is permitted. Two devices generally appear suitable to maintain the status of an amateur where sponsorship is involved. These are the concept of a trust and moneys paid in escrow.

(1) TRUSTS

In September 1982 the International Amateur Athletic Federation (I.A.A.F.) decided to permit national federations to conclude sponsorship arrangements on behalf of amateur athletes. Athletics is one example of many amateur sports.[32] The proviso, however, was that to preserve amateur status athletes could only benefit from sponsorship monies to a limited extent. Beyond certain specified costs and expenses the balance of sponsorship funds accruing to an identifiable athlete were to be held in trust for that athlete. The balance comprised the sum left after deduction of the National Federation's commission and legitimate expenses. The specific rule (52 viii) in the I.A.A.F. 1983/4 Handbook states:—

> "The following persons are ineligible to take part in competitions under I.A.A.F. rules. . . . Any person who (viii) allows his name, picture or athletic performance to be used for advertising, except when this is connected with a contract of sponsorship or equipment entered into by his national governing body and any resulting payment or benefit goes to the national governing body. The national governing body after deducting any percentage considered appropriate, can pay the remaining part of such sponsorship payment or benefit to an athlete's fund."

Since athletes funds are essentially a device using a trust to preserve amateur status, sponsorship moneys invested in the fund become payable to the athlete, who is the beneficiary of the trust, when he or she ceases to be an amateur. This might arise on his or her retirement from competition. Where the athlete dies before the requirement stipulated, then his or her entitlement will be paid to the personal representatives of the deceased. The other terms which the I.A.A.F. recommends are applied by its members to the "Athletes' fund," as set out in rule 17 of the 1983/4 I.A.A.F. handbook.

[32] In view of recent trends, however, athletics may no longer be an amateur sport by the time this book is published.

Rule 17 requires the existence of the trust and the terms applying thereto, to be confirmed in writing. Insofar as the U.K. is concerned, it is the responsibility of the B.A.A.B. as the I.A.A.F.'s domestic federation, to prepare the terms of the athletes' fund and to submit these to the I.A.A.F. Trusts may be implied in certain circumstances without the existence of writing. There are said to be three essentials (often called the three certainties) for the creation of a valid trust. These are: first, certainty of words. No particular form of words is necessary. Secondly, certainty of subject-matter, *i.e.* the property to which the trust is to attach must be identified. Thirdly, certainty of objects. Objects such as "philanthropic," "patriotic" or "public purposes" are so vague that they are unlikely to satisfy the test of certainty.

(a) *Beneficiary's interest in trust property*

The beneficiary will have the right to enforce both the terms of the trust and obligations imposed upon the trustees. If the terms of the trust are such that moneys, *i.e.* the trust property will be payable to him or her on retirement, then that obligation may be enforced.

The trust property, *i.e.* money will not normally be regarded as belonging to the beneficiary until such time as it vests. Thus if it vests on retirement it would not be available to his or her creditors until that time. Certain tax considerations apply, however, since income accruing to the fund will generally be taxable in the hands of the trustees and no allowances as in the case of a normal person are available.

(b) *The duties of a trustee*

The duties of trustees which may be enforced by the beneficiary include the following. The trustees must strictly perform the terms of the trust. An amateur athlete solely entitled to the trust money could compel the trustee to transfer the money to him on retirement if that is when it is to vest.[33] The trustee is under an obligation to keep proper accounts and supply information to the beneficiary. A trustee is under a further obligation, subject to the terms of the trust, to invest funds which are not immediately required.

---

[33] Note the rule in *Saunders* v. *Vautier* (1841) 4 Bear. 115.

(c) *Disabilities of the trustees*

There are a number of onerous obligations (often referred to as disabilities) imposed on a trustee. Some of the more relevant ones to the amateur are as follows. A trustee must not profit from his position. Thus he must not use his position or any knowledge derived from it for his personal advantage. A trustee is not normally entitled to remuneration for performing the trust. This need not apply where the benificiary consents. A trustee must not purchase trust property; use the trust property for his own benefit or lend to a co-trustee.

(2) ESCROW

Escrow applies only to deeds, *i.e.* written documents dealing with some form of property or obligation[34] made under seal. An intended deed may be delivered in escrow which has the effect that the intended deed will not become operative until the specified conditions have been fulfilled.

Delivery in escrow may be used in much the same way as a trust to avoid tainting amateur status. Its advantage over trusts is that the onerous obligations imposed on trustees will not apply. Thus it would be possible for the sponsor to prepare, sign and seal a contract under which he was obliged to pay money to an amateur. The contract could be delivered to the sponsor's solicitor, bank, or agent in escrow, the condition necessary for release of the funds being retirement of the sponsee from the amateur sport. Until such time as this condition was fulfilled the money would not belong to the amateur.[35] The sponsor would be bound by the transaction if the condition was fulfilled and could not withdraw or change his mind before the condition was fulfilled.[36]

[34] See *Goddard's Case* (1584) 2 Co. Rep. 4b & 5a, 76 E.R. 396.
[35] *Vincent* v. *Premo Enterprises (Voucher Sales)* [1969] 2 Q.B. 609.
[36] *Alan Estates* v. *W.G. Stores* [1982] Ch. 511.

7. Express Terms Licensing Sponsorship Rights

The section in the long form standard agreement headed "Grant," lists the various promises and licences which the sponsor is to acquire. Certain obligations are expressly undertaken by the sponsee in the grant section and other parts of the standard agreement relating to these promises and licences. It is important to understand the rationale of such express terms. The promises and licences will vary from contract to contract. The following are some of the more usual promises and licences which might be acquired in sport, arts or leisure sponsorship.

Title identification

Title identification or similar association involves naming the sponsorship object[1-2] after the sponsor or his products, or directly linking the sponsor's name with the sponsorship object. For example, the Football League Cup in the United Kingdom has been re-named, for a limited period, the Milk Cup. The Cornhill Tests in cricket are well known. Other examples include the 1982 Rolling Stones European Tour where each section of the tour had a different title sponsor. A film or book may also be named after a sponsor.[2] There are many examples of title identification existing at a local level such as a brass band changing its name to that of the local brewery company.

The co-operation of the sponsee in ensuring that full credit is given to the title sponsor is essential. It is recommended that the sponsor includes a suitable clause in his agreement which states that the sponsee shall use the full sponsored title in all publicity or other material issued in relation to the

[1] See p. 114.
[2] See p. 34.

sponsorship. This should include procuring the use of the full sponsored title in any publicity material issued by co-sponsors and exerting its best efforts to ensure that the press and media give due credit to title sponsors.

The response and co-operation of the media in giving recognition to a title sponsor is a difficult matter. The sponsee is unlikely to be in a position to do much more than ensure that accurate information is available in the form of press kits and maintain a good relationship with the press. Such a relationship is probably easier to establish and maintain on a local basis than nationally. There is no directive from the Press Council giving guidance to newspapers on the levels of recognition, which it is recommended are given, to title sponsors. In each case it is a matter for editorial discretion. In certain cases there may be considerable advantages in introducing a media sponsor as a co-sponsor to an event. The *Observer*, for example, has joined forces with co-sponsors in the transatlantic yacht race. Capital Radio has co-sponsored a play and the *Sunday Telegraph* operates a joint sponsorship with the Victoria Wine Company in relation to cricket and Rugby Union. Where a media sponsor is involved one can be fairly certain that the sponsor will receive recognition and the full sponsored title will be used.

Where the media is television or radio, then specific guidelines exist. The sponsor should be obliged to comply. These guidelines are discussed at greater length in Chapter 15, below.

The sponsee will, in all probability, have responsibility for agreeing the terms of any broadcast contract for coverage of a sponsored event. It makes sense to require the sponsee to clarify the question of title credit with the broadcaster.

Tobacco and alcoholic beverages may create separate problems with title identification, particularly in relation to youth events.

Advertisements on stadium boards, banners, players, etc.

Few would argue that advertising on boards, banners, players, or clocks, etc., which is picked on by the television camera, is regarded by sports sponsors as the most important sponsorship right.

The sponsorship agreement, in the case of boards or banners erected at a venue, will need to determine between the parties who has responsibility for producing, erecting, protecting, maintaining and removing them. Usually this is a responsibility imposed upon the sponsee. The right to stadium advertising boards may be granted to the sponsor on an exclusive basis for the sponsor's products or services. If this is the case, any competitive advertising at the venue will need to be removed or concealed. This may, or course, create problems as the venue may be subject to prior contractual commitments. To conceal existing boards may expose the sponsee to potential claims from existing contractors. If such boards are not removed or concealed then the sponsee may have failed to comply with his contract with the sponsor.

Television regulations specifically limit advertisements, and are dealt with in Chapter 15. A clause should appear in the sponsorship contract making it clear that any advertising submitted by the sponsor which is likely to appear on television must comply with broadcast regulations. The broadcast contract will normally be negotiated by the sponsee and will specify any particular restrictions that do exist, *e.g.* the number of boards or banners, or names which may appear on them. Some sponsees will have entered into long term contracts with the broadcasters dealing with what may be displayed, for example, the Race Course Association and the B.B.C./I.T.V.

Advertisements on players themselves are only likely to arise in sports sponsorship. Player advertising is again substantially affected by broadcast regulations and therefore discussed later. Amateur status and what is permitted under the rules of the controlling sports bodies is also important. This is also discussed elsewhere. Suffice it to say here that in certain sports, players are prohibited from advertising a sponsor's name on clothing.

An obligation placed on the sponsee to procure the inclusion of a sponsor's name on clothing may create difficulties particularly in "one-off" sponsored events. Tennis is perhaps the clearest example where it frequently occurs that individual players will be separately sponsored from the competitions in which they participate. Before the sponsee undertakes to include identification on players clothing he will need to ensure, for example, that the rules of entry into its competition are such that only identification supplied by the organiser may be worn. Inclusion of such a provision in the rules of any professional sport is likely to be contentious as one is in effect "taking from Peter to feed Paul." The inclusion of a sponsor's name on tickets or the acquisition by the sponsor of advertising space in a programme requires little original thought or peculiar obligations by either party. As with stadium advertising boards the sponsor should, of course, be required to supply artwork in good time to meet the print deadline of the sponsee. Where the positioning of the advertisement in relation to others, or exclusivity, or colour as opposed to black and white, is required then responsibility for these matters should be specifically set out in the contract.

Advertisements, by way of "on screen credits" during broadcasts usually for timing or computer companies are subject to special rules.

Use of names, photographs, logos and other insignia

The association between the sponsor and sponsee is likely to be enforced by the sponsor receiving a licence to use the name and/or logo of the sponsee on his products or in advertisements. The sponsor might use the words "Royal Shakespeare Company" in a publicity programme or include the World Cup mascot on soft drinks cans.

There are a number of very important points to make in connection with the licensing of such rights. Sponsorship is usually a short term relationship, certainly when compared to the life of a sports federation or arts body. What may be licensed to the sponsor in terms of names, logos, etc., may, if it is not properly controlled, inflict long term damage on the sponsee. Similarly from the sponsor's viewpoint, if he does not understand precisely what he is acquiring then he may sustain serious commercial damage.

Mascots, symbols, legends or slogans fall into two basic categories. Although the underlying legal basis of this distinction is analysed in depth later,[3] the practical distinction is that certain mascots, logos, legends and slogans are capable of existing as property and others are not. For example, a name alone, be it the Royal Shakespeare Company or the Football League Milk Cup, can only be "owned" in a proprietary sense in limited circumstances. The name Coca-Cola, for example, is registered as a trade mark and therefore exists as a type of property. If a mascot or other mark does not exist as property then any permission or licence given to the sponsor must reflect that fact.

[3] See Chaps. 9, 10 and 11.

Before the sponsor enters into a sponsorship he would be wise to require the sponsee to disclose which mascots, logos or other marks have either been registered as trade marks or exist as other categories of intellectual property such as copyright. Certainly in terms of large sponsorship projects this information will be essential. The sponsor may, assuming there is time, always ask the sponsee to extend a trade mark registration programme or agree to extend it himself in the name of the sponsee.

Where the sponsee owns proprietary rights in mascots, logos or other marks then he will wish to protect his ownership thereof by ensuring that the sponsor does nothing to damage or prejudice his title or interest. The practical consequences under English law require that the sponsor should submit samples of any merchandise on which a trade mark is used, for prior approval regarding quality. The sponsee may also wish to check that an appropriate trademark notice such as an ® or ™ or copyright notice has been used. This will demonstrate the sponsee's concern that where the name, etc., is being used as a hallmark of quality, such quality is maintained and that third parties are given due notice of subsisting proprietary rights. Reference may be made to the full standard form contract for other matters which it is customary to include as obligations on the part of the sponsor.

The risks of not understanding whether a particular mascot, logo or other mark exists as property will arise in the market place. A sponsor might go to the expense of printing millions of its soft drink cans with a legend such as "Espana 82" only to find that the sponsee's representation in the contract that it had exclusive rights to this term was a misunderstanding on the sponsor's part.

As with title identification the sponsee should be required to use the respective mark itself and to use its best endeavours to procure use by the media including television. Similar principles to those discussed in relation to mascots, logos and slogans will apply to the use of photographs, portraits and other images.

Official supplier and similar status

Status as an official supplier or official sponsor is frequently acquired in relation to sponsored events. For example, the Organising Committee of the 1984 Los Angeles Olympics has appointed an "official supplier" of typewriters. Official supplier status may also be acquired in relation to a sports federation. For example, the English Basketball Association might appoint an "official supplier" of basketballs. The scope for official supplier status in the arts world is perhaps more limited.

The right for a sponsor to describe itself as an official supplier should be linked with an obligation on the part of the sponsor to supply its respective products or services for use in relation to the event and or organisers or other bodies. The sponsee on the other hand should be required to utilise the goods or services supplied. Without these further obligations the transaction is likely to lack credibility.

Endorsements

Specific endorsements of a sponsor's goods or services rarely form any part of a sponsorship package unless individuals are involved. The act of the sponsee accepting the sponsorship is, in view of the proximity of the parties, a form of endorsement. Sports, arts or leisure bodies in contast to individuals are unlikely to issue statements recommending one brand of goods to another. Use of their logos and official supplier status will undoubtedly convey this impression.

Where endorsements are acquired in isolation then there is no sponsorship relationship and therefore it falls outside the terms in this book. Where endorsements are acquired as part of a sponsorship package then an express term should be included in the contract which obliges the sponsee to observe a particular standard of behaviour. Thus, if the sponsee were to appear in court on a drunk and disorderly charge, the sponsor should be in a position to withdraw from the sponsorship. Where an express term is not included it is submitted that the court might imply such a term.[4]

Use of recordings

Sponsors may acquire rights to use recordings which are linked with the sponsee. Some events, for example, will have official music or a theme tune which, like the event, title and official logo, will be promoted within the media. Many events will also be recorded on video and sponsors often require

[4] *The Moorcock* (1889) 14 P.D. 64.

access to video footage for use in connection with point of sale and/or publicity material.

Where use of recordings is permitted by the sponsor then the sponsor should assume that such material will be subject to existing proprietary interests and the sponsee should therefore be obliged, once the sponsor has identified the material that he wishes to use, to obtain any consent or clearance that may be required. Further, the sponsee should undertake responsibility for payment of any fees or royalties that may be due to organisations such as the Performing Rights Society Limited.

General

As already discussed most rights and licences which the sponsor is to acquire will last for a year or so and then revert to the sponsee. A general obligation should therefore be imposed on the sponsor to protect what belongs to the sponsee, *i.e.* the sponsor should be required to submit sample art work of intended promotions and generally do everything he can to uphold the name and reputation of the sponsee. This would, in most cases, include not associating any of the rights or licences with obscene or pornographic material and to ensure that the sponsor did not utilise the rights in an illegal manner. Certain jurisdictions, for example, would preclude the sponsor from promoting its sponsorship via lotteries. The sponsor will normally be precluded from interfering with the general policies and administration of the sponsee.[5]

It is increasingly common for sponsors to require sponsees to effect insurance which will be sufficient to cover any liability on the part of the sponsee to make refunds to the sponsor, where the rights and promises are not delivered due to an insurable fortuity.

[5] See p. 93.

8. The Meaning of Property

No finite definition exists under English law of property. Property, according to one learned textbook, "deals with the legal relations between people and things."[1] That legal relation may affect only the parties themselves or it may affect others. If, for example, someone agrees to buy a gold watch for £50, takes delivery, but fails to pay the price, a debt exists. The relation of the buyer to the seller is personal and does not affect anyone else.[2] Once the price has been paid ownership of the watch passes to the buyer. The law will protect that ownership against everyone else by ensuring (subject to certain exceptions which are not dealt with here) that the owner can recover possession from others who borrow it or steal it or otherwise acquire it without the owner's consent. A relation which affects only the parties themselves is called a personal relation. A relation which affects others is called a real relation.

Ownership, possession and title

If someone buys a watch then they become the owner. As owner possession of the watch may be given to others such as the jeweller when it is being repaired. Possession and ownership are not the same. Title to a thing may prove ownership or degrees of ownership. Ownership of a house, for example, is established either by examining the vendor's title as shown at Her Majesty's Land Registry where the property is registered or by deducing title from the deeds and other documents if title to the land is not registered. There are degrees of title. For example, in registered land there is title absolute and good or possessory leasehold title. Absolute title to things arises from creating them such as writing a book,

[1] Lawson, *Law of Property* (2nd ed., 1982), p. 1.
[2] That is not to say it cannot exist as property.

manufacturing them or by being the registered owner of them.

Categories of property

Although property is not a finite concept there are, nevertheless, a number of categories into which different types of property fall. The first categorisation is between realty and personalty. Realty is real property or land other than leaseholds. Personalty (or chattels) is divided between chattels real which are leasehold interests in land and chattels personal. Chattels personal are further sub-divided into choses (things) in possession such as goods and choses (things) in action such as debts. A simplified categorisation might be as follows[3]:

(a) land,
(b) goods, *i.e.* tangible moveables other than money,
(c) choses in action,
(d) money, and
(e) funds.

Of these categories, (a), (b) and (c) have particular relevance to sponsorship.

Land

Land includes not only a defined geographical area but also the air space above it and subsoil beneath it. Land also includes houses and permanent structures. A permanent advertising hoarding affixed to land would be regarded as a fixture and therefore part of the land. This is discussed briefly later in the book.[4]

Goods

The Sale of Goods Act 1979, s.61(1) defines goods as all chattels personal other than money or choses in action. A car, watch, programme and television set are all goods.

Choses in action

Choses in action are intangibles. It is comparatively simple to appreciate that a gold watch is an item of property because

[3] Lawson, *Law of Property* (2nd ed., 1982), p. 20.
[4] See p. 254.

it has a physical existence. A debt, however, or the goodwill attaching to a business or copyright in a painting or a song are also capable of existing as property although they have no physical existence. The property in a debt is identified with the right to enforce payment. Tickets to a sports event are choses in action in so far as they permit the holder to enforce his right of entry to the event.

In order for choses in action to qualify as property they must satisfy one underlying condition; that is that they must be capable of being transferred from one person to another. If they are not so transferable then they are not "things" or property. On this basis, a crossed personal cheque in favour of X could not be a chose in action since, if X purported to endorse the cheque in favour of Y, Y could not compel X to make the payment. In contrast, a banker's draft to pay X "or order" would be a chose in action and therefore property since X could endorse the draft to Y and Y could directly enforce the obligation of the bank to make payments.

It is important to appreciate that even though a promise or debt is not transferable, that debt may still be enforced between the parties. If A supplies goods to B then A will be able to claim the price of those goods from B, assuming that a contract exists.

Property and sponsorship

Property is relevant from the sponsor's viewpoint in two main ways:

1. Sponsorship attaches to an "individual, event, happening, property or object,"[5] for example, a book, film, play, race, club, art exhibition, brass band, racehorse, etc. Some, but not all of these items may exist as property. Where they do exist as property then rights ownership is comparatively straightforward to establish.

2. Once the sponsor has identified the object of his sponsorship, *i.e.* the individual event, happening, property or object, he then has to find a means of associating himself with it. The association will usually consist of a combination of contractual promises such as a credit for the sponsor to be included at the end of a sponsored film. The association will probably also involve matters which go beyond simple contractual promises and are exclusive licences to use

[5] See the definition on p. 4.

trademarks or copyright belonging to the sponsee. The sponsor might, for example, receive an exclusive licence to use the logo of a theatrical company in its sales brochures. The logo must exist as property for the sponsor to acquire an exclusive licence to use it. Exclusive licences are discussed further below.

From the sponsees viewpoint property is important because of the three main characteristics that attach to ownership. These are respectively:

(a) the right to make physical use of it. Thus, if the sponsee owns the theatre where a play is to be performed, prima facie he has the right to erect advertising banners which will be seen during the performance. This right also enables the sponsee to prevent others using what belongs to him without his consent;

(b) the right to the income from it in money in kind or in services. A sponsee who licenses a sponsor to install an advertising board on his land is entitled to ask for a fee for giving his permission; and

(c) the power of management and control including alienation. This feature of ownership is closely related to (a) above. It enables a sponsee to license the sponsor to use the logo in which copyright subsists, for example, on certain products or only in certain territories or for a specific time. It also gives the sponsee the right to sell the property outright.

The sponsee does not have to own property to create the sponsorship relationship. For example, the sponsor may decide to sponsor an individual athlete. Humans are not regarded as property since that has connotations of slavery. This does not prevent sponsorship. It may have an affect upon it however, as discussed below under exclusive licences.

Sponsorship objects

The distinction has already been made between the individual event, happening, property or object such as a book, play or sports event and the promises and licences which will exist in relation to these. The promises and licences are the hooks upon which the sponsor will hang his marketing coat. For the purposes of the text the individual event, happening, property or object is referred to as the sponsorship object. The combination of the sponsorship object and the promises and licences together comprise the sponsorship assets. The sponsee should identify his sponsorship assets since they are what he or she is able to offer to the sponsor.

Licences and exclusive licences

A licence makes lawful that which could otherwise be unlawful.[6] A sponsee might, for example, grant a licence to a sponsor to erect stadium advertising boards on his land or to use a logo in which copyright subsists. In each of these examples the sponsee owns property, in the first case, land, and in the second case, copyright. The sponsor could not therefore exercise rights over the sponsee's property without his authority (there are of course exceptions which are not discussed here).

It is probable, although by no means essential, that the licence will arise under a contract. A licence granted without a contract would be revocable at will on reasonable notice. Revocation of a licence granted by a contract would be governed by the terms of the contract.[7]

A licence itself cannot be regarded as property since it does not create an assignable right.[8] It may arise in relation to a sponsorship object which is property.

An exclusive licence, as its name suggests, is a licence conferring some form of exclusivity. Much of sponsorship involves granting exclusive licences. Exclusivity is often conferred in relation to product categories, of which the following are examples: an exclusive licence within the soft drinks category to install stadium advertising at a venue; an exclusive licence within the soft drink category to sell drinks at a venue or an exclusive licence to use the slogan "Official Supplier" within the soft drink category.

The grant of an exclusive licence, depending upon the precise wording used in the contract, implies that the sponsor is in a position to stop others from exercising the licence. Going back to the beginning of this chapter, an exclusive licence between the sponsor and the sponsee is a real relation because it affects others and not just the parties themselves. Where the exclusive licence is granted in relation to property

---

[6] *Thomas v. Sorrell* (1673) 1 Free. K. B. 85.

[7] See p. 72.

[8] *Clore v. Theatrical Properties Ltd. & Westby & Co. Ltd* [1936] 3 All E.R. 483 C.A.

belonging to the sponsee then under normal principles of ownership[9] the sponsee will be able to prevent others from exercising the licence. Thus, he or she could prevent others entering upon his or her land and erecting advertising boards or using his or her logo by bringing an action for copyright infringement. To quote from a recent judgment of Oliver L.J.[10] "the expression exclusive right can be misleading if not subject to some analysis."

A licence purporting to confer exclusivity upon sponsors of the Rolling Stones European Tour regarding the use of the likeness of the Rolling Stones on point of sale material could not be defended. An individual has no property under English law in his image or likeness.[11] Thus, a famous boxer could not prevent a film being made of him whilst boxing at the former National Sporting Club in Covent Garden since he had no property in his features.[12] A sponsee might, however, be in a position to grant exclusive rights to use photographs of the Rolling Stones taken at a particular concert. This would require the sponsee to be in control of the venue and to include a condition on any tickets permitting access which prohibited taking photographs. It also assumes that the sponsor takes the photographs himself and that he therefore will own copyright.[13]

In a recent case a United Kingdom company was licenced by the owners of the United States television series "Kojak" to use the name Kojak on lollipops. It seemed a sensible commercial arrangement since the Kojak from the television series had a great liking for such sweets. Linking the name Kojak with lollipops would almost inevitably enhance sales of the lollipops. The licence given to the United Kingdom company was "exclusive" and a royalty on sales was to be paid. A problem arose, however, in that another United Kingdom company had, without any consent from the creators of the television series, used the name "Kojakpops" in relation to lollipops. Substantial numbers of "Kojakpops" were sold. Because the unlicensed company had built up such a reputation in the market place they were able, on the basis of their good will, to stop the company which had the licence to sell "Kojak" lollies in the United Kingdom.

[9] See p. 111.
[10] *R.C.A.* v. *Pollard* [1983] F.S.R. 9 at 17.
[11] In contrast to specific paintings or photographs, see p. 134.
[12] *Palmer* v. *National Sporting Club Ltd.* (1905) 10 MacG.C.C. 55.
[13] See p. 135.

The reason for this decision is set out in the judgment of Walton J.[14] "It seems to me that in general the licences granted by Universal City Studios [the owners of the "Kojak" series] . . . insofar as they relate to this country. . . . there being no copyright simply in the name "Kojak". . . . are really writs in water." It is thought that the simile with writs in water is intended to emphasize that the licence although included in a written contract was of no value whatsoever.

Promises distinguished from licences

Certain of the rights passing to the sponsor will effect only the parties themselves and will never escape from the boundaries of the contract. These are personal rather than real relations[15] They include advertisements in an official programme or the right to receive a verbal credit prior to the start of a sponsored play. The dividing line between promises and licences can be thin. If the sponsee undertook to produce and erect on his land a stadium advertising board featuring the sponsor's name, that is a promise. If, however, the sponsee gave the sponsor permission to enter upon his land and erect his own stadium advertising board, that is a licence. If the sponsee agreed that he would erect on his land a stadium advertising board belonging to the sponsor then that is both a promise and a licence. It is a promise because it requires performance by the sponsee and a licence because it would be unlawful for the sponsor's advertising board to remain on the sponsee's land without permission.

Licences often merge with promises in this way. Thus, in one case, the organisers of a dog show purported to grant exclusive rights to take photographs at the show. Swinfen Eady L.J. in giving judgment stated "no-one possesses a right of preventing another person photographing him any more than he has the right of preventing another giving a description of him."[16] The organisers of the dog show were therefore unable to prevent other people taking photographs. The licence was to enter the dog show; the promise was exclusivity regarding photographs. The term "right" has been used occasionally in the text of this book rather than "promises."

[14] *Tavenor Rutledge* v. *Trexapalm* [1977] R.P.C. 275.
[15] See p. 111.
[16] *Special and General Press Agency* v. *Our Dogs Publishing* [1917] 2 K.B. 125 at 128.

Exclusivity and promises

The judgment given in the *Our Dogs* case is illuminating. It offers a solution to a sponsee who wishes to grant exclusivity in relation to sponsorship objects which are incapable of existing as property, for example, human beings. This chapter began with the distinction between real and personal relations.[17] If a contract were made with everyone who might be affected by a particular promise then exclusivity may be granted, notwithstanding the absence of property. Thus, in the *Our Dogs* case if it had been made a term of the contract (*i.e.* ticket) permitting access to the dog show that no photographs could be taken, then exclusive rights could have been granted to one person.

Granting exclusive rights on the basis that other people could be prevented from exercising their normal rights through an action for breach of contract has limited effectiveness. One could not, for example, prevent spectators at an event which was not confined to some geographical area over which the sponsee had control (such as the London Marathon course) from taking photographs. No contract will exist between spectators and the organisers at such public events, and therefore there is no opportunity to incorporate restrictive conditions. Damages might be difficult to assess against a person who is in breach of contract.

There are a number of miscellaneous circumstances in which a promise or licence acquired on an exclusive basis by the sponsor might be defended. These circumstances tend to overlap with other issues such as defamation, consumer protection and trespass, and are discussed later.[18]

---

[17] See p. 111.
[18] See Chap. 12.

9. Sponsorship Assets as Intellectual Property

The previous chapter examined in general terms the importance of property to sponsorship. This chapter, together with the two that follow, examines the extent to which specific sponsorship assets are capable of existing as intellectual property. Intellectual property was discussed in the previous chapter under the heading of "Choses in Action." Like property itself, no finite definition of intellectual or industrial property exists. It includes, for the purposes of this book, copyright, trade marks and goodwill protected by the action of passing off.

The law which applies to copyright, trade marks and passing off is detailed and complex. These chapters perhaps more than any others have involved a subjective judgment by the authors on the practical issues that tend to arise in sponsorship rather than a general discussion of the law in these areas. To that extent the reader should be alerted to the limitations of this text.

The specific sponsorship assets discussed in this text are by no means exhaustive.

Copyright

Copyright prevents the unauthorised copying, reproduction or repetition of certain material which is identified in the Copyright Act 1956. The protected material is divided into two parts. Part I copyright covers literary, dramatic, musical and artistic works and Part II covers sound recordings, cinematograph films, television and sound broadcasts and typographical arrangements. Part I copyright might broadly be distinguished from Part II on the basis that it protects the fruits or products of original, creative or intellectual endeavour such as an author's right to prevent other people exploiting his book. In contrast, Part II copyright covers material which is not necessarily creative but nevertheless requires protection for economic reasons as money will usually have been invested in producing it.[1]

Copyright does not protect ideas themselves[2] unless and until such ideas have been reduced to some permanent or semi-permanent form such as a sketch or drawing.

One characteristic which distinguishes copyright from trade marks discussed in the next chapter is that no registration of copyright is required to secure protection under the Act.[3] Subject only to satisfying the criteria set out in the Copyright Act an artist, author, composer, publisher, and many other recognised categories are afforded immediate protection against unauthorised exploitation of their works.

Copyright rarely involves only one copyright interest in particular material. A sponsored music video might, for example, contain the concurrent copyright interests of the composer, choreographer and production house, together with the interests of the musicians under the Performers Protection Acts.

The term for protection of copyright material varies with the different material and sections of the Act. Detailed consideration is not given here. However, a broad summary of the term is as follows:

   (a) Literary, dramatic and musical works, whilst unpublished, are protected during the life of the author, plus 50 years or, if he or she dies after the publication, 50 years after the date of publication.[4]

   (b) Artistic works are protected during the life of the artist plus 50 years. In the case of engravings, however, if the work is published after the death of the artist then copyright subsists for 50 years after publication. In the case of photographs, copyright subsists for 50 years after publication.[5]

   (c) Sound recordings are protected for 50 years from the date of the first publication.

---

[1] Originality is not stated as a requirement in Part II copyright, but is implied; see Cornish, *Intellectual Property: Patents Copyright, Trade Marks and Allied Rights* (1981), p. 331.

[2] *Kenrick & Co.* v. *Lawrence & Co.* [1890] 25 Q.B. 99.

[3] *Cf.* the Washington Registry, where some form of public record exists, and also the Registered Designs Act 1949.

[4] Copyright Act 1956, s.2(3).

[5] *Ibid.* s.3.

(d) Cinematograph films are protected for 50 years from registration under the Films Act 1960 or if not registrable, 50 years from the date of first publication.[6]

(e) Broadcasts are protected for 50 years from the original date of broadcast.[7]

(f) Typographical arrangements are protected for 25 years from the first publication date.[8]

Ownership

INITIAL OWNERSHIP

Initial ownership of copyright, as one might expect, tends to be with the creator or author of the protected material in Part I copyright, such as books, songs, artwork, etc.,[9] and with the maker or the person having economic control in Part II copyright, e.g. a film company that undertakes production of a film will own copyright in the film. The B.B.C. or I.B.A. will own copyright in their respective broadcasts.

The owner of literary, dramatic, musical and artistic works and recordings, films and typographical arrangements must be a qualified person, who is the author, composer or maker as appropriate. Qualification in this context is defined in section 1 of the Act broadly as being a British or Irish subject or person domiciled in the United Kingdom or another country to which the act extends. Qualification for broadcasts is set out in section 14(2) of the Act.

This general rule on initial ownership is subject to three important exceptions.

1. For Part I copyright[10] in the case of a photograph, painting, drawing, portrait or engraving, the person who commissions the work and who has paid money or monies, will be the owner. This also applies where a sub-contractor undertakes the work. Thus a component part for an engraving of the death mask of a Nigerian king, made by a sub-contractor, was a commissioned work.[11] In Part II copyright, a similar presumption arises but only in the case of sound recordings.[12]

---

[6] *Ibid.* s.13.
[7] *Ibid.* s.14(2).
[8] *Ibid.* s.15(2).
[9] *Ibid.* ss.1–9.
[10] *Ibid.* s.4(3).
[11] *James Arnold & Co.* v. *Miafern* [1980] R.P.C. 397.
[12] Copyright Act 1956, s.12(4).

121

2. Copyright in a work which is created by an author in the course of his employment under a service contract or apprenticeship with a proprietor of a newspaper, magazine or periodical is split between the proprietor and the author. The proprietor will own copyright insofar as publication in the newspaper, magazine or periodical is concerned and the author obtains what is left. This may include hardback and overseas rights.

3. An employer is entitled to copyright in material produced by an employee in the course of his employment under a contract of service or apprenticeship.[13]

Initial ownership may of course be dealt with by prior agreement of the parties. Thus if an author is commissioned to write a book, the sponsor could always contract with the author on the terms which vested copyright in the sponsor.

ASSIGNMENTS

After initial ownership has been determined a sponsor might take an assignment or licence of the copyright. Assignments transfer ownership from one party to the other. Assignments of copyright in favour of the sponsor are rare. Examples do exist of sponsors taking an assignment of copyright in sponsored books, films and videos. This may enable the sponsor to engage in parallel economic opportunities.

As already mentioned, sponsors may look at potential sponsorship projects with an eye to recovering directly some or all of their investment. For example, sponsors of the soccer World Cup acquired the right to use the official World Cup logo on their products and in promotions related thereto. This right, if exploited fully as a merchandising opportunity, achieved greater sales. Some sponsors sub-licensed their rights for valuable consideration.

An assignment of copyright must be in the form prescribed by section 36 of the Act to take effect as a legal assignment.[14] The Act prescribes that the assignment must be in writing and signed by or on behalf of the assignor.[15] An assignment may take effect both with respect to existing copyright and future

---

[13] *Ibid*. s.4(4).

[14] Without such formalities then the assignment may nevertheless take effect in equity. See *Nicol* v. *Barranger* 1917–1923 MacG.C.C. 219.

[15] Copyright Act 1956, s.36(3).

copyright.[16] Although writing is required no particular form of words need be used.[17] An assignment may be for one particular country or limited to a specific period of time or to specific rights such as film or video only.[18] There are similarities between an exclusive licence and assignments.

LICENCES AND EXCLUSIVE LICENCES

The sponsor is more likely to take a licence in copyright than an assignment. For example, he may acquire a licence for two years to use the official logo of a theatre on his stationery. Licences in copyright may be express or implied from all the circumstances of the transaction. It will usually be in the interests of the sponsee to deal with the licence in writing as he will require the sponsor to undertake certain responsibilities to ensure that nothing is done to prejudice his copyright interest. There is no formal requirement that the licence must be in writing. However, in the case of an exclusive licence the discussions below in relation to section 19(9) should be considered. A licence may be implied in particular circumstances. Thus a letter to the editor on a theme of public interest was taken to imply a licence on the part of the newspaper to publish it.[19]

The licence given to the sponsor may be exclusive or non-exclusive.[20] Where the licence is exclusive and falls within section 19(9) of the Act, the exclusive licensee may be in a position to take independent action against infringers in the case of interlocutory injunctions.[21] In other cases the owner or licensee will need to join each other as parties to the proceedings, unless the leave of the court is obtained.[22] Section 19(9) of the Act requires that the exclusive licence be in writing and signed by or on behalf of the copyright owner or prospective owner. Further, it must authorise the licensee to the exclusion of all others to undertake those matters which but for the licence would be the exclusive prerogative of the owner.

[16] *Ibid.* s.37(1), (2) and (5).
[17] See *Savory Ltd.* v. *World of Golf Ltd.* [1914] 2 Ch. 566.
[18] See *Hospital for Sick Children (Board of Governors)* v. *Walt Disney Productions Inc.* [1968] Ch. 52, where film rights were limited to silent film rights. See also Copyright Act 1956, s.36(2).
[19] See *Springfield* v. *Thame* (1903) 89 L.T. 242 and see also p. 72.
[20] See p. 115.
[21] *Warwick Film Productions* v. *Eisinger* [1963] 1 W.L.R. 756.
[22] Copyright Act 1956, s.19(3).

The owner's and the exclusive licensee's rights to damages are concurrent.[23] This means that there is essentially one right of action in respect of the infringement and both the owner and exclusive licensee have a financial interest in stopping it. Their respective financial interests can only properly be determined by examining the agreement itself. Damages will be based on each party's interest but will not be duplicated.

An action for conversion under section 18 of the Copyright Act may be bought by the exclusive licensee alone and he may retain all damages under section 18.[24] This position which has the potential effect of enabling an exclusive licensee to make a large profit out of the transaction is unlikely to continue and has been criticised by the Whitford Committee Report and more recently in the Government Green Paper on copyright.[25]

Exclusive licencees and non-exclusive licencees not meeting the requirements of section 19(9) may not as a rule take independent action against infringers.

PRIOR DEALINGS IN COPYRIGHT

Both United Kingdom assignees and licencees of copyright suffer from the absence of any public record or register of title to copyright.[26] If one were transferring a house rather than copyright, the prospective purchaser, could, if the property were registered, inspect the property register which would reveal all dealings with the house. An assignee of copyright becomes the owner and as with other types of property,[27] he can defeat any subsequent purported assignments or non-exclusive licences which conflict with his ownership. An assignee and those deriving title through him will not take subject to prior licences granted by or under the title of the copyright owner where he has no notice of them and has given value and acted in good faith.[28] Since there is no register of transfers an assignee will take subject to prior assignments which he did not know about. Special rules relate to exclusive licences however, under section 19(4). This subsection

---

[23] *Ibid.* s.19(2)(*a*).
[24] *Ibid.* s.19(2)(*b*).
[25] *Reform of the Law Relating to Copyright, Designs and Performers' Protection*, Cmnd. 8302 (1981) Chap. 14, para. 3.
[26] See p. 120, n.3.
[27] See Chap. 8.
[28] Copyright Act 1956, s.36(4).

prevents an exclusive licensee bringing infringement proceedings against a subsequent exclusive licensee. The first exclusive licensee's remedy is against the owner for breach of contract, *i.e.* breach of exclusivity. Thus, if copyright owner A grants an exclusive licence to B and then again to C, B cannot sue C for infringement because of section 19(4), but he could sue A for breach of contract. A sponsor who seeks an assignment of copyright should insist that the sponsee warrants that he owns the copyright and has not granted any prior assignments or licences.

ACTION AGAINST INFRINGERS

In a sponsorship contract, it would be customary for the sponsor to pay a once only rights fee for all rights and licences which comprise the sponsorship package. The sponsor has a great deal of incentive to protect his investment. Most sponsorship contracts therefore place a responsibility on the sponsor to police the market for infringers. The right to take legal action is controlled by sections 17 and 18 of the Copyright Act [29] which state that infringement of copyright shall be actionable at the suit of the owner. Applying the usual commercial balance to a sponsorship deal, the sponsor may be required to police the market but he will almost invariably expect the owner, *i.e.* sponsee, to take action against infringers. As discussed below, responsibility for the conduct of proceedings is a different issue from how the cost of those proceedings are to be dealt with.

Most sponsors who acquire an exclusive licence to use a mark or other copyright material in relation to their products, or an exclusive licence within a particular territory will be able to take direct action against infringers.[30]

Infringement of copyright

Sponsors generally associate themselves with a person or event in anticipation of receiving media coverage. It is in the sponsor and sponsee's overall interest to gain wide exposure of event titles, marks, music and other features of the sponsored event. That exposure may be through the Press, radio, television, videogrammes and other media. Such

[29] See p. 124.
[30] But note s.19(4).

exposure is likely to increase both the circumstances and rewards of piracy.

INFRINGING ACTS

Consideration must be given to the separate sections of the Act to determine whether an infringement has taken place. Thus Copyright in a literary, dramatic or musical work is infringed by[31]; (i) reproducing the work in any material form; (ii) publishing the work; (iii) performing the work in public; (iv) broadcasting the work; (v) causing the work to be transmitted to subscribers to a diffusion service; (vi) making any adaptation of the work[32] and (vii) doing in relation to an adaptation of the work any of the acts specified in relation to the work in paragraphs (i) to (v) above. Copyright in artistic works is infringed by the same acts stated at points (i), (ii), (iv) and (v) above.[33] In addition it is an infringement to make a reproduction in three dimensions of a two dimensional work and vice versa.[34] In the case of two dimensions to three dimensions, however, it is a defence under section 9(8) that it would not appear to non-experts to be a reproduction.

Copyright is infringed in relation to sound recordings by (i) making a record embodying the recording; or (ii) causing the recording to be heard in public; or (iii) broadcasting the recording.[35] Copyright in relation to cinematograph films is infringed by (i) making a copy of the film; (ii) causing the film, insofar as it consists of visual images, to be seen in public or insofar as it consists of sounds to be heard in public; (iii) broadcasting the film; or (iv) causing it to be transmitted to subscribers to a diffusion service.[36] The acts restricted by copyright in a television or sound broadcast are complex and include making a recording other than for private purposes, causing it to be seen or heard in public by a paying audience and rebroadcasting it.[37] In relation to published editions of works, copyright is infringed by the making, by any photographic or similar process of a reproduction of the typographical arrangement of the edition.[38]

[31] Copyright Act 1956, s.2(5).
[32] As defined in the Copyright Act 1956, s.2(6).
[33] Copyright Act 1956, s.3(5).
[34] *Ibid.* s.48.
[35] *Ibid.* s.12(5).
[36] *Ibid.* s.13(5).
[37] *Ibid.* ss.14(4) and 14(8).
[38] *Ibid.* s.15(3).

In any infringement situation three matters require consideration. The first is identifying who committed the infringing act. The second is the exceptions or general defences which may be available. The third is whether it is the sponsor or the sponsee who should be required to take the appropriate action.[39]

PARTIES RESPONSIBLE FOR INFRINGEMENT

The person or body responsible to the copyright owner for the infringement will be the person who commits the restricted act. A sponsor who acquired an exclusive right to use the theme tune of a sponsored event in advertisements would reasonably expect that the sponsor's major competitor could be prevented from using the theme. Proceedings based upon copyright infringement might be instituted against the competitor directly, the competitor's advertising agency if the latter was responsible for the reproduction or the radio station which broadcast the tune.[40] In each case where an infringement is suspected, the restricted acts must be considered. In addition certain other parties may be brought into the action by virtue of sections 5 and 16 of the Copyright Act. These sections are necessary, since in the main the restricted acts apply only to copying or reproducing the work. This would not catch the importer or dealer.[41]

It is quite possible for the sponsee and sponsor to agree to share the costs of infringement proceedings in advance and since it is in both parties' interests to stop infringers this may be an equitable compromise. What happens to damages recovered might also be agreed in advance. However, a formula is provided in the Act[42] where this is not the case. The formula allows for an apportionment between the owner and exclusive licensee as the court may consider just.[43] Criminal remedies are also available in certain circumstances as set out in section 21 of the Copyright Act. It is an offence, for example, to make for sale or hire a copy of a work in which copyright subsists.[44]

---

[39] This has already been discussed at p. 125.
[40] See *I.T.C.A. Ltd.* v. *Performing Rights Society Ltd.*, *The Times*, November 23, 1982.
[41] See *Infabrics* v. *Jaytex* [1981] 2 W.L.R. 646 and also "Remedies," and "The Burden of Proof," p. 207.
[42] Copyright Act 1956, s.19(5) and (6).
[43] See also "Remedies" and, in particular, "The Burden of Proof," p. 207.
[44] Copyright Act 1956, s.21(1).

The scope of the offence in relation to films and sound recordings has been extended by the Copyright Act 1956 (Amendment) Act 1982 and provisions for increased penalties and improved powers of search and seizure have been made by the Copyright (Amendment) Act 1983.[45]

International recognition

There are a number of conventions in existence which recognise copyright in certain material. It may be possible to rely upon the protection available under the domestic laws of a convention country to bring proceedings against unlicensed third parties.

The most important of these international agreements are the Berne Convention and the Universal Copyright Convention (U.C.C.). The United States and the Soviet Union became signatories to this latter agreement. There are also a number of agreements in existence regarding the protection of television broadcasts. The conventions are introduced into British law by order in council pursuant to the Copyright Act 1956.[46] Where it is sought to secure protection under the U.C.C. the symbol © must be used in proximity to the work, together with the name of the author and the year of first publication. This is only a formal requirement, however, when the work is first published outside a convention country by a foreign author, *i.e.* an author of a convention country but not of the convention country in which protection is being sought. Use of the copyright symbol and the name of the author or publisher might have relevance to various presumptions that arise in relation to proceedings.[47] A special notice exists for protecting the rights of producers of phonograms or of performers, or both, in relation to phonograms: the symbol "P."[48]

Defences

Not every defence has been discussed here—only the ones that it is thought might apply in a sponsorship context.

---

[45] Infringement may now result in imprisonment and a maximum fine of £1000. See Copyright (Amendment) Act 1983.

[46] s.32.

[47] Copyright Act 1956, s.20, and see *Warwick Film Productions* v. *Eisinger* [1963] 1 W.L.R. 756, and *Wham-O Manufacturing Co.* v. *Lincoln Industries Ltd.* [1982] R.P.C. 281, where the symbol was absent.

[48] International Convention for the Protection of Performers, Producers of Phonograms and Broadcasting Organisations.

(a) *Statutory*

Literary and dramatic works. Fair dealing—for purposes of research, of private study[49] or for the purposes of criticism or review (provided that a sufficient acknowledgment is given to the original work[50]) or for the purpose of reporting current events where the report is contained in a newspaper, magazine or similar periodical or in a broadcast or cinematograph film. This strikes a balance between the public interest and the economic interest of the copyright owners. In one case[51] the defendant wrote a book criticising the cult of scientology relying upon his own experiences but also repeating substantial extracts from books written by the plaintiff who was the founder of the cult. The defendant sought to rely upon section 6(2), *i.e.* fair dealing for purposes of criticism or review. The court held that in this case it was a valid defence to the plaintiffs action for copyright infringement. It is submitted that on the basis of section 6(1) it would always be permissible for a newspaper or magazine to write an article about a sponsored event and use the relevant event logo in that article. It would not be permissible to use the logo of the sponsored event on a guide book or programme without a licence. In the latter case, apart from taking potential income away from the copyright owner the implication in using the logo on the guide or programme is that the publication has the sanction of the organisers.

The reading or recitation in public by one person of any reasonable extract from a published work, provided that an acknowledgment is given and it is not broadcast,[52] is not an infringement of copyright.

Also permitted is the inclusion of a short passage of a published work in a collection intended for use in schools.[53]

Finally, the reproduction in the form of a film or other recording where the matter was originally licensed to be broadcast and for the purpose of making the broadcast[54–55] is not an infringement.

---

[49] Copyright Act 1956, s.6(1).
[50] *Ibid.* s.6(2) and (10).
[51] *Hubbard* v. *Vosper* [1972] 2 Q.B. 84. See also the recent case of *Independent Television Publications Ltd.* v. *Time Out; British Broadcasting Corporation* v. *Time Out, The Times*, May 10, 1983.
[52] Copyright Act 1956, s.6(5).
[53] *Ibid.* s.6(6). See the qualifications in that section.
[54–55] *Ibid.* s.6(7).

Musical works. Copyright in a musical work is not infringed by a person (*i.e.* manufacturer) making a record of the work or an adaptation of it in the United Kingdom pursuant to the statutory licence.

Artistic: (i) inclusion by way of general background in a film or broadcast[56]; and (ii) three D from two D if they do not appear to non-experts to be reproductions.[57]

Sound recordings. There is no infringement of copyright where a sound recording is played in public, provided that it is played in premises either where people sleep, *e.g.* hotels, mainly as part of their amenities or for a charitable or welfare organisation.[58]

(b) *Public policy*

The court may refuse to give relief on general grounds of public policy where the particular material in which copyright is claimed is obscene or defamatory, etc. Thus the court refused relief where a film was purported to be derived from the plaintiff's novel, and the novel was of a highly immoral tendency.[59]

Copyright and particular sponsorship objects

(1) BROADCASTS

For the purpose of broadcasts it is important to distinguish sponsorship of an event which is broadcast from sponsorship of the broadcast itself. Many sports and leisure events occur in the United Kingdom through sponsorship. The two existing broadcasting authorities, which are the B.B.C. and the I.B.A. will broadcast events which are financed or part-financed by sponsors subject to certain restrictions. These restrictions are dealt with below. In general, they will not broadcast programmes, films or documentaries which are themselves financed by sponsors. The difference in the eyes of broadcasting authorities is more than one of semantics and is discussed below.[60]

[56] *Ibid.* s.9(5).
[57] *Ibid.* s.9(8).
[58] *Ibid.* s.12(7).
[59] *Glyn* v. *Weston Feature Film Co.* [1916] 1 Ch. 261 at 269–270.
[60] p. 233.

Broadcasts themselves, whether in radio or television are unlikely to give rise to issues of ownership. A sponsor may have a copyright interest in a film or other material which is broadcast, but it is most unlikely that he will have any copyright in the broadcast itself.[61] The owner of copyright in a broadcast originating in the United Kingdom will be either the British Broadcasting Corporation or Independent Broadcasting Authority under sections 14(1) and 49(10) of the Copyright Act 1956. Foreign broadcasts may be protected under section 28.

(2) BOOKS

Books are literary works within section 2 of the Act; see p. 120 for the protection afforded to literary works. The publishers' interest will be separately protected under section 15 of the Act.

(3) FILMS AND VIDEOS

Sponsorship may represent a way of part financing the production of a film. The sponsor could receive credits and use the film to convey a particular message. Sponsored films may run into difficulties, however, in so far as their exhibition on television is concerned. These difficulties relate to the current I.B.A. and B.B.C. regulations which may prevent sponsored films being shown. This should be contrasted with indications of a more flexible approach with cable television. These are discussed below.

The definition of a cinematograph film is contained in section 13 of the Copyright Act. Essentially it is a sequence of visual images recorded on material of any description so as to be capable, by the use of that material, of being shown as a moving picture.[62] This definition consists of two essential elements. The first is a "sequence of visual images" and the second is a "recording capable of being shown as a moving picture." A live broadcast is not a film although a recording made from the broadcast may be protected as one. The definition clearly covers videograms, *i.e.* video cassettes or discs. It also covers films made for television such as *Starsky and Hutch*.[63] Copyright existing in the film also covers

[61] Copyright Act 1956, s.16(7).
[62] *Ibid.* s.13(10) for the full text.
[63] See the *Spelling Goldberg* case *infra*.

131

soundtrack which is written for the film and incorporated within it.[64] The first owner of copyright in a film is the maker. The maker is the person who undertakes arrangements for making the film.[64] This will often be the production company although it will be a question of fact who undertakes the arrangements in each case.

Many sponsors are keen to utilise films or video of sponsored events for in-house promotional purposes or otherwise for advertisements or in-store promotions. Permission must be obtained from the owner and others with a copyright interest except where the film will not be seen or heard in public. Taking a single frame from a film and using it in an advertisement without the permission of the owner is as much an infringement of copyright in the film as taking a more substantial part of it. Thus a pin-up taken from a still of a television film of *Starsky and Hutch* infringed copyright in the film.[65]

The meaning of "public" in this context is normally determined by looking at the nature of the audience. Showing a video of a sponsored event to employees could well be regarded as being 'in public." Thus, in *Ernest Turner* v. *P.R.S..*,[66] playing music to 600 employees working in a factory was held to be "in public." If it were exhibited in stores as part of a general corporate promotion then it would almost certainly be "in public." Similarly if it were shown to the sponsor's dealers as part of a sales drive it would probably be shown in public. The cases have been decided mainly in relation to other parts of the Act. These decisions are applicable by analogy to films. Thus "in public" included playing music in a hotel lobby,[67] playing music to 185 Rangers supporters and 25 guests,[68] and a jukebox in a restaurant.[69] In contrast, the performance of a play before an audience consisting mainly of nurses and doctors was held to

---

[64] Copyright Act 1956, s.13(10).
[65] *Spelling Goldberg Productions Inc.* v. *B.P.C. Publishing* [1981] R.P.C. 283.
[66] [1943] 1 Ch. 167.
[67] *Performing Rights Society* v. *Hawthorns Hotel (Bournemouth)* [1933] Ch. 855.
[68] *Performing Rights Society* v. *Rangers F.C. Supporters Club* [1975] R.P.C. 626.
[69] *Vigneux* v. *Canadian Performing Rights Society Ltd.* [1945] A.C. 108.

be in private.[70] This should be regarded very much as a borderline case.[71]

(4) NON BROADCAST RIGHTS AND NARROWCASTING

The concept of sponsored programming for cable television is a new area. The legal position on ownership is currently problematic. The government[72] has accepted the findings of the Hunt Report[73] and is proposing to authorise a rapid expansion of cable as a means of distributing programmes. The legal problems were briefly discussed in the Government Green Paper[74] New legislation is currently being considered contemporaneously with reform of copyright law generally.[75]

At the present time distribution of a programme by cable direct from a ground station is not broadcasting since it falls outside the definition contained in the Wireless Telegraphy Act 1949. The only protection against diffusion by cable currently contained in the Copyright Act are the rights of the owners of literary, dramatic, musical and artistic works[76] and Cinematograph films.[77] The owners of these works or materials are entitled to prevent cable distribution. There is a problem, however, even in relation to owners of this material since once they have licensed the B.B.C. or I.B.A. to broadcast then they are taken to have licensed the B.B.C. and I.B.A. to diffuse the work by cable without further payment.[78] Further, in relation to such works or material it is not a restricted act where the diffusion is part of an incidental service in hotels, flats and other places where persons reside or sleep.[79]

It seems likely[80] that the Government will introduce

---

[70] *Duck* v. *Bates* (1884) 13 Q.B. 843.

[71] Note also the case of *Canadian Admiral Corporation Ltd.* v. *Rediffusion Inc.* [1954] Ex. Cr. 382, which held that programmes which were shown to subscribers of a cable service, was not in public.

[72] See the Development of Cable Systems and Services Cmnd. 8866 (1983).

[73] Report of the Inquiry into Cable Expansion in Broadcasting Policy. Cmnd. 8679 (1982).

[74] Cmnd. 8302 (1981). Reform of the Law Relating to Copyright Designs and Performers' Protection.

[75] Cmnd. 8866 (1983) para. 163.

[76] Copyright Act 1956, ss.2 and 3.

[77] *Ibid*. s.13.

[78] *Ibid*. s.40(3).

[79] *Ibid*. s.48(3).

[80] See Reform of Law relating to *Copyright, Designs and Performer's Protection*, Cmnd. 8302 (1981).

legislation which grants the "diffuser" copyright in his diffused work.[81] The other likely amendment is that the implied licence will, in favour of the B.B.C. and I.B.A., remain, but only insofar as simultaneous diffusion of B.B.C. and I.B.A. broadcasts are concerned. Re-diffusion would be subject to separate payment.[82]

(5) PAINTINGS

Copyright will exist in paintings as artistic works under section 3 of the Act. For a discussion of the protection available see p. 138.

(6) PHOTOGRAPHS

Many sponsors are licensed to use photographs of a sponsored event or individual in connection with the promotion of their products. Where the photographs are of individuals, special considerations apply which are discussed in detail later. The general principle, however, is that photographs are artistic works under section 3(1)(a) of the Copyright Act, irrespective of artistic quality. The person who takes a photograph will own copyright in it unless it is commissioned. This produces the surprising result that a sponsor of a sporting event will often pay a fee to an agency which takes a photograph of a soccer player and nothing to the player himself. The case of *Palmer* v. *National Sporting Club* is clear authority for the absence of any rights on the part of the sportsman in this regard.[83]

Unless special considerations apply which are discussed below the sponsor, will be able to use the photograph as he wishes. He must make sure that either he or the sponsee owns copyright. In a recent case photographs of various pop groups including the Carpenters and Beatles were used in relation to the promotion of blank cassettes. Copyright in the photographs belonged to the record companies and it was held that copyright had been infringed by the use of the photographs in the advertisements for the cassette.[84] In another case the Lady

---

[81] *Ibid.* para. 22.
[82] Cmnd. 8302 (1981) para. 19.
[83] See p. 116.
[84] *A. & M. Records Inc.* v. *Audio Magnetics Inc. (U.K.)* [1979] F.S.R. 1 and also the Adam Ant case, *Merchandising Corporation of America Inc.* v. *Harpbond Ltd.* [1983] F.S.R. 32.

Anne Tennant was able to maintain an action against the *Daily Mail* when photographs which she had taken of H.R.H. Princess Margaret and Roddy Llewellyn were used without her permission.[85]

Ownership of copyright in photographs is subject to an exception regarding commissioning. If photographs are commissioned for value then it will be the commissioner who will own copyright. It seems from one early case decided under the predecessor to the current Act that the consideration for the commissioning need only be minimal. In the case of *Stackmann* v. *Paton*,[86] the headmaster of a school lined his schoolchildren up to have their photographs taken. It was held that he had given "good" consideration and therefore owned copyright in the photograph. It would be unlikely that this case would be decided the same way today.[87] Indeed there were previous cases which held that the mere attendance of celebrities at photographic sessions was not adequate consideration.

Assuming that the copyright position is clear and all fees in relation to the acquisition of copyright or a licence therein have been paid, are any additional consents required?[88] Could the sponsor, for example, commission a photographer to take shots of a soccer star in a sponsored match and use those photographs in relation to a promotion without the soccer star's consent? The basic answer to this question is yes. United Kingdom law does not recognise a right of privacy.[89] A sportsman or similar celebrity is usually in no better position than anyone else to prevent a photograph being used for promotional purposes without his consent.[90]

No real person has a proprietary right in his own features or image which will enable him or her to prevent others using photographs for commercial gain. Such rights cannot therefore be licensed to a sponsor. In *Sports and General Press Agency Ltd.* v. *"Our Dogs" Publishing Company Ltd.*[91]

---

[85] *Lady Anne Tenant* v. *Associated Newspapers Group* [1979] F.S.R. 298.
[86] [1906] 1 Ch. 774.
[87] *Copinger and Skone James on Copyright* (12th ed., 1980), p. 336.
[88] This is subject to what is said in the following chapter on trade marks and passing off.
[89] Contrast, for example, U.S. law which does, *e.g.* California Code, s.3333, and note that such a right was considered but rejected by the Younger Committee.
[90] See *Ellis* v. *H. Marshall & Son* (1895) 64 L.J.Q.B. 757.
[91] [1917] 2 K.B. 125.

which concerned the organisers of a dog show granting exclusive rights to take photographs, Swiften Eady L.J. recognising that the "Ladies Kennel Association" had been put to trouble and expense in organising the show which was their property and which included the right to take photographs themselves and to grant the same to others, stated that "In my opinion it is not accurate to speak of the right of taking photographs as property."[92] "In my judgment no-one possesses the right to prevent another person photographing him any more than he has the right to prevent another person giving a description of him, provided the description is not libellous or otherwise wrongful."[93]

Where the photograph is of something which already enjoys protection under some other part of the Copyright Act such as an artistic work, sculpture[94] or painting then the copyright owner may be able to prevent photographs being taken and reproduced. A suite of furniture of a distinct design was not considered to be a work of artistic craftsmanship,[95] nor was the face of Adam Ant an artistic work when made up.[96] One could envisage this applying where photographs of a famous painting are sold as postcards. A special exception exists, however, under section 9(3) of the Act which provides that copyright in artistic works on public display, is not infringed by taking photographs of them. However, it is often a term of admission to such places that no photographs will be taken.

(7) PLAYS

Plays are "dramatic" works within section 2 of the Act. A dramatic work is defined in section 48(1) as a "choreographic work or entertainment in dumb show if reduced to writing in the form in which the work or entertainment is to be presented." It will be noted that what is protected is the written word. Thus a film cannot be a dramatic work but the script or storyboard can be. For the protection afforded to dramatic works, see literary works at p. 138.

---

[92] p. 127.
[93] See also *Palmer* v. *National Sporting Club* (1905) 10 MacG.C.C. 55.
[94] See, for example, *Wham-O Manufacturing Co.* v. *Lincoln Industries Ltd.* [1982] R.P.C. 281, where the wooden models of a frisbee were held to be sculptures.
[95] *Hensher (George)* v. *Restawile Upholstery (Lancs)* [1976] A.C. 64.
[96] *Merchandising Corporation of America Inc.* v. *Harpbond Ltd, supra.*

(8) RECORDS

Copyright will exist in records and tapes under section 12 of the Act. For the protection available see p. 149.

(9) SATELLITE BROADCASTING

The legal implications of satellite broadcasting were again considered in the Green Paper.[97] It argues (without coming to any conclusion) that the "up leg" stage in relation to direct broadcast satellites may require protection. It is felt that the "down leg" stage is already covered under broadcasting. Pirating of the signal transmitted between point to point satellites is already protected by the Wireless Telegraphy Act 1949.

(10) SCULPTURES

Copyright will exist in sculptures as works of artistic craftsmanship under section 3 of the Act. For the protection available to artistic works see p. 138.

(11) SPORTS EVENTS

No copyright exists in a sports event.[98]

Sponsorship licences and copyright

(1) TITLES AND SIMILAR SLOGANS

Rights for an event to be named after a sponsor such as the "Milk Cup" or "Marlborough Grand Prix" are important. Within a similar category are rights promoting some official status to an event or body such as "Official Supplier of Soft Drinks to the World Cup" or "The Official Audio Company to the Youth Orchestra."

Although it has been argued that copyright can exist in titles or similar slogans,[99] decided cases have shown little enthusiasm for affording copyright protection to a title. Thus

---

[97] Cmnd. 8302.
[98] The only exception might be "wrestling" contests which occasionally appear to be acted according to a script or a fixed fight.
[99] See *Lamb* v. *Evans* [1893] 1 Ch. 218.

copyright has not been found to exist in titles such as "Exxon,"[1] "where there's a will there's a way,"[2] "Splendid Misery,"[3] and "The man who broke the bank in Monte Carlo."[4]

The reason why copyright is unlikely to exist in titles and slogans appears to be that they cannot in themselves amount to "literary" works under section 2(1) of the Act. Clearly the brevity of such titles or slogans has much to do with the refusal of the courts to afford them protection.[5] A great deal of original thought and effort may go into the creation of event titles and similar slogans, notwithstanding their brevity and one might argue that the economic investment in their creation should justify protection under the Copyright Act.

(2) USE OF MARKS

The official 1982 soccer World Cup mascot which was a small orange device called "Naranjito" became familiar throughout the world. In addition to being seen by television audiences it was featured in the Press and other media. The World Cup sponsors such as Coca-Cola included it on millions of their products.

Marks usually start their life as sketches or drawings and therefore, irrespective of their artistic quality but subject to their originality, will be protected as artistic works under section 3(1) of the Copyright Act. Thus copyright in the posters used to advertise the film *Jaws* was infringed by reproducing the work in a material form on T-shirts.[6] Where, however, marks start life in some three dimensional format such as a piece of sculpture or work of art uniquely associated with a theatre or gallery then they may be protected under section 3(1) as original works of artistic craftsmanship. The death mask of the Nigerian king was an artistic work.[7] The work was merchandised on scarves and similar objects. An

---

[1] *Exxon Corporation* v. *Exxon Insurance Consultants International Ltd.* [1982] Ch. 119.

[2] *Broemel* v. *Meyer* (1912) 29 T.L.R. 148.

[3] *Beckett* v. *Attwood* (1881) 44 L.T. 660.

[4] *Francis Day and Hunter Ltd.* v. *Twentieth Century Fox Corporation Ltd.* [1940] A.C. 112.

[5] See P. Circis, (1981) 131 New L.J. 618.

[6] *Universal City Studios Inc.* v. *Mukhtar & Sons* [1976] 1 W.L.R. 568.

[7] *James Arnold & Co.* v. *Miafern* [1980] R.P.C. 397. See also *Wham-O Manufacturing Co.* v. *Lincoln Industries Ltd.* [1982] R.P.C. 281.

infringement will occur where a "substantial part" and not necessarily the whole work is copied.[8] Where part is copied it must be a part in which copyright can exist in its own right. Thus, copying two straight lines would not be an infringement.[9]

However marks start their lives, the sponsee who intends licensing them should always think about proving his title to copyright.[9a] It is particularly important therefore to obtain a written assignment of copyright from the artist pursuant to section 36 of the Act. Although section 20 of the Copyright Act creates various presumptions in favour of ownership, the sponsee may be required to produce evidence of his title to prospective sponsors before they sign their agreements. It will also help the position of the sponsee in securing withdrawals or settlements from "pirates" if he can produce a formal document establishing his title.

Where marks are translated into a three dimensional format such as a doll or brooch section 3(1)(a), 9(8) and 48 of the Copyright Act may apply. Thus, in the case of *Kings Features Syndicate Inc.* v. *Kleeman,*[10] the plaintiffs owned copyright in the "Popeye the Sailor" cartoon strip. The defendants imported dolls and brooches which were made in the shape of "Popeye." The court held that the dolls and brooches infringed copyright in the drawings belonging to the plaintiff. The Act requires, however, that the three dimensional model be taken from the original work.[11] It is also an infringement to produce a two dimensional work from a three dimensional object.[12] In the case of *Spelling Goldberg Productions Inc.* v. *B.P.C. Publishing,* copyright in the single frame of a film was infringed by making a poster from it. If a three dimensional object were taken from a still of the film, copyright would not have been infringed since section 9(8), which prevents three dimensional copying of two dimensional artistic works, does not apply to films, since they are not artistic works.[13]

The marks may incorporate titles such as "World Games" as an integral part. Words themselves, as already discussed,[14]

---

[8] *L.B. (Plastics)* v. *Swish Products* [1979] F.S.R. 145.
[9] *Merchandising Corporation of America* v. *Harpbond Ltd.* [1983] F.S.R. 32.
[9a] *Merchant-Adventurers* v. *M. Grew* [1972] 1 Ch. 242.
[10] [1941] A.C. 417.
[11] *L.B. (Plastics)* v. *Swish Products* [1979] F.S.R. 145.
[12] Copyright Act 1956, s.48.
[13] See *James Arnold & Co.* v. *Miafern* [1980] R.P.C. 397.
[14] See p. 137.

are unlikely to be protected by copyright. Where they are incorporated into some graphics or artwork or are heavily stylised, then they may be protected as artistic works. Thus in *Karo Step*[15] copyright existed for the words "Karo Step" which were stylised and surrounded by a few distinctive graphics. Where a legend or name is combined with an artistic device, the sponsor must understand what rights he is acquiring. The official symbol of the 1982 soccer World Cup, for example, had the legend "Espana 82" underneath. The entire device was licensed to sponsors. More than one sponsor complained about competitive unlicensed merchandise bearing the words "Espana 82." It was impossible to prevent the unauthorised merchandise flooding the market since no copyright could exist in the legend "Espana 82" when used on its own. Since the sponsors thought they had acquired "exclusive" rights to the entire device, some felt aggrieved.

Registered designs

In considering the degree of protection and commercial monopoly available to a sponsor for three dimensional items it may be important to establish whether any additional or superior protection is available under the registered design legislation.[16] Conceptually the registered design legislation seems to have been intended to protect the interests of manufacturers of industrial items which fell short of being protected as patents, due to lack of inventiveness and were not really artistic works under the Copyright Act. The registered design legislation permits registration of certain designs under section 1(3) of the 1949 Act. Once registered, the owner of the design may prevent others from applying his design industrially.

The exclusivity available is for up to three consecutive periods of five years each, *i.e.* 15 years in total. After expiry of the protected period other manufacturers may step in and apply the design industrially.[17] Industrial application is defined as the production of more than 30 articles or non-handmade goods manufactured in lengths or pieces.[18]

---

[15] [1975] R.P.C. 255.
[16] See the Registered Designs Act 1949 and ss.10 and 44 of the Copyright Act 1956, amended by the Design Copyright Act 1968.
[17] Registered Designs Act 1949, s.10(5).
[18] *Ibid.* s.36, as amended by the Copyright Act 1956, s.10(5).

During the 15 year period the owner has wide exclusive rights to make, import or sell the protected design.

Registered design legislation conflicts with the protection already available for artistic works which start their life as drawings or other protected works under section 3 of the Copyright Act. Indeed the effect of the overlap produces the result that under the present law no superior protection appears to be available to the sponsee or sponsor in registering a character such as a "Naranjito" doll as a registered design except where it did not start life as a drawing, photograph or other object protected under the Copyright Act.[19] The other possible advantage of registering a mark as an industrial design is where the character will be animated or placed in different positions. Since copyright only protects particular drawings, problems may arise if the marks are slightly changed and then reproduced on T-shirts, etc. Since a registered design protects the article itself rather than copying from the drawing, it is at least arguable that registration may provide additional protection. Generally, however, since exclusivity is conferred under the Copyright Act for the life of the artist plus 50 years, that is preferable to 15 years exclusivity under the registered design legislation. It is important, therefore, to ensure that the article such as the doll which is applied industrially starts life as a sketch or drawing. A recent case[20] has held that once any article is applied industrially then the maximum period of protection is 15 years. This decision is against previous authorities.[21]

(3) USE OF NAME, IMAGE, VOICE OR LIKENESS

The main distinction between this section and the previous one is that mascots, symbols, etc., will usually exist as artistic works or drawings with the consequence that copyright protection will be available. It is comparatively easy to establish that any similar mascots or symbols on the market

---

[19] It should be noted here that works of sculpture are not registrable anyway: Designs Rules 1949 (S.I. 1949 No. 2368) r.26.

[20] *Hoover plc.* v. *Hulme (STO)* [1982] C.M.L.R. 186. See also (1982) New L.J. 1082.

[21] See *Sifam Electrical Instrument Co.* v. *Sangamo Weston* [1971] 2 All E.R. 1074, applying *Dorling* v. *Honnor Marine* [1965] Ch. 1. In the *Sifam* case the face of an ammeter, which was not registrable under the 1949 Act, was given protection for the full term of 50 years from the artist's death. These cases were decided under the 1949 and 1956 Acts.

have been copied from the original since the chances of two people simultaneously producing the same design is very small. No independent copyright or other property exists, however, in a name, image, voice or likeness under English law.

Thus in a case already mentioned[22] it was stated that "no one possesses a right of preventing another person photographing him any more than he has a right of preventing another person from giving a description of him." In another case a woman was unable to prevent the sale of picture postcards depicting her driving a pair of ponies and similar scenes.[23]

In another case, Jack Palmer and Gunner James Moir entered into a written contract to box for a purse of £350 at the National Sporting Club, Covent Garden. No written agreement was entered into with the club itself. The National Sporting Club entered into a contract with a film company in which they purported to grant "exclusive cinematographic rights to take bioscope pictures of the Moir-Palmer boxing match." Palmer objected to being filmed, the basis of his objection being that in America the practice was that boxers received a share of income from the sale of the film. It was held that Palmer had no right to prevent his being filmed in the fight and further was not entitled to any income arising from sales of the film.[24]

The effect of the distinction is simply demonstrated. It would be reasonable to expect a sponsor of a football club to obtain the right to use photographs of the team when promoting his sponsorship. Since, however, the team have no right to prevent people coming to the ground and taking photographs of them (except where the taking of photographs was expressly prohibited as a condition of the contract for entry of the public to the grounds[25]) no general exclusivity can be conferred on the sponsor with respect to the use of the team's image or likeness.

It has been seen that copyright does exist in photographs.[26]

---

[22] *Special and General Press Agency* v. *"Our Dogs" Publishing Co.* [1917] 2 K.B. 125.

[23] *Corelli* v. *Wall* (1906) 22 T.L.R. 532.

[24] *Palmer* v. *The National Sporting Club Ltd.* (1905) 10 MacG.C.C. 55, also *Corelli* v. *Wall* (1906) 22 T.L.R. 532, and (1905) 41 MacG.C.C.

[25] See *Special and General Agency* v. *"Our Dogs" Publishing* [1917] 2 K.B. 125.

[26] See p. 134.

Copyright in photographs only prevents others using a particular photograph. It does not prevent someone else taking a different photograph of the same object on the same day and from the same angle. Thus in one case no infringement of copyright took place where two different photographers took photographs of the same furniture from the same angle. It was suggested that the arrangement of furniture was an artistic work but this argument was rejected.[27] In a more recent case the argument that a heavily made up face was a "painting" and therefore an artistic work was also rejected.[28] It is therefore more difficult for sportsmen, actors or others who will be of interest to sponsors because of their media value to prevent personality piracy. Where a particular photograph is copied, such as that of the Carpenters and the Beatles, then the situation is different.[29]

There have been debates for some time in the United Kingdom[30] on the introduction of a right of "privacy" or "publicity" as exists in certain continental jurisdictions such as France and in the United States.[31] Such a right might recognise that an individual has some form of proprietory interest in his own personality, i.e. name, image, likeness. This right could enable an individual to prevent others using his "personality" without his consent. There is in the authors' view a great deal of logic and argument in favour of the introduction of such a right.[32]

A recent United States case well illustrates the American solution. It is submitted that if the same case were heard in the United Kingdom no remedy would be available.[33] A professional baseball player granted a chewing gum manufacturer the exclusive right to use his photographs in advertisements. The player then granted another chewing gum manufacturer the right to use his photograph. The court recognised, in an action by the first chewing gum manufacturer, that the

---

[27] *Jarman & Platt* v. *Barget (I)* F.S.R. 260 C.A.
[28] See also *Merchandising Corporation of America Inc.* v. *Harpbond Ltd.* [1983] F.S.R. 32.
[29] See *A. & M. Records Inc.* v. *Audio Magnetics Inc. (U.K.)* [1979] F.S.R. 1 at p. 154 above.
[30] See, for example, the Younger Committee Report, Cmnd. 5012 (1972).
[31] See "Celebrity Endorsements" by Michael E. Jones (1979) 15 N.Eng. L.Rev. at 521.
[32] See Wayne de Nicols, "Personality Piracy" 78 L.S. Gaz. 150.
[33] *Haelan Laboratories Inc.* v. *Topps Chewing Gum* (1979) 202 F.2d. 816 (1953).

baseball player had a "right of publicity" which allowed him to receive payment for the authorised use of his name or likeness and collect pecuniary damages when an advertiser used his likeness without authorisation. Similarly in another case *Uhlaender* v. *Henricksen*[34] it was stated that "a celebrity must be considered to have invested his years of practice and competition in a public personality which eventually may reach marketable status. The identity embodied in his name, likeness, statistics and personal characteristics is the fruit of his labours and is a type of property."

It will be a matter for the sponsor to agree in his contract with the sponsee (and the sponsee in turn to decide exactly what rights he has over teams, etc.) what rights, if any, he will receive with regard to names, images, likeness, etc. The range of possibilities start with the sponsor being entitled to use photographs of, for example, a sponsored football match, musical event or cultural exhibition. At the opposite end of the scale the sponsor might receive a full endorsement in the sense that an individual or group of individuals such as a football team might proclaim "we believe Fiat cars are the best."

It may be assumed that however discreet or subtle the use of a name, image or likeness by the sponsor, it is intended to persuade the public that the rock star, basketball player, or team has freely selected the sponsors products or services as being the ones which he, she or they genuinely prefer. The selection of a particular image will depend upon the message which the sponsor wishes to convey. Thus in the days when tobacco companies were keen to promote the supposed health benefits of cigarettes, R.J. Reynolds Tobacco entered into direct endorsement contract with an athlete. The athlete's image was shown in association with the following endorsement "when the pace gets me fatigued a camel [which is an R.J. Reynolds brand of cigarette] gives me a lift."[35]

It is conceivable that the endorsement may be given by a fictional character as well as a real one. For example, Johnny Weismuller, who portrayed Tarzan, endorsed a product known as "Wheaties" in the character of the Tarzan role. A sponsor of a film or play might well require the lead character to endorse his products.

English law, despite denying the existence of a proprietary

[34] 316 F.Supp. 1277 at 1282.
[35] See *R.J. Reynolds Tobacco Co.* v. *F.T.C.* 192 F.2d. 535 (7th circuit 1951).

right in a personality, has applied existing common law remedies such as passing off, defamation and the Routh-Webster Injunction (which are all discussed below) to provide some form of protection against "personality piracy." In the authors' view, the English courts have not always been ready to understand and support modern marketing practices. However, it is important that evidence of such practices should be available to the court.[36] One is therefore left with a complicated hotch-potch of remedies. It is surely a peculiar state of the law when a fictional character, such as Popeye which can only exist as a drawing[37] is given protection against unauthorised use but a real character, for example, Sebastian Coe, is not.

Name

No copyright exists in either a real or fictitious name.[38]

Signature

Copyright may exist in a signature.[39]

Image or likeness

No copyright exists in the image of a person, in or out of character. Copyright may exist, however, in a photograph of that person or in a sketch or drawing under section 3(1) of the Copyright Act[40] or a cinematograph film.[41] Copyright will only protect the particular sketch or photograph or frame of film, thus if someone else independently makes their own sketch, photograph or film, then the person featured will have to look to some remedy other than copyright.[42]

---

[36] See, for example, *Lego v. Lego Lemelstrich Ltd.* [1983] F.S.R. 155 where evidence of a market research survey was adduced to establish that the public were confused by the use of the name "Lego" in relation to irrigation equipment.

[37] See *Klarman v. King Features Syndicate, supra.*

[38] See p. 138.

[39] See *Copinger and Skone James on Copyright* (12th ed., 1980), see p. 34, n. 2.

[40] See p. 134.

[41] *Spelling Goldberg Productions Inc. v. B.P.C. Publishing* [1981] R.P.C. 283.

[42] *Jarman & Platt v. Barget (I)* [1977] F.S.R. 260, C.A.

Although copyright itself is unlikely to be of much assistance, the Performers Protection Acts which are closely related to copyright may be. This legislation affords certain protection to specific classes of individual essentially whilst they are "performing" copyright works. The protection makes it an offence to reproduce, broadcast or transmit without the written consent of the performer.[43] *The Act makes infringement a criminal offence.* No civil right of action based upon breach of statutory duty is available either for performers or record companies. Thus in a recent case the Court of Appeal felt bound by a previous decision[44] and refused relief for record companies who had acquired exclusive rights regarding record performances of Elvis Presley.[45] The relief sought was against "bootleggers."[46]

The Performers Protection Acts comprise the Dramatic and Musical Performers Protection Act 1958 and the Performers' Protection Act 1963 (the Dramatic and Musical Performers' Protection Act 1972 merely increased the penalties). The protection extends to actors, singers, musicians and dancers[47] in their performances of dramatic, literary, musical or artistic works.[48] There are two important conditions for the Acts to apply, the first being that protection extends only to the defined categories of individuals and secondly, the protection only applies whilst they are performing the protected works. No general right of privacy is conferred.

Once these conditions have been satisfied and the performance is protected it becomes an offence knowingly to include that performance in a record,[49] film or parts of a film.[50] Film would include a video, and therefore would apply to the unauthorised recording on video of a rock concert or broadcast[51] or in material transmitted to subscribers to a diffusion service.[52] This would cover, for example, transmis-

---

[43] Dramatic and Musical Performers Protection Act 1958, ss.(1)(*a*), (2)(*a*) and 3.

[44] *Ex p. Island Records* [1978] 1 Ch. 122.

[45] *R.C.A. Corporation* v. *Pollard* [1983] F.S.R. 9.

[46] See also *Peter Shelley* v. *Peter Cunane*, as yet unreported, for which leave to appeal to the Court of Appeal has been granted. (1983) 133 New L.J. 377.

[47] See the Performers Protection Act 1963, s.1(1).

[48] See the Dramatic and Musical Performers Protection Act 1958, s.1(1).

[49] *Ibid.* s.1(*b*).

[50] *Ibid.* s.2.

[51] *Ibid.* s.3.

[52] Performers Protection Act 1963, s.3(1).

sion to subscribers to a diffusion service (e.g. a cable network) or over wires or other paths so as to be seen by the public,[53] or to use the record or film in a public performance.[54]

It will be seen, therefore, that the Performers Protection Acts provide limited protection to certain categories of individual, insofar as it will be necessary to obtain their written consent before using their performance.[55] The importance of the protection, however, is more in how it will be developed in the future rather than its existing scope. The Government Green Paper has recognised that the performers should have a civil remedy alongside the criminal one.[56] The Government also recognise in the Green Paper the possibility of extending the scope of the Act as recommended by the Whitford Committee Report[57] to include variety artists performing non-copyright works. This is undoubtedly a small step towards recognising a right of privacy or publicity since the next category which must be included is sportsmen and women. The lobby created in this regard by the Sportsmans Rights Society Limited should be noted.

The relevance of the Performers Protection Acts to protecting a name, image or likeness may be summarised as follows: actors, singers, musicians and dancers or other persons who act sing deliver, declaim, play in, or otherwise perform, literary dramatic, musical, or artistic works are the only individuals currently protected. Even within these protected categories the prohibited acts do not include taking photographs or reproducing drawings. It would be an offence, however, to make a video of a sponsored musical concert for commercial purposes. A sponsor of a play would need to obtain the consent of the actors to make a commercial video even though he has obtained legitimate access to the venue and has secured consent from others with a copyright interest such as the playwright. This would not apply, however, to the sponsor of a sporting event since sportsmen do not fall within the list of protected categories specified above, (Sportsmen will also not be performing copyright works and therefore in contrast to a concert where the music

---

[53] *Ibid.* 3(1)(*a*) and (*b*).

[54] Dramatic and Musical Performers Protection Act 1958, ss.1(*b*) and 2(*c*).

[55] The consent may also be given by their representative, *e.g.* agent; *ibid.* s.7.

[56] The maximum fine is currently £1000, Performers' Protection Act 1972 and Criminal Law Act 1977, s.28.

[57] Cmnd. 6732 (1976).

itself will probably be subject to copyright under section 3(1) of the Copyright Act 1956, no legislative protection exists).

It would also seem that the Performers Protection Acts are of no use in preventing the image of musicians, singers, etc., being reproduced on promotional merchandise such as T-shirts without their consent.

Voices

No copyright exists in a voice as such,[58] although copyright would exist in a sound recording and television broadcast under sections 12 and 14 of the Copyright Act respectively. An advertisement using a voice similar to that of a famous cricket commentator to advertise a particular make of bat would not be an infringement of copyright but editing the voice of a real commentator recorded from the television would be an infringement of copyright but not against the commentator, but B.B.C. or I.T.V. respectively.

Direct endorsements

Any direct endorsement by a sportsman, pop group, actor or other person, should depend upon their consents. John McEnroe, for example, is not going to stand up and proclaim the virtues of a particular tennis racquet unless he chooses to do so on the basis of an agreement reached with the manufacturer.

The consent may be obtained through a sponsorship agreement. Problems may arise, however, when the sponsor is not contracting with the individual or group of individuals who actually perform the endorsement but with a club or representative body. In football, for example, if the club agrees that its team will turn up three times a year to proclaim the virtues of driving a particular car, the sponsor should satisfy himself that the club has the right to contract in this manner with regard to its team. The Professional Football Players Union, the P.F.A. is particularly keen to ensure that its members retain as many commercial rights as possible which can produce direct income for its members. These are matters involving contract rather than property.

Situations can arise when a direct endorsement occurs without any consent. In the famous case of *Tolley* v. *Fry*[59] an

[58] *Sim* v. *Heinz (H.J.) & Co.* [1959] 1 W.L.R. 313.
[59] [1931] A.C. 333.

148

amateur golfer, Tolley, was shown in an advertisement with a bar of Fry's chocolate protruding from his back pocket. Tolley's caddy was proclaiming the virtues of Fry's chocolate to Tolley. No consent was obtained from Tolley and he obtained damages for defamation. In these circumstances, the famous individual involved is in no better position in preventing an unauthorised use than one who is unknown to the public.

The direct endorsement will not necessarily involve the use of a name, image, likeness or voice. In sponsorship contracts the right to use phrases such as the "official football of the World Cup" is clearly designed to create the impression that the World Cup organisers selected one particular ball in preference to another. In a United States case[60] the following words were used by a wholesaler: "Official Golf Ball. This golf ball is standard and official as required by the United States Golf Association, the Royal and Ancient Club and other governing bodies." The official Golfing Authority will be unable to prevent the use of such a slogan under United Kingdom copyright law unless it comprises a literary work under section 2(1)[61] which the Golf Authorities owned.[62]

(4) USE OF OFFICIAL MUSIC

Just as specific marks are often created for use in connection with specific events, so too is official music. The 1982 soccer World Cup, for example, had a theme tune which was officially adopted by the Organising Committee. This music went out during the transmission of the televised matches by the Spanish Broadcasting Network.

Copyright will exist in a musical work subject to section 2(1) of the Copyright Act. The author of a protected musical work is given wide powers to control its exploitation.[63] Similarly where a record is made from the work then copyright will exist in the sound recording.[64] A sponsor, therefore, who acquires exclusive rights to use the official music of a sponsored event in advertisements or in relation to the promotion of his products, can feel reasonably secure that his exclusivity can be protected.

[60] *Federal Trade Commission* v. *Allied Golf Company* (1924) 7 F.T.C. 250.
[61] See p. 137.
[62] Subject to what may be said in the chapters that follow.
[63] s.2(5).
[64] s.12.

It should be noted, however, that section 8 of the Copyright Act provides a statutory licence to make a record or adaptation thereof in the United Kingdom for the purpose of retail sale,[65] subject to the existing record having previously been made in or imported into the United Kingdom by or with the licence of the owner and for the purpose of retail sale[66] and 15 days notice has been given to the copyright owner[67] and a six and one-quarter per cent royalty is paid.[68] Despite this statutory licence a number of individual deals are being negotiated at different rates of royalty. The terms of this statutory licence only permit a record to be made. It is not an authorisation to use the existing one.

A sponsor will usually acquire the exclusive right to use the official music or record in a promotional sense. The statutory recording licence does not permit the making of a record which will be used for promotional purposes. This is illustrated by the case of *Chappell & Co. v. Nestlé & Co.*[69] Nestlé, who manufactured chocolate, purchased gramaphone records containing a musical work and an advertising slogan. The records were offered by Nestlé to the public at the price of 1s.6d. and three six penny chocolate bar wrappers. It was held in an action against both Nestlé and the company that produced the records that such a use was not a retail sale under section 8(1) and therefore the company which produced the records had infringed copyright in the records which belonged to the plaintiff.

---

[65] s.8(1)(*c*).
[66] s.8(1)(*a*) for full text as further conditions attach.
[67] s.8(1)(*b*).
[68] ss.8(1)(*d*) and 8(2).
[69] [1960] A.C. 87.

10. Trade Marks

Copyright in a drawing of a character that may be merchandised in connection with a sponsored event or used on the sponsors products, may give rise immediately to proprietory interests without formalities such as registration. Proprietory interests in names as we shall see, require use in the market place before the common law will recognise and protect goodwill attaching to them. Trade marks come somewhere between copyright which exists immediately the criteria set out in the Copyright Act is satisfied and common law rights which only exist after the reputation known as "get up" has been established. After a stringent process of examination and other requirements have been met it may be possible to register a name, character or logo as a trade mark. That trade mark may then be licensed to the sponsor.

Within the context of sponsorship, trade marks are important in two main areas. Firstly, in relation to a logo, character or name of an event, and secondly, names of sponsors registered as trade marks when used by the sponsee in connection with a sponsored event. The latter use is only of relevance insofar as the sponsor may seek to ensure that the sponsee does nothing to prejudice ownership of a company name or logo registered as a trade mark.[1]

There are a number of factors to consider in weighing up the desirability of trade mark registration, not the least of which is whether superior protection is available to that existing under copyright or common law. Registration of a trade mark in contrast to copyright and common law protection involves the payment of a registration fee. An international trade mark registration programme for an event such as the 1982 soccer World Cup could cost in excess of £100,000. Careful planning and thought is therefore required before embarking on such expense. A short section of this

[1] See p. 71 below.

chapter has been set aside to deal with the practical matters of planning such a trade mark registration programme on an international basis.

The main advantages of registering a name or device as a trade mark are: first, protection may be secured for names and other matters which would not be protected under copyright or by the common law. Secondly, monopoly over a name or device may be secured before it has established itself in the market place and common law remedies such as passing off apply. Thirdly, once registered, proceedings against infringers may be more straightforward than under copyright or common law, since registration is proof of ownership. It is similar to being able to show that you own a house because your name appears on the register of title at H.M. land registry and proving title of unregistered land by deducing title through the various deeds and other documents.

Registration of trade marks

(1) WHY REGISTER?

The object of registering a trade mark within the overall context of sponsorship is to ensure that the sponsee owns property in the mark and is therefore able to protect the licences acquired by the sponsor, insofar as copyright and common law rights may be deficient. The main areas of deficiency are names, whether real or fictional, slogans, etc. Logos, designs and characters representing the sponsee or sponsored events are also often registered as trade marks even though copyright may exist. This occurs particularly where the sponsorship object is international such as a worldwide tennis tournament and it will be necessary to rely upon foreign courts and foreign procedures to protect the licences. Such courts may not recognise copyright and other remedies to the same extent as does United Kingdom law. Sponsors and other licensees of logos may also find some reassurance in paying money to use the mark after they know it has passed the stringent requirements of trade mark registration.

(2) DEFINITION

A mark is defined in the Trade Marks Act 1938 as a mark (being a device, brand, heading, label, ticket, name, signature, word, letter, numeral or any combination thereof). To be a trade mark within the terms of the Act it must be used or proposed to be used in relation to goods for the purpose of indicating a connection in the course of trade between the goods and some person having the right either as proprietor or as registered user to use the mark.[2] On this basis the use of the trade mark "Coca-Cola" (Reg. T.M.) on cans shows that the Coca-Cola Company has manufactured or licensed a bottler to manufacturer its product. A trade mark may be a two or three dimensional object.[3]

(3) FORMAL REQUIREMENTS FOR REGISTRATION

Application for registration may be made under Part A or Part B of the Trade Mark Register.[4] Part A has more stringent conditions for eligibility than Part B. The remedies available under Part B are more restricted than Part A.[5] It is unlikely that an applicant would deliberately apply for registration in Part B. Where he is unable to satisfy the conditions of Part A the registrar of trade marks (to whom applications will be made) may direct that the application may only be granted in part B.

The remainder of this Chapter is concerned with applications made under Part A, unless otherwise indicated.

Registration of a mark depends upon the proprietor[6] satisfying the criteria set out in section 9(1) of the Act. The criteria require the mark to contain or consist of at least one of the following:

(a) the name of a company, individual or firm represented in a special or particular manner;

(b) the signature of the applicant for registration or some predecessor in his business;

(c) an invented word or invented words;

(d) a word or words having no direct reference to the character or quality of the goods and not being according to ordinary signification, a geographical name or a surname; or

---

[2] Trade Marks Act 1938, s.68(1).
[3] *Smith, Kline & French Laboratories' Application* [1968] R.P.C. 415.
[4] Trade Mark Act 1938, s.1(2).
[5] See Cornish, *Intellectual Property: Patents, Copyright, Trade Marks and Allied Rights* (1981) p. 561 and Greene M.R. in *Saville Perfumery* v. *June Perfect* (1941) 58 R.P.C. 147.
[6] Trade Marks Act 1938, s.17.

(e) any other distinctive mark but a name, signature, word or words other than such as fall within the descriptions in the foregoing paragraphs (a), (b), (c) and (d) shall not be registrable under the provisions of this paragraph except upon evidence of its distinctiveness.

Some examples of how these have relevance to sponsorship include: company wishing to launch a new product under the name of a sponsored individual, *e.g.* Stirling Moss driving gloves, or World Games pens; or a company wishing to use the symbol of a sponsored tournament on its products or in advertisements.

Taking the definition of a trade mark and the criteria for registration together, a number of points emerge.

(a) *Intention to use the mark*

It is the proprietor of the mark who must intend to use it on the goods covered by the application.[7] Where the proprietor does not intend to use the mark himself on the goods in question then the application must be accompanied by an additional application for the licensee *i.e.* sponsor to be registered as a user of the trade mark.[8] The registered user agreement must be filed at the time of the application if the proprietor has no intention to use the mark. The other exception to the requirement of "intention to use" the mark is in the case of a person filing on behalf of a company which is about to be incorporated.[9]

The requirement of intention to use is fundamental to registration. It is not sufficient that the proprietor intends to license the trade mark unless it is accompanied by the registered user agreement as outlined above. Thus where a company was formed to licence the name "Pussy Galore" which arose out of an Ian Fleming novel, the application failed since there was no intention on the part of the company to use the name. All it intended to do was to issue licences.[10] Intention to use also means intention to use within the United Kingdom. Where an application was made to register the name "Rawhide" in the United Kingdom which came from a United States television cowboy series, the judge doubted any

---

[7] *Ibid.* s.17(1).
[8] *Ibid.* ss.28 and 29(1).
[9] *Ibid.* s.29(1)(*a*).
[10] "*Pussy Galore*" *Trade Mark (Registration)* [1967] R.P.C. 265.

intention to use if the series was never shown in the United Kingdom.[11]

The Registrar has an overriding discretion to refuse the application to register a registered user, where it appears that granting the application would facilitate trafficking in the mark.[12] This discretion was recently exercised in the Hollie Hobbie Trade Mark case, and the Registrar's decision was confirmed by Whitford J. in the High Court and by the Court of Appeal.[13] Hollie Hobbie was a device consisting of a young girl in calico and lace with the name Hollie Hobbie underneath. It was originally used on greeting cards but due to its popularity had subsequently been licenced on T-shirts and numerous other products. The owners of the device American Greetings Cards sought to register it as a trade mark in the United Kingdom in a number of different categories. The applications were accompanied by registered user agreements since American Greetings Cards did not intend to use the device themselves, only to license it. The applications were rejected on the basis that granting the applications would have facilitated trafficking in the trade mark.

The decision of Whitford J. affirming that of the registrar appears to have been influenced by a number of factors. These included the fact that some twelve applications in different categories were filed at once and that the term of the licences was less than the seven year term which is the initial period of protection under the Act. Dillon J.[13a] in the Court of Appeal rejected the argument that any deception was required in the anti-trafficking provision and indicated that trafficking meant " . . . disposing of the mark, or the reputation in the name, as of itself a marketable commodity in circumstances where there is no trade connection between the proprietor of the mark and the goods or business in relation to which the mark will be used." This case has serious repercussions on the desirability and tactics of applying for trade mark registrations for sponsored events.

A private members' bill was introduced into the House of

---

[11] Re Cheryl Playthings' Application, sub. nom. "Rawhide" Trade Mark [1962] R.P.C. 133.

[12] Trade Marks Act 1938, s.28(6).

[13] Re American Greetings Corporation's Application [1983] 1 W.L.R. 912; [1983] F.S.R. 138.

[13a] [1983] 1 W.L.R. 912 at 919.

Lords by Lord Campbell of Alloway Q.C., as the Trademarks Act 1938 (Amendment) bill to provide protection of
service marks by registration.[14]

The objection of lack of intention of the applicant to use
the mark is raised more frequently than any other where
sports federations undertake trade mark registration programmes. The problem is understandable when the application
is made in relation to goods as diverse as cameras and soft
drinks. The sports federation will be seeking to cover the
product categories of potential sponsors. Registered user
agreements are impossible to produce in many cases since at
that stage the sports federation will be filing in anticipation of
future sponsors (this problem is discussed briefly under
planning the programme).

Intention to use is not a requirement in one exceptional
case which is called defensive registration.[15]

(b) *Use in relation to goods.*

The mark must be used in relation to goods, the effect
being that one could not, for example, register a name used in
relation to banking or insurance services. Where services are
applied directly to goods before they reach the consumer,
then it may be possible to register a trade mark for the
service.[16] The current international classification of goods
covers some 42 classes including seven service categories but
these may not be applied for in the United Kingdom.[16a]

(c) *The mark must be distinctive*

Trade marks enable the consumer to distinguish those
goods bearing the trade mark from other similar goods.
Obviously the consumer can distinguish a hammer from a
pork pie but what about one pork pie from another?
Distinctiveness is an important requirement of all trade
marks. If a mark is in everyday use then it would clearly be

---

[14] This bill passed the House of Lords and was sent to the House of Commons but fell with the dissolution of parliament. It was reintroduced in
the House of Commons by Mr. Stephen Dorrell M.P. on July 20, 1983.
A second reading was due on November 11, 1983.

[15] Trade Marks Act 1938, s.27.

[16] See Cornish, *Intellectual Property: Patents, Copyright, Trade Marks and
Allied Rights* (1981) p. 517 and *Aristoc* v. *Rysta* [1945] A.C. 68.

[16a] But see n.14 above.

unfair to confer a monopoly via a trade mark on one trader for his products to the prejudice of all others. One might imagine in the pork pie example that words such as "Prime Pork Pies" could not be registrable for this reason. Distinctiveness may be present in a particular combination of colours.[17]

Distinctiveness means that the mark must have been adapted to distinguish the proprietor's goods from others.[18] Adapted in this context means[19] that the mark was selected by the proprietor for the purpose of distinction and such distinction operates in fact.[20] Part B applications must be capable of being distinctive rather than adapted to distinguish.[21]

It will be seen below that specific evidence of distinctiveness need only accompany the application where it is made pursuant to section 9(1)(e), unless it is a device.[22] In other cases the registrar may decide of his own volition that the mark is not distinctive and call for evidence on that point. Certain words can never be distinctive notwithstanding actual use, e.g. Elextrix for vacuum cleaners.[23]

(d) The mark must not be deceptive

Deception may occur in a number of different ways, for example, the use of the mark "Orlwoola" on clothing which is not made of wool[24] or a name which suggests that goods have a false geographical origin such as Forrest London for clocks made in Coventry.[25] The prohibition against registering deceptive marks is contained in section 11 of the Act. This section also prohibits marks which would be contrary to law or morality or of scandalous design.

---

[17] *Smith, Kline & French Laboratories' Trade Mark Application* [1976] R.P.C. 512 and *Unilever's (Striped Toothpaste) Trade Mark Application* [1980] F.S.R. 280.

[18] Trade Marks Act 1938, s.9(2).

[19] *Ibid.* s.9(3)(a) and (b).

[20] See *Yorkshire Copper Works* v. *Registrar of Trade Marks* [1954] 1 W.L.R. 554.

[21] Trade Marks Act 1938, s.10.

[22] See above.

[23] *Re Elextrix's Application* [1959] R.P.C. 283. See also *Re York Trailer Holdings* [1982] 1 W.L.R. 195.

[24] *Re Trade Marks Act 1905* (1909) 25 T.L.R. 695; *sub. nom. Re "Orlwoola" Trade Mark* 53 S.J. 672.

[25] *Re Hill's Trade Mark* [1893] R.P.C. 113.

Additional rules have been made under the Act which provide that a number of marks are prohibited from registration or may only be registered at the registrar's discretion or where some form of consent has been obtained.[26] Prohibited marks include the use of such words as royal or imperial if they imply royal patronage.[27] Marks which the registrar may refuse include words such as "patent" and "registered," representations of the royal family, the words "Red Cross" and "Geneva Cross."[28] Marks which require consent from the apparent owner include flags, coats of arms and similar insignia. This category would appear to include the marks of bodies such as Football Association and International Olympic Committee.

(e) *The mark must not be the same as or resemble an existing trade mark*

The test of similarity between two marks is whether a "tangible danger of confusion" would arise.[29] For example, Tablones was held to be too near Tabloids.[30] There is an exception, however, for honest concurrent use.[31]

(f) *Registrar's discretion*

The registrar has a discretion notwithstanding that the proposed mark satisfies all the statutory tests to refuse an application or to accept it subject to such amendment, modification, limitation or condition as he may think fit[32] or to add a disclaimer.[33] From the authors' experience the three amendments that are requested most frequently are first that the list of goods covered by the application be restricted. Secondly that the registrar will require a disclaimer attaching to some part of the mark. The disclaimer might be that

---

[26] The Trade Mark Rules 1938 made pursuant to s.40 of the Trade Marks Act 1938.

[27] Trade Mark Rules 1938, r. 16.

[28] *Ibid.* r. 15.

[29] Lord Upjohn in *"Bali" Trade Mark* [1969] F.S.R. 288.

[30] *Re Capsuloid Co. Ltd.'s Application* [1906] R.P.C. 782.

[31] Trade Marks Act 1938, s.12(2) and see *"Bostitch" Trade Mark* [1963] R.P.C. 183.

[32] Trade Marks Act 1938, s.17, and see *Alfred Dunhill's Trade Mark Application* [1982] R.P.C. 145.

[33] Trade Marks Act 1938, s.14.

registration of this mark confers no exclusive right to the use of a football devise.[34] Thirdly, in particular marks which have some sporting association, that they are only used in relation to sports goods.[35]

(4) Registered users

It has already been observed that where the proprietor of a trade mark does not intend to use it himself, then it will nevertheless be valid provided that a registered user agreement, *i.e.* formal licence, is recorded on the Trade Mark Register. The licence may be granted by the proprietor for some or all the goods covered by the registration and may be subject to conditions or restrictions such as duration, territory, royalty, minimum guarantees, etc.[36] In the Hollie Hobbie[37] Trade Mark case[38] the fact that the registered user agreements were for a period less than the seven years' protection secured on first registration seemed relevant to the judge's finding that trafficking would be encouraged if the applications were granted. It was accepted, however in the High Court, that the term of the registered user agreements need not always coincide with the life of the trade mark, particularly when linked to other relevant provisions. Registration enables the registered user to obtain substantially the same rights and privileges as the proprietor. He may, therefore, sue infringers when the proprietor neglects or refuses to do so within two months of receiving a notice[39] but like the proprietor may be sued for "passing off."

To obtain registration the proprietor and proposed registered user must apply in writing. The application must be accompanied by a declaration giving various details of the proposed licence such as goods, restrictions, special conditions, etc.[40] The registrar may then record the registered user on the register subject to any restrictions or conditions which

---

[34] See, for example *Re Diamond T. Motor Car Co.* [1921] R.P.C. 373.
[35] See *Tonino Trade Mark* [1973] R.P.C. 568 where, on similar principles, Tonino was only permitted on the basis that it would be used for Italian wines as it had an Italian sound.
[36] Trade Marks Act 1938, s.28(1).
[37] *American Greetings Corporation's Application* [1983] 1 W.L.R. 912; [1983] F.S.R. 138.
[38] See p. 155.
[39] Trade Marks Act 1938, s.28(3).
[40] *Ibid.* s.28(4).

he thinks proper and subject to the agreement not being against the public interest.[41]

It is important to establish the business connection between the proprietor and user. This may be achieved by the proprietor retaining quality control over the goods the registered user produces.[42] Thus in a sponsorship agreement where the sponsor acquires the right to include a trade mark such as the World Cup mascot on his products or promotional items, the sponsee should ensure that he can see and approve samples and that quality is maintained.

It is possible to license a trade mark without complying with the formality and expense of the registered user agreement.[43] Indeed, it is often common in the world of sponsorship not to register a user agreement. The profit margins and administrative effort may not justify going through the whole procedure. One must always bear in mind, however, where applications are not accompanied by registered user agreements, that there must be an intention on the part of the applicant to use the mark itself, otherwise the application will be deficient. Quality control, however, must be included in any licence agreement to establish the business connection otherwise the trade mark may be subject to objection for "non-use".[44] An unregistered user will not be able to take direct action against infringers since that is the exclusive province of proprietors and registered users. An unregistered licensee must therefore ensure that his agreement with the proprietor compels the proprietor to take action against infringers since he will be unable to take action himself.

(5) THE REGISTRATION PROCESS

There are two stages in the process of registration, the first being the application and the second, registration. It may take an application anything from 18 months to achieve registration in the United Kingdom to five years in certain countries such as Italy. It is only once the mark has actually achieved

---

[41] *Ibid.* s.28(5).
[42] See Cornish, *Intellectual Property: Patents, Copyright, Trade Marks and Allied Rights* (1981) p. 556 and note that a quality control provision was included in the Hollie Hobbie licence agreements.
[43] See, for example, the *Bostitch* case ([1963] R.P.C. 183).
[44] See Cornish, *Intellectual Property: Patents, Copyright, Trade Marks and Allied Rights* (1981) p. 557.

registration that it will acquire protection as a trade mark and only then that the proprietor will be in a position to enforce his rights against third parties.

When it is decided to register a trade mark either a solicitor or a firm of Chartered Patent Agents should be consulted. Applications may be filed by agents and agents may be required to produce written evidence of their authority.[45] Advice will be obtained about distinctiveness and the other pre-requisites to achieving registration. It is also probable that the solicitor or trade mark agent will recommend a search of the trade mark register for similar marks.[46] This may avoid unnecessary expense particularly on large trade mark programmes. It is important to search in all the classes to be covered by the prospective application. If very similar trade marks are registered then it might be sensible to alter the applications before they are filed to ensure that the two marks can be distinguished. This will occur before fees are paid and may therefore save money. It is only marks which achieve registration or for which applications to register have been filed which will be revealed by the search.

The process of planning registration begins with a decision on which goods the intended trade mark is likely to be used. This may be a stab in the dark with sponsorship since the identity of the sponsors and their products may not be known at that stage. Classification of goods is dealt with by the Trade Mark Rules.[47] The goods are divided into a number of different classes, e.g. soft drinks are in class 32, clothing is in class 25. There is a separate fee payable per class of goods so that one fee would be payable for mineral waters and orange squash in class 32 and a separate fee for sports clothing in class 25. In 1983 application fees per class when filing through a professional agent were approximately £135.[48]

Having decided on the goods (it is frequently the practice to file for "all goods within a class 25," etc.) a search against existing registered trade marks should be instituted. If the search reveals nothing which is very similar, then the application forms will be signed by the proprietor.[49] Applica-

---

[45] Trade Marks (Amendment) Rules 1982 (S.I. 1982 No. 718).
[46] This service is no longer offered by the Registry itself: *ibid.*
[47] 1938, 4th Sched.
[48] See the Trade Mark (Amendment) Rules 1983 (S.I. 1983 No. 181). for registry fees.
[49] s.42 enables a person to seek preliminary advice from the registrar as to prima facie distinctiveness. This is little used in practice.

tions may be subsequently amended with the consent of the registrar.

The registry then conducts a search of both existing registrations and pending applications to consider the other grounds for objection discussed above. On the basis of his examination the registrar may suggest amendments, modifications, conditions, limitations or disclaimers or approve the mark. The proprietor is not obliged to accept the amendments and similar conditions suggested by the registrar and he may ask for a hearing. Evidence is normally presented in writing. However, it is possible to have an oral hearing at which one can attempt to overcome the objection or other proposed conditions by argument.

Once the registrar has accepted the mark it is then advertised in the *Trade Marks Journal.* Anyone who wishes to object to the mark may lodge an opposition.[50] The registrar will consider the merits of the opposition and the applicant will be given the chance to comment upon it. If the registrar upholds or rejects it, it is possible for the dissatisfied party to appeal against the decision.

Certain firms offer clients continuous monitoring facilities against marks advertised in Trade Mark Journals throughout the world. These facilities locate marks which may be similar to those of their clients. The clients then have the option to file an opposition.

Assuming any further objections are overcome the mark becomes a registered trade mark as from the date of application.[51] The registration period is seven years[52] renewable for successive periods of 14 years[53] on payment of a renewal fee. Once registration takes place that is prima facie evidence of the validity of such registration.[54]

(6) VALIDITY AFTER REGISTRATION

Even after a mark has been registered as a trade mark its validity may be challenged. This may become difficult after seven years as proceedings are barred except in the case where

---

[50] Trade Marks Act 1938, s.18(2). The person who objects need not, but usually will have a similar mark himself.
[51] *Ibid.* s.19(1).
[52] *Ibid.* s.20(1).
[53] *Ibid.* s.20(2).
[54] *Ibid.* s.46.

the original registration was obtained by fraud or it is deceptive within the meaning of section 11 of the Act.[55]

Any person "aggrieved" which has been interpreted as meaning a trader of the same or similar goods[56] may apply to have a trade mark removed where the original entry was made without sufficient cause or where it wrongly remains on the register.[57] Application is made either to the court or to the registrar at option of the applicant.[58]

The applicant will need to establish grounds for removal such as lack of distinctiveness or that it is deceptive[59] or other specific grounds for removal which are contained in the Act. Thus a mark may be removed where it can be established that there was never a bona fide intention to use the mark at the time of application and no bona fide use has since taken place, or where a continuous period of five years has elapsed with no bona fide use.[60]

Transmission of trade marks

A trade mark may be assigned for some or all of the goods for which it is registered[61] with or without the goodwill of the business.[62] It would seem that the assignment need not be in the form of a written document.[63] The assignment, however, must not confuse or cause deception.[64] This might arise where, for example, the assignor retains a similar unregistered mark. It is necessary, where the assignment of the mark is not accompanied by the goodwill in it to apply to the registrar within six months of the assignment for directions on advertising the assignment.[65] The assignment will be entered

---

[55] *Ibid.* s. 13(1). s.11 is discussed at p. 157.

[56] Therefore the Society of Friends, *i.e.* Quakers, could not challenge the validity of the registration of Quaker for wines and spirits, since they did not trade in them (*Ellis & Co.'s Trade Mark* [1904] R.P.C. 617).

[57] Trade Marks Act 1938, s.32(1).

[58] *Ibid.* s.54.

[59] See *General Electric Co. (of U.S.A.)* v. *General Electric Co.* [1973] R.P.C. 297.

[60] See *Hermes Trade Mark* [1982] R.P.C. 425 and the Trade Mark (Amendment) Rules 1982 (S.I. 1982 No. 718), r.8.

[61] There is an exception for associated marks in the Trade Marks Act 1938, s.23.

[62] *Ibid.* s.22(1).

[63] *Ibid.* s.25.

[64] *Ibid.* s.22(4).

[65] *Ibid.* s.22(7).

on the register.[66] The penalty for failing to register is that the assignment cannot then be admitted as evidence of title except in special circumstances or where the court directs otherwise.[67]

Infringement

The provisions which determine infringement are complex. There are three basic acts which give rise to an infringement. First, use of a registered trade mark or something closely resembling it, in the course of a trade without the permission of the owner.[68] Such use must be in relation to goods covered by the registration and be likely to confuse or deceive.[69] Use in a three dimensional form such as the reproduction of a doll or puppet of a two dimensional character is only an infringement where the registration covers the three dimensional form.[70] The case of *Re James Trade Mark Application* has recently been applied to reject an application to register the shape of a Coca Cola bottle on the rationale that a mark is something apart or extra, in concept, from the goods to which it is affixed or impressed.[70a] This should be constrasted with the decision of Whitford J. in *Sobrefina S.A.'s Trade Mark Application*.[71] A mark may cover the whole surface of an object such as stripes on toothpaste. Use in relation to goods, covers use in advertisements promoting those goods.[72] Use in an editorial context in newspapers which, as already mentioned may be desirable to promote the mark in relation to a sponsored event, would not constitute an infringement. Use of a tobacco mark "Conquest" on dummy cigarette packets

---

[66] *Ibid.* s.25(1).

[67] *Ibid.* s.25(3).

[68] *i.e.* proprietor or registered user; *ibid.* s.4(1).

[69] For a discussion on s.4(1), see *Gallagher* v. *The Health Education Bureau* [1982] F.S.R. 464, a decision of the High Court of Ireland.

[70] *Smith, Kline & French Laboratories' Application* [1968] R.P.C. 415, distinguishing *re James Trade Mark, James* v. *Soulby* (1886) 33 Ch.D. 392 where Lindley J. stated "A thing itself cannot be a mark itself."

[70a] The Coca-Cola Company (Trade Mark Application No. 1057232) Intellectual Property Decisions (1983) Vol. 6, p. 12.

[71] [1974] R.P.C. 672 at 860. See also *Re Unilever's (Striped Toothpaste) Trade Mark Application* [1980] F.S.R. 280.

[72] *Hardmuth (L. & C.) (Great Britain)* v. *Bancroft & Partners* (1953) 70 R.P.C. 179.

in an anti-smoking campaign was held to be an infringement.[73]

To constitute an infringement the use must be as a trade mark. The distinction between what is or is not trade mark use is subtle. Coins which contained the logo "Espana 82" which was a registered trade mark in Spain did not constitute an infringement because the trade mark was used to commemorate the event and not to distinguish one coin from the other.

The second act which gives rises to an infringement is the licensee of a trade mark, which could include a sponsor, exceeding the express terms of his licence.[74] Thus where a sponsee licenses a sponsor to use a trade mark on goods of a certain quality and that quality is not maintained, then this would be an infringement.[75] Another example might be where the sponsor or some other licensee is prohibited from altering the trade mark but does so by combining it with his own logo.[76] Other examples are given in the Act.[77] To constitute an infringement, however, there must be an express term of the licence agreement which is breached.

Thirdly, infringement occurs by using a trade mark, or one deceptively similar thereto, to import a reference to its owner (*i.e.* proprietor or registered user) without permission.[78] This is intended to cover the situation where the trade mark is used to compare one type of goods with another in comparative advertising, *e.g.* X cars are better than Y cars.

Certain activities are specifically excluded from constituting an infringement. There are also a number of non-statutory defences which may be pleaded by the potential infringer.[79]

(1) MATTERS NOT CONSTITUTING AN INFRINGEMENT

These include the following:
  (a) Prior use of an identical or similar unregistered mark

---

[73] *Gallagher v. Health Education Authority* [1982] F.S.R. 464, a decision of the High Court of Eire based upon interpretation of similar provisions to the Trade Marks Act 1938 in the Irish Trade Marks Act 1963.
[74] Trade Marks Act 1938, s.6.
[75] *Ibid.* s.6(2)(*a*).
[76] *Ibid.* s.6(2)(*b*).
[77] *Ibid.* s.6(2)(*d*).
[78] *Ibid.* s.4(*b*) for the full text.
[79] See Kerly, *The Law of Trade Marks and Trade Names* (11th ed. 1983), p. 275.

does not constitute infringement,[80] and prior is defined as use before the other mark was registered. It should be borne in mind in this context that where a mark is likely to be merchandised, it is advisable to treat it with a high degree of secrecy. The occasions in which a mark such as the World Cup mascot is copied and then immediately used and registered by "pirate" operators is alarming. Copyright may be used to protect the marks appropriation in those countries in which copyright is recognised. In one case a company applied to register the "Oscar" film device as a trade mark. It was held that the Academy of Motion Pictures, Arts and Science who owned copyright in the silhouette of the Oscar could prevent the registration.[81] Although it is the prior use and not the "motives" of such a pirate which are relevant, one might hope that the trade mark registrars will become aware of the general problems associated with such piracy.

(b) Concurrent registrations for the same or very similar marks.[82]
(c) Bona fide use by a person of his own or his predecessors names or place of business.[83]
(d) Bona fide use by a person to describe the character or quality of his goods.[84]

(2) NON STATUTORY DEFENCES

(a) Validity of registration.[85]
(b) No infringement on the basis of dissimilarity. It is a question of fact to determine in each case whether two marks are the same or closely resemble one another. The 1982 soccer World Cup logo was frequently pirated. The pirate would alter the colours or arrangement of the logo slightly and argue that the alteration made the mark sufficiently different to avoid there being an infringement. This is not the case, however, as

---

[80] Trade Marks Act 1938, s.7(1).
[81] *OSCAR Trade Mark* [1979] R.P.C. 173.
[82] Trade Marks Act 1938, s.4(4).
[83] *Ibid.* s.8(*a*).
[84] *Ibid.* s.8(*b*) except where this "imports a reference."
[85] See p. 153.

altering the colours will not be a defence.[86] The Act itself provides[87] that where a trade mark is registered without limitation on colour that it shall be deemed to be registered for all colours. It is also no defence if the defendant alters the trade mark by adding his own name or some other feature to it.[88] Infringement includes not only taking the whole mark, but also one or more of its essential features.[89]

(c) Acquiescence, consent, delay or estoppel on the part of the proprietor to the infringement. Section 4(3)(a) gives effect to these Common Law defences. Acquiescence seems to mean not merely letting the infringement take place but encouraging or inducing it.[90] Delay must be inordinate.[91]

Trade marks and sponsorship licences

(1) TITLES AND SIMILAR SLOGANS

The procedure for registration begins with an examination of section 9 to decide into which category the application falls.[92] There is an advantage where the mark falls within the first four categories.[93] In these categories, although the mark must be distinctive, it is not necessary to produce evidence thereof unless the point is taken by the registrar. Evidence of distinctiveness may necessitate the production of samples[94] which will present problems where such use has not occurred. Even if such evidence is available it must be doubted whether words such as "World Cup" could ever acquire distinctiveness. In contrast, words such as the "F.I.F.A. Soccer World Cup" are probably capable of acquiring distinctiveness through use.

---

[86] *British Petroleum Co.* v. *European Petroleum Distributors* [1968] R.P.C. 54, but contrast *Smith, Kline & French Laboratories' Application* [1968] R.P.C. 415 where the colours were the grounds upon which the mark was distinctive.

[87] Trade Marks Act 1938, s.16.

[88] *Lever Bros. (Port Sunlight)* v. *Sunniwite Products* (1949) 66 R.P.C. 84.

[89] See Kerly, *The Law of Trade Marks and Trade Names* (11th ed., 1983), p. 250.

[90] *Ibid.* Chap. 15, s.40.

[91] Twelve years was not sufficient in *Electrolux* v. *Electrix*, (*No.* 2) (1953) 71 R.P.C. 23.

[92] See p. 153.

[93] Trade Marks Act 1938, s.9(1)(a)–(d), and (e) for device marks.

[94] *Ibid.* s.9(3)(b).

In the authors' view, it is undesirable to license a title of itself to a sponsor on an exclusive basis. A title will be the first thing that is pirated and therefore the expense and administrative effort in policing the market place is considerable. As has already been discussed, copyright is not much help with titles.

Of the categories which do not necessarily require evidence of distinctiveness to accompany the application a title might fall within two of the four as a "word mark."[95] Registration, on this ground, will depend on establishing that the mark either consists of an invented word or that it has no reference to the character or quality of the goods covered by the application and is not a geographical name or surname.

(a) *Invented words*

An invented work is one which does not "convey any . . . obvious meaning to ordinary Englishmen."[96] Thus "Kodak"[97] was held to be an "invented word" but "Tarzan" was not.[98] The distinction between these cases is that at the time of application "Tarzan" had already became part of the language and had even appeared in dictionaries. In contrast, "Kodak" was an entirely new word.

Merely mis-spelling a word or combining two or more familiar words will not make the word invented.[99] Invented words are likely to have more relevance to fictional characters within a book, play, or film than to a title. Characters such as Darth Vador from *Star Wars*, which may be heavily merchandised, would seem ideal candidates for registration as invented words.

(b) *No reference to character or quality*

Titles may be registered as trade marks without evidence of distinctiveness accompanying the application where they have no direct reference to the character or quality of the goods. Whether a title would be taken as referring to the character or quality of the goods is a question of fact. Words such as

---

[95] *Ibid* s.9(1)(c) and (d).

[96] Parker J. in *Philippart* v. *Whiteley* [1908] 2 Ch. 274 at 279.

[97] *Kodak Ltd.* v. *London Stereoscopic & Photographic Co. Ltd.* [1903] R.P.C. 337.

[98] *Tarzan Trade Mark* [1970] R.P.C. 450 and see Kerly, *The Law of Trade Marks and Trade Names* (11th ed., 1983), p. 108.

[99] See the *Orlwoola* case, p. 157.

"Scotchlite" for reflector lights[1] or "Tastee-Freez" for ice cream[2] were held to refer to the character or quality of the goods, whereas the word "National" used to describe cash registers[3] and "Radiation" for gas appliances were not.[4]

The title to a sponsored book such as "Rothmans International Yearbook of Football" would not in the author's view be registrable without evidence of distinctiveness since the title refers to the character *i.e.* book. Words like "Federation Cup" (which is a sponsored tennis competition) might not be registrable for tennis clothing without evidence of distinctiveness, but it might be possible to register for computer equipment. A geographical name may not be registered under this heading.[5] Thus a competition such as the "Americas Cup" would require evidence of distinctiveness.[6]

Titles which do not fall within section 9(1)(c) or (d) will only be registrable once distinctiveness is established. The word "Tarzan" was held not to achieve distinctiveness in relation to films or magnetic recordings.[7] In contrast the word "Sheen" proceeded to registration in respect of sewing cottons as it was capable of being distinctive and was actually being used as such.[8] Titles such as "Americas Cup," "*Star Wars*," "Pharoah Exhibition" or "Tall Ships" should be registrable on evidence of distinctiveness. If not registrable under Part A, then Part B might be considered. Descriptive titles such as "Official Supplier" will not in the author's view be registrable.

(2) USE OF MASCOTS, SYMBOLS AND SIMILAR DEVICES

A device mark is more likely to be registered by the sponsee as a trade mark than a word mark such as a title. There are also important marketing considerations in choosing between a word mark and a device. For example, it is common sense that given the choice of a T-shirt with an interesting graphic device on it such as the Rolling Stones tongue and lips logo or

[1] *Re Minnesota Mining and Manufacturing Application* (1948) 65 R.P.C. 229.
[2] *Tastee Freez International Application* [1960] R.P.C. 255.
[3] *National Cash Register Co.'s Application* [1917] R.P.C. 354.
[4] *Re Radiation Ltd.'s Patent* [1942] R.P.C. 123.
[5] See *Re York Trailer Holdings Ltd.* [1982] 1 W.L.R. 195.
[6] But contrast *Magnolia Metal Co.'s Trade Mark* [1897] 2 Ch. 371. Where an application for the name "Magnolia" was not refused merely because there happened to be a town in the United States called Magnolia.
[7] *Tarzan Trade Mark* [1970] R.P.C. 450.
[8] *Re Coats (J. & P.) Ltd.'s Application* [1936] R.P.C. 355.

just the words Rolling Stones, a consumer would have more interest in the T-shirt with the device.

Section 9(1)(e) of the Trade Marks Act 1938 requires evidence of distinctiveness for word marks which do not fall within sub-paragraph (a) to (d) of section 9. Although devices are registrable under section 9(1)(e), proof of distinctiveness need not, in contrast to certain word marks, accompany the initial application unless they are descriptive devices. This is important in many sponsorship situations where actual use will not take place until near the sponsored event. It is this advantage that is no doubt responsible for dressing up certain word marks to look like devices.[9] The 1982 soccer World Cup applications were for devices, however, the device had the words "Espana 82" underneath. The complete work was registered as a device. It is unlikely however that the proprietor of the device could stop other companies using the words "Espana 82" on the basis of registration of the whole device.

Although evidence of distinctiveness need not accompany the application a device mark must nevertheless be adapted to distinguish.[10] One problem here is that existing registrations for similar devices may exist. If, for example it is sought to register a rabbit device it is inevitable that there will be numerous rabbit devices on the United Kingdom register. The chosen rabbit device will need to be different in some way from the others. A search of existing registrations before the design is finalised and the application made will help.[11]

Devices which describe the goods to which their application relates will not be registrable as they are not distinctive.[12] A drawing of a cricket bat would not be registrable for cricket bats or balls. A device consisting of several cricket bats worked up into a particular and distinctive design might be registrable.[13] If the device is common but does not describe the goods, then it might also be registrable.[14]

---

[9] In *Re Woodward's Trade Mark, Woodword Ltd.* v. *Boulton Macro Ltd.* [1915] R.P.C. 173. "Gripe Water" with a few embellishments around the lettering was held to be a word mark.

[10] Or capable thereof for Part B.

[11] See Kerly, *The Law of Trade Marks and Trade Names*, (11th ed., 1983), para. 8–58 for devices common to a particular trade and distinctiveness.

[12] *Re Renold Chains' Application* [1966] R.P.C. 487, C.A.

[13] See Kerly, *The Law of Trade Marks and Trade Names* (11th ed., 1983), Chap. 8, para. 8–59 and "*Welsh Lady*" *Trade Mark* [1964] R.P.C. 459.

[14] A magnolia flower was held distinctive for a metal alloy: *Re Magnolia Metal Co.'s Trade Marks* [1897] 2 Ch. 371.

(3) USE OF NAME, IMAGE, VOICE OR LIKENESS

(a) *Name including signature*

A name will be registrable only on proof of distinctiveness under section 9(1)(*e*) of the Act. There are three exceptional cases where evidence of distinctiveness will not be required.

First, in the case of a real name represented in a special and particular manner, *i.e.* not just printed in block letters.[15] The special and particular manner requirement was satisfied in the case of Robin Hood where certain of the letters had small devices of an archer and target incorporated within them.[16] The name of a purely fictional character will not be registrable under this exception. Where, however, the name is fictitious as opposed to fictional or it has some basis as a real character in history even though that may have been glamorised it will be registrable.[17]

The protection afforded by registration of a name is only likely to exist in the particular form in which it is registered. No exclusivity of the words "Robin Hood" would therefore have been conferred by the registration except where it is used with the archer and arrow in the lettering.

The second exception is a signature.[18] Thus the signature of John McEnroe for tennis racquets may be protected through registration as a trade mark.

The third exception—invented words—has already briefly been discussed under names of fictional characters.[19]

In all other cases evidence of distinctiveness must be produced. Thus names such as "Slazenger,"[20] "the Rolling Stones" or "Globe Theatre," will all require evidence of distinctiveness to accompany the application.

(b) *Image or likeness*

An image or likeness in the form of a portrait or

---

[15] Trade Marks Act 1938, s.9(1)(*a*).
[16] *Re Standard Cameras' Application* (1952) 69 R.P.C. 125 and see Kerly, *The Law of Trade Marks and Trade Names* (11th ed., 1983), para. 8–09.
[17] Kerly, *The Law of Trade Marks and Trade Names* (11th ed., 1983), para. 8–10.
[18] Trade Marks Act 1938, s.9(1)(*b*).
[19] See p. 168.
[20] *Re Slazenger Ltd.'s Application* [1914] R.P.C. 501.

photograph may be registered as a device.[21] The photograph or other likeness must be distinctive, *i.e.* not generally used by the trade.[22] Registration will require the consent of the person whose image is depicted.[23]

(c) *Voice*

Trade marks and the infringement thereof can only exist in printed or other visual representation of the mark.[24] Therefore no trade mark can be registered with respect to a noise and no infringement of the mark can occur through reproduction in sound alone, *e.g.* on commercial radio.

International perspective

As with copyright, trade marks are effected by international agreements. The two most important agreements are probably the International Convention for the Protection of Industrial Property which was concluded in Paris in 1883 and is thus often referred to as the Paris Convention. The most important feature of this convention, of which Great Britain is a party, is that it allows six months' priority application in member countries.[25] If a trade mark is filed in Great Britain then that same mark may be filed in another convention country within six months and the date of filing will be treated as the date of the original application in Great Britain. This enables pirate registrations to be usurped and may have considerable practical significance in countries where the first person to register is treated conclusively as the owner. This applies in many South American countries and continental Europe. The Paris Convention also permits registration of service marks, although such registration cannot be achieved within the United Kingdom.[26]

---

[21] See Kerly, The Law of Trade Marks and Trade Names (11th ed. 1983), para. 8–57 and *Rowland* v. *Mitchell, Re Rowland's Trade Mark* [1897] 1 Ch. 71. where the plaintiff's portrait enclosed in an oval line was registered in relation to cough lozenges called "Army and Navy Paregoric Tablets."

[22] *Re Anderson's Trade Mark* (1884) 26 Ch.D. 409.

[23] Unless long since dead: *Re Carroll's Application* (1899) 16 R.P.C. 82.

[24] Trade Mark Act 1938, s.68(2).

[25] International Convention for the Protection of Industrial Property 1883, Art. 4.

[26] But see p. 156, n.16 *re* private member's bill.

The second important convention is the International Registration of Marks of Manufacture and Commerce which was concluded in Madrid in 1891 and is since frequently called The Madrid Arrangement. The most important practical significance of this agreement (of which Great Britain is not a party) is that once a registration is achieved in a convention country by a national of that country then that registration may be deposited with the International Office for the Protection of Industrial Property in Berne, Switzerland. Upon such deposit the mark will be protected in all countries who are parties to the Madrid Arrangement without the necessity of registration under the applicable National System (and unless the mark conflicts with a mark already registered or is not registrable under domestic law). Not only does this procedure save time but it also potentially results in saving a large amount of money.

Trade mark notice

It has become customary to include "TM" next to any mark which is in the process of registration and "R" when it has actually achieved registration.

This is neither a formal requirement for protection under the Trade Marks Act 1938 nor the Paris Convention. It should be borne in mind, however, that where "R" does have a statutory meaning such as in the United States or Sweden one should take care not to falsely represent the mark as being registered.

Planning a trade mark registration programme for a large sponsored event

Trade marks in contrast to other potential remedies such as copyright and passing off can involve the sponsee in substantial initial costs. There are a number of matters which the sponsee ought to consider before engaging on a trade mark registration programme.

(1) INTENTION TO USE THE MARK

Where an applicant for registration is a trading company, e.g. Football Marketing Ltd. the trade mark registrar is unlikely to be immediately suspicious of the company's "intention of use" of the mark.[27] Where the applicant is an unincorporated entity such as a football federation the registrars suspicions may immediately be aroused as to the intention of the federation to trade in the goods. Where registered user agreements are filed, one should not file 12 at a time as occurred in the Hollie Hobbie case.

(2) SHORT TERM MARKS

The time available for registering the marks and their commercial life, *i.e.* the period in which they are likely to earn income, must be taken into account in all registration programmes. There is no point in applying to register a mark where the application will not proceed to registration before the event takes place. Few jurisdictions allow interlocutory relief, *i.e.* action to be taken against infringers of the mark between the period of application and registration. This period can extend from six months to three or four years.

The longer the commercial life of the mark the greater the justification to register it. For certain premier events, however where the marks have an extremely high short term value, marks should be registered to protect the client's use of those marks in the market place.

A client will often invest thousands of pounds in promotions using the marks in association with their own products. For example many millions of soft drink cans may be printed with a mascot of a sports event. If the client's use cannot be protected against pirates then the client, if he signs the contract in the first place, may query what he has paid for.

(3) PARIS CONVENTION

The Paris Convention and similar conventions allow six months' priority in filing applications where the original application is filed in a convention country. The effect of this is that where, for example, an application were filed in Spain, it is then possible to file applications in other convention countries and the date of application in those countries will be treated as the same date as the original application.

Applications, however, under the Paris Convention are

---

[27] See p. 154. But it should always be borne in mind that if a registered agreement is not filed then it is necessary to plan how to establish an intention by the applicant to use the mark.

expensive in that they impose additional filing requirements in each convention country. The expense of filing applications under the Paris Convention can only be fully justified in limited circumstances. One of those sets of limited circumstances is in South American countries where the first applicant is treated conclusively by the registrar as the owner of the mark. The date is therefore critical.

(4) COMMON LAW COUNTRIES

Common Law countries such as the United Kingdom, Australia, New Zealand and Canada have sophisticated intellectual property laws, coupled with a very arduous process for registering trade marks. In these countries costs could be saved by relying on copyright and passing off protection rather than on trade mark registrations particularly for short term marks. It is important, therefore, to ensure that proper copyright assignments are obtained from the outset.

(5) PROPER PLANNING

In many countries the costs of filing multiple trade mark applications, i.e. five categories at one time, is proportionally less than single applications. It is therefore important to plan the registration programme well in advance. The following questions will need answering in planning any programme:
  (a) is the mark a short term or long term mark?
  (b) if short term, when will the event take place and what is the marks commercial life?
  (c) who designed the mark and is a copyright assignment in existence?
  (d) which are the important markets for the mark?
  (e) which are the important clients for the mark and are they attaching any particular importance to a specific territory?
  (f) which are the important merchandising categories?
  (g) is Latin America one of the important territories?
From the answers to these questions it should be possible to prepare a plan and budget.

11. Passing Off

Passing off, unlike copyright and trade mark infringement, is a common law remedy. Thus the courts and not parliament are responsible for its development. Since the courts have nurtured passing off to its present condition, one might anticipate that growth will continue wherever circumstances justify its application. In the area of licensing, its growth has become somewhat stunted as will be seen from the text that follows.

The scope of passing off can only be determined by examining the decided cases. There is some argument[1] that a general remedy of "unfair competition" with its roots in "passing off" exists. This has been used to explain cases where it appeared that the basic ingredients of passing off were missing but a remedy was nevertheless found. Re-classifying such cases as unfair competition is confusing. The tort of "passing off" as a common law remedy should retain the flexibility within itself to adapt to changing social and economic conditions.[2] In the author's opinion, there is no all-embracing definition of "passing off," only a number of principles which are applied with reasonable consistency.[3]

The requirements

(1) GOODWILL IN THE COURSE OF TRADE

Passing off involves the appropriation or damage to goodwill. A useful definition of goodwill was made by Lord

---

[1] See, for example, Lawson, *Advertising Law* (1978), p. 94.

[2] See Diplock L.J. in the "Advocaat" case, *Erven Warnink* v. *Townend* [1980] R.P.C. 31, the House of Lords judgment at 94, where he suggested that the original cases such as *Spalding* v. *Gamage (A.W.) Ltd.* [1914] 2 Ch. 405. were merely examples of the application of a more general instance of passing off; see Hobb [1980] E.I.P.R. 49.

[3] See, for example, the five points set forth in Diplock L.J.'s judgment in *Erven Warnink* v. *Townend* [1979] A.C. 731.

Macnaghten in 1901: "It is the benefit and advantage of the good name, reputation, and connection of a business. It is the attractive force which brings in custom. It is the one thing which distinguishes an old-established business from a new business at its first start."[4] It follows, therefore, that goodwill must be established in the first place before anything can happen to it. Where, for example, a boxer sought to restrain another boxer from using the title "Welter Weight Champion of Trinidad" his action failed since the boxer himself and the title were unknown in the United Kingdom.[5]

The extent or quantum of goodwill which is necessary before passing off will apply, is difficult to assess and therefore difficult to prove as evidence. Much will depend upon the facts of the case. It has been suggested that the goodwill must have a substantial value.[6] This does not seem a requirement, certainly as far as interlocutory injunctions are concerned. The courts have been required to intervene in what may seem very parochial circumstances indeed. Thus in one case a company was prevented from using the name "Mr. Chippy" on the basis that one trader had built up sufficient goodwill in this name after three weeks substantial trading with one van.[7] Goodwill may exist in relation to goods or services.[8]

Even where goodwill exists that goodwill may be confined geographically to a particular area. Thus passing off did not apply in relation to a newspaper in Glasgow which had the same name as one in London.[9] It may also relate to a particular class of goods or services. Thus the makers of "Zoom" ice lollies could not prevent another company marketing "Zoom" bubble gum.[10] Sponsorship is concerned

---

[4] *Commissioners of Inland Revenue* v. *Muller & Co.'s Margarine Ltd.* [1901] A.C. 217 at 223.

[5] *Serville* v. *Constance* [1954] R.P.C. 146. But Harman J. indicated that if malice had been proved, slander of title or injurious falsehood might have been established.

[6] Per Frazer L.J. of Tulleybelton in the "Advocaat" case, [1980] R.P.C. 31.

[7] *Stannard* v. *Reay* [1967] R.P.C. 589. Note, however, that where the trader is using a very common name like "Oven Chips" it will take much longer to create distinctive goodwill in such a common name: *McCain International* v. *Country Fair Foods* [1981] R.P.C. 69.

[8] See *Office Cleaning Services* v. *Westminster Window and General Cleaners* [1946] R.P.C. 39 and contrast Trade Marks.

[9] *George Outram & Co. Ltd.* v. *London Evening Newspapers Co. Ltd.* (1911) 27 T.L.R. 231, and see also *Brestian* v. *Try* [1958] R.P.C. 161.

[10] See *Lyons Maid* v. *Trebor* [1967] R.P.C. 222.

with marketing products or enhancing a corporate image. This involves use of the media and sophisticated marketing techniques to secure exposure. At the level of a soccer World Cup, titles, mascots and symbols will be promoted internationally. The sponsors will wish to capitalise on the goodwill attaching to these. Sponsors will therefore include such items on their own products or in publicity material. Sponsorship often therefore exists within an international market in relation to a wide range of goods or services.

Goodwill may have been created by the combined effort of the initial rights owner, *i.e.* sponsee, the media and the sponsors.[11] This creates potential problems in locating ownership of goodwill in the United Kingdom as between the parties. Goodwill may however be owned jointly by the parties just as goodwill in the name "Champagne" is owned by all the producers of that wine from the Champagne district of France.[12]

(2) GOODWILL IN THE UNITED KINGDOM

It is not easy to extract the principles which a United Kingdom court will apply in protecting goodwill which has been built up abroad. Some of the decided cases are difficult to reconcile and most have been decided at the level of an interlocutory injunction at which difficult points of law are not normally discussed.[12a] It is suggested, however, that the following guidelines might be applied. It is not necessary for the sponsorship object to exist in the United Kingdom, for goodwill to arise here. In the case of *Maxims* v. *Dye*[13] a Parisian restaurant secured an injunction against a British restaurant of the same name. This case conflicts with an earlier decision where the Crazy Horse Saloon failed to obtain an injunction in similar circumstances on the grounds that it had no place of business in the United Kingdom.[14] It has been argued that this latter case was wrongly decided.[15] Customers of merchandise connected with the sponsorship

---

[11] For goodwill created through exposure on television, see *Adidas* v. *O'Neill* [1983] F.S.R. 76, a decision of the Supreme Court of Ireland.

[12] *J. Bollinger* v. *The Costa Brava Wine Co.* (*No. 3*) [1960] Ch. 262.

[12a] See *American Cyanamid* v. *Ethicon Ltd.* [1975] A.C. 396.

[13] [1977] 1 W.L.R. 1155.

[14] *Bernadin (Alain) Et Cie* v. *Pavilion Properties* [1967] R.P.C. 581.

[15] See Cornish, *Intellectual Property: Patents, Copyright, Trade Marks and Allied Rights* (1981), p. 482, n. 48.

must actually exist in England or Wales. The customers must be real in the sense that a market identified with the get up must have been created either through actual sale or promotion and advertising.[16] There must be an appropriation or some other damage arising from the passing off. This is, in fact, a normal requirement for passing off since if damage results goodwill must have existed in the first place.[17]

(3) GOODWILL IN RELATION TO PARTICULAR PRODUCTS/ SERVICES

Passing off protects goodwill. The most obvious circumstance in which goodwill needs protection is where one trade sets up with the same name in the same line of business and appropriates the first trader's customers, for example, two similarly named restaurants each serving deep dish pizzas.[18] Where the parties are not in the same line of business then appropriation of customers is unlikely. However, damage still might occur either in the particular line of business or more generally to the goodwill attaching to a name or get up as a whole. In commerce, as evidenced by what have become known as trade mark extension programmes (whether or not trade marks are involved), goodwill can exist in certain names distinct from the line of business in which that goodwill has been built up. Mary Quant, for example, started in clothing but the trade name is now used on a variety of items ranging from cosmetics to crockery. There are at least three areas in which the English courts have so far intervened through passing off to protect goodwill without confining it to particular products or services.

The first is where damage to reputation might result. Thus, the court refused to allow a moneylender to use the name "Harrod" since this might damage the reputation of the store Harrods.[19] In another case, Annabel's nightclub was able to

---

[16] *Sheraton Corp. of America* v. *Sheraton Motels* [1964] R.P.C. 202; *Home Box Office Inc.* v. *Channel 5 Home Box Office* [1982] F.S.R. 449; *Athletes Foot Marketing Associates Inc.* v. *Cobra Sports Ltd.* [1980] R.P.C. 343; *Lettuce* v. *Soll-Morcum* [1980] E.I.P.R. 169; and *Établissements Panhard et Levassor* v. *Panhard Levassor Co. Ltd.* [1901] 2 Ch. 513.

[17] See the *Athletes Foot* case n.16 *supra*.

[18] *My Kinda Town Ltd.* v. *Soll* [1983] R.P.C. 15.

[19] *Harrods* v. *Harrod* [1924] R.P.C. 74.

179

prevent a rather dubious escort agency using the same name.[20]

The second is where a professional reputation such as that of the medical profession or accountants might be damaged. Thus, the British Medical Association (B.M.A.) were able to stop the defendants using the B.M.A. logo in relation to drug stores.[21]

The third is where what might be described as household names are sought to be used, thereby either depriving the owner of the household name from extending his business into new areas or creating confusion amongst the general public who might assume that the household name and product were linked. Thus the owners of "Marigold," which had become a famous brand of rubber gloves, secured an injunction against a company about to use the same name in relation to toilet tissues.[22] Also, the owners of the brand "Red Label," used in relation to whisky, were able to prevent another company using the name "Red Label" in relation to cigarettes.[23] A similar result was reached where the name "Lego" which had become famous for children's building bricks was used by another company in relation to garden sprinklers.[24]

Goodwill, however, may be confined to a particular line or area of business. In one case, for example, the owners of the television series "The Wombles" could not stop a company using the name "Womble Skips."[25]

This requirement is sometimes called the "Common Field of Activity Doctrine."[26] The underlying principle of the common field of activity doctrine, where goodwill is confined to a particular sector of the market, would appear to be sound. To give one company a monopoly of a name would unduly fetter trade and be meaningless if damage to goodwill is unlikely to occur. The recent case of *Lego* v. *Lego*[27]

---

[20] *Annabel's (Berkeley Square)* v. *Schock (G.)* [1972] R.P.C. 838.

[21] *British Medical Association* v. *Marsh* [1931] R.P.C. 565, but contrast *Clark* v. *Freeman* (1848) 11 Beav. 112, and see also *Dr. Barnado's Homes; National Incorporated Association* v. *Barnardo Amalgamated Industries and Bernadout* [1949] R.P.C. 103.

[22] *L.R.C. International* v. *Lilla Edets Sales Company* [1972] R.P.C. 560.

[23] *Walker (John) & Sons.* v. *Rothmans International* [1978] F.S.R. 357.

[24] *Lego System Aktieselskab* v. *Lego M. Lemelstrich* [1983] F.S.R. 155.

[25] *Wombles* v. *Wombles Skips* [1977] R.P.C. 99.

[26] See Wyn Parry J. in the "Uncle Mac" case, *McCulloch* v. *Lewis A. May (Produce Distributors)* [1947] R.P.C. 58.

[27] [1983] F.S.R. 156.

suggested however that the common field of activity doctrine no longer exists.[28] The common field of activity test can be illustrated by the following cases. The radio broadcaster, Uncle Mac, was unable to prevent a company trading upon his reputation by selling a product under the name of "Uncle Mac's Puffed Wheat."[29] The pop group Abba were unable to restrain their image from being merchandised on T-shirts, pillow cases, etc.[30] This line of English cases has not been followed in certain parts of the Commonwealth. Thus in one case which expressly disapproved the common field of activity test in *McCulloch* v. *Lewis A. May*, a well-known pair of ballroom dancers were able to restrain a company from using their photograph on a record cover.[31]

In a sponsorship relationship the World Cup mascot might, for example, be included on soft drink cans to associate the manufacturer with the World Cup, in the eyes of the public. It is a different situation from the use of the Coca-Cola trade mark, for example. The Coca-Cola trade mark is a sign to the consumer that the can contains a soft drink with a particular taste and quality. The use of the World Cup mascot is not necessarily a sign of quality, but it might be. Its purpose is to establish a connection in the eyes of the consumer between the World Cup and Coca-Cola.

The English courts have so far refused to apply passing off to protect the business of licensing which by analogy would also apply to many sponsorship situations. The goodwill which is to be protected in licensing is not only the licences which have already been granted, but the ability of the licensor to earn income from granting additional licences. In certain cases that ability may exist generally in relation to a name without linking it to any special product. Damage to the goodwill occurs wherever an unlicensed company uses the particular name or get-up, since this deprives the licensor of potential income. Where the unlicensed use of the mascot or logo is used on inferior products, it might also damage the goodwill generally on the basis of damages to reputation.[32]

---

[28] Relying for this proposition on *Erven Warnink* v. *Townend* [1979] A.C. 731.

[29] *McCulloch* v. *Lewis A. May (Produce Distributors)* [1947] R.P.C. 58.

[30] *Lyngstad* v. *Anabas Products* [1977] F.S.R. 62.

[31] *Henderson* v. *Radio Corporation Pty.* [1969] R.P.C. 218. Copyright in the photograph was not in issue.

[32] See *Children's Television Workshop Inc.* v. *Woolworth (N.S.W.)* [1981] R.P.C. 187, known as the *Sesame Street* case.

(4) SUBJECT-MATTER OF GOODWILL

Goodwill may exist in almost any distinctive feature or characteristic of a business: names such as "Harrods"[33] or "Albert Hall Orchestra"[34]; or "John Letters" for gold clubs[35]; or in distinctive shapes or packaging such as a red cellophane sweet wrapper[36]; or the colour grey applied to a gas cylinder[37]; or characters derived from films or books, "The One Armed Swordsman"[38]; or the three stripes used on sportswear[39]; or slogans, visual images, radio, television or newspaper advertisements[40]; and mascots and logos and nom de plumes.[41]

Where a name or other mark has a common or everyday meaning then it will be more difficult to show that any goodwill can exist in that name alone. There are numerous companies who will, for example, manufacture footballs under the slogan "World Cup Football." Such a term can hardly distinguish one football from another.[42] In contrast a name like Champagne, although used by a number of traders in relation to sparkling wine produced in the Champagne district of France, will distinguish that wine which is of exceptional quality from other sparkling wine.[43]

---

[33] *Harrods* v. *Harrod* [1924] R.P.C. 74.

[34] *Hall of Arts* v. *Albert Hall* [1934] R.P.C. 398.

[35] *John Letters & Co.* v. *J. Letters (Craighton)* [1967] R.P.C. 209 a decision of the Court of Session, Scotland.

[36] *White Hudson & Co.* v. *Asian Organisation* [1964] 1 W.L.R. 1466.

[37] *Sodastream Ltd.* v. *Thorn Cascade Co.* [1982] R.P.C. 459, C.A.

[38] *Shaw Brothers (Hong Kong)* v. *Golden Harvest* (H.K.) [1972] R.P.C. 559.

[39] *Adidas Sportsclubfabriken Adidass Lea K.G.* v. *O'Neill & Co.* [1983] F.S.R. 76, a decision of the Supreme Court of Ireland. Passing off did not succeed, however, since the defendant had sufficiently distinguished his goods.

[40] Per Scarman L.J. in *Cadbury Schweppes Pty.* v. *Pub Squash Co. Pty.* [1981] 1 W.L.R. 193; contrast with *Lang Brothers* v. *Goldwell* 1982 S.L.T. 309, a Scottish decision where, with overtones of Compton Mackenzie and "Whiskey Galore," a number of Scottish whiskey producers succeeded in a passing off action on what seemed dubious grounds against an English concoction called "Wee McGlen." "Wee McGlen" was supported by an advertising campaign with a Scottish flavour, *i.e.* pipes and thistles.

[41] *Marengo* v. *Daily Sketch and Sunday Graphic* [1948] W.N. 92.

[42] Contrast *Spalding* v. *Gamage (A.W.) Ltd.* [1914] 2 Ch. 405 where footballs were described as "Orb Footballs."

[43] *Bollinger (J.)* v. *Costa Brava Wine Co. (No. 3)* [1960] Ch. 262.

Strong evidence in the form of a number of years trading will be necessary before a common descriptive name can acquire identifiable goodwill. Thus in a recent case one company brought "oven chips" onto the market but was unable to prevent others using the name provided the use was prefixed by their own company's name.[44]

(5) THE REPRESENTATION

A representation may amount to passing off where there is a false suggestion that goods or services are those of, or are connected with, some other person. The false representation or suggestion may take any number of forms. Its effect, or at least probable effect, will be to damage goodwill. The false representation is usually achieved through taking a name, such as "Orb Footballs"[45] or by imitating the packaging or design, or get up such as using red cellophane wrappers.[46]

It seems relevant to finding a false representation that it confuses the customer so that he buys someone else's goods believing that they are or have a connection with the goods he wishes to buy.[47] A false representation may arise where the quality of goods which are imitated or copied is inferior. For example, razor blades were advertised as "Genuine U.S. Gillette Razor Blades" but were in fact, secondhand. In this case Gillette were able to obtain an injunction, as it was a Gillette policy never to sell resharpened secondhand blades.[48] There is authority that mere trinkets will never be protected by passing off since all the public are concerned with in such cases is what the object looks like and not where it comes from. Thus a company which manufactured an ornamental dog was unable to stop a company manufacturing a similar ornament. There was no deception since the public did not mind where the goods came from.[49]

Although the representation must be false the defendants'

---

[44] *McCain International* v. *Country Fair Foods* [1981] R.P.C. 69, C.A. Contrast *Reddaway (Frank) & Co. Ltd.* v. *George Banham & Co. Ltd.* [1896] A.C. 199.

[45] *Spalding* v. *Gamage (A.W.) Ltd.* [1914] 2 Ch. 405, the goodwill of which belonged to someone else, *supra*.

[46] *White Hudson & Co.* v. *Asian Organisation* [1964] 1 W.L.R. 1466, *supra*.

[47] See *My Kinda Town* v. *Soll* [1983] R.P.C. 15.

[48] *Gillette Safety Razor Co.* v. *Franks* (1924) 40 T.L.R. 606.

[49] *British American Glass Co.* v. *Winton Products (Blackpool)* [1962] R.P.C. 230. See also *Lorimar* v. *Sterling* [1982] R.P.C. 395 discussed below.

motives are irrelevant, except that if he is innocent, it is doubtful that anything more than nominal damages would be awarded against him.[50] Where the defendant is not himself perpetrating the passing off, for example where he is supplying others, then he will be liable only where his intention to deceive can be established.[51] People he supplies such as retailers or wholesalers will be liable even if they are innocent. A dishonest motive may assist a court in finding passing off but it is by no means conclusive.[52]

Whether a false representation exists or not will depend upon how the representation is interpreted by the consumer. "The first question is whether (the defendant) has sailed too close to the wind or has shown a true mariner's judgment."[53] In a recent case one soft drink company had built up substantial goodwill through sales and advertising a particular brand of squash called "Solo." The label on the squash was distinctive and another company bought out a brand called "Pub Squash." The labels had broadly similar characteristics as did their containers but they were by no means identical. Passing off was not established since there was no false representation. The critical test is whether the consuming public was confused or misled by the get up into thinking that "Pub Squash" was the product of Cadbury Schweppes, (the makers of "Solo").[54] Evidence of confusion produced at the trial will assist the plaintiff's case.[55]

In sponsorship situations even after goodwill is established, there may be problems in finding a false representation. Does a customer, for example when he buys a T-shirt containing the mascot of the sponsored event and the sponsor's logo, believe that there is a connection between the sponsored event and the T-shirt? The common sense answer would seem to be, yes, unless the consumer was aware that under English law it may be possible to reproduce such a logo without the consent of the owner. In certain sponsorship situations the

---

[50] See Cornish, *Intellectual Property: Patents, Copyright, Trade Marks and Allied Rights* (1981), p. 485.

[51] *Ibid.* p. 485.

[52] See *Cadbury Schweppes Pty.* v. *Pub Squash Co. Pty.* [1981] 1 W.L.R. 193.

[53] Cornish, *Intellectual Property: Patents, Copyright, Trade Marks and Allied Rights* (1981), p. 486.

[54] See Scarman L.J.'s judgment in the *Pub Squash* case *supra*, and see also *Ardath Tobacco Co. Ltd.* v. *Sandorides Ltd.* [1924] R.P.C. 50 where the mark "99" was used on cigarettes was held not to be passing off of the mark "999".

[55] *Hulton Press* v. *White Eagle Youth Holiday Camp* [1951] R.P.C. 126.

most vigorous controls are maintained on quality of product. Once the consumer knows that if he buys a sweatshirt, for example, with the Rugby Football Union logo on that it will be of high quality, there must clearly be a false representation by anyone who reproduces that logo without a licence on inferior products. In a series of recent South African cases bought by the owners of the television soap opera "Dallas," the question arose whether the public would associate the television programme with various products incorporating the name and/or personalities taken from the programme and sold by a merchandising agent. Passing off failed since no such association would be assumed and therefore no deception would result.[56]

(6) DAMAGE

Goodwill is a type of property. It is not essential for the purpose of obtaining an injunction to prove actual damage although it will be necessary to establish that the false representation, if it is permitted to continue, will inflict damage on that goodwill. The usual way in which damage is occasioned has been discussed above (appropriation of customers or damage of trading reputation). The circumstances in which damage will not arise through passing off are those where no goodwill exists[57] or there has been no false representation.[58]

Finding damage in a sponsorship or merchandising situation where the mark or insignia has not yet been licensed, will require the courts to acknowledge that raising income through licensing a mark to different sponsors is a business in its own right. The damage that will result where the mark is pirated before it has been licensed will be either loss of potential income from prospective sponsors or damage to the sponsor's trading reputation.[59]

---

[56] *Lorimar Productions Inc.* v. *Sterling Clothing Manufacturers (Pty.)* [1982] R.P.C. 395. Contrast as a trade connection requirement in Trade Marks discussed by Dillon L.J. at 919 in *Re American Greetings Corp.'s Applications* [1983] 1 W.L.R. 269.

[57] See p. 179, and note the recent decision of *I.P.C. Magazines* v. *Black and White Music Corp.* [1983] F.S.R. 348 where interlocutory relief was not available to the owners of the character "Judge Dredd" to prevent the release of an unlicensed record about Judge Dredd. Contrast with *News Group Newspapers* v. *Rocket Record Co.* [1981] F.S.R. 89.

[58] See p. 183 and *Walter* v. *Ashton* [1902] 2 Ch. 282.

[59] See p. 179.

Ownership

(1) OWNERSHIP OF GOODWILL

Goodwill is owned by the person who creates it in the market place. Goodwill in the name "Kojakpops" was owned by the company who had established the name in the United Kingdom market and not the company who had acquired what purported to be an exclusive licence from the owners of the "Kojak" television series.[59a] Where goodwill is jointly owned between the sponsee and sponsor then joint action may be possible.[60]

(2) ASSIGNMENT

Since goodwill which may be protected by passing off exists in a particular characteristic or get up of a business, it is not possible to separate the business from the goodwill. Goodwill is assignable therefore only in circumstances in which the whole business goes with it.[61] A licence to use the mark or other "get up" is permissible. There is a potential risk, however, over a long period of time that the goodwill may become associated with the licensee who may ultimately enforce his rights against the original owner.[62] Goodwill may be lost and therefore assignment impossible where no trade has taken place for a number of years.[63]

Passing off and sponsorship licences

(1) TITLES AND SIMILAR SLOGANS

Goodwill may exist in a title. Passing off may arise when someone else appropriates or damages existing goodwill built up in a title. Typical examples include "White Eagle Holiday Camp" which was held to be passing off "Eagle" which was a

---

[59a] *Taverner Rutledge* v. *Trexapalm* (1975) 119 S.J. 792, *supra.*

[60] See *Dent* v. *Turpin* (1861) 2 John & H. 139.

[61] See *Star Industrial Co.* v. *Yap Kwee Kor* (*trading as New Star Industrial Co.*) [1976] F.S.R. 256, P.C.

[62] *Oertli (T.) A.G.* v. *Bowman (E.J.) (London)* [1956] R.P.C. 341.

[63] See *Star Industrial Co.* v. *Yap Kwee Kor* (*trading as New Star Industrial Co.*) [1976] F.S.R. 256, P.C., in contrast to *Ad Lib Club* v. *Granville* [1972] R.P.C. 673.

childrens' comic.[64] Here the plaintiffs also operated a holiday camp and there was evidence of confusion.[65]

It must be remembered however, that each case will be decided on its facts and passing off will not arise unless the basic ingredients are present. Therefore, the organisers of the Miss World Competition (which is often sponsored) were unable to restrain the release of a film entitled "The Alternative Miss World." The film recorded the exploits of transvestites and others competing for the title "The Alternative Miss World" in a tent on Clapham Common.[66] The reason that the action failed appears from the judgment of Lord Denning M.R. to be the absence of a false representation. The public interpretation of the two events was likely to be that they were entirely different. The prefix "The Alternative" to Miss World would, on a common sense view, distinguish the one from the other. *Athletics Weekly* were unable to prevent another company using the title "Athletics Monthly." On the facts it was revealed that the two publications were totally different in size and format and the title alone was insufficient to create a false representation that the publications were linked.[67] "The Dagenham Girl Pipers" were unable to restrain a newly established band called "The Famous London Girl Pipers," again, it seems, on the basis that there was no false representation that the two bands were associated.[68]

Many titles to sponsored events particularly in sport will involve the use of very common or descriptive names. World Cup or World Athletics Championships are examples. The courts are unlikely to be convinced that any goodwill can ever exist in such names so that passing off can apply. In the *Athletics Monthly* case this was confirmed in relation to the word "Athletics." Where the title is prefixed by other words, however, such as "1982 F.I.F.A. Soccer World Cup" goodwill may be built up by the owners of the competition, *i.e.* F.I.F.A. It was assumed by Lord Denning M.R. in the

---

[64] *Hulton Press* v. *White Eagle Youth Holiday Camp* [1951] R.P.C. 126.

[65] See also *Mothercare* v. *Robson Books* [1979] F.S.R. 466.

[66] *Miss World (Jersey)* v. *Street (James) Productions* [1981] F.S.R. 309, C.A., and also *Morecambe and Heysham Corporation* v. *Mecca* [1966] R.P.C. 423.

[67] *World Athletics and Sporting Publications* v. *A.C.M. Webb (Publishing) Co.* [1981] F.S.R. 27, C.A.

[68] *Dagenham Girl Pipers* v. *Vishnu Pather* [1952] R.P.C. 1.

Alternative Miss World case that goodwill existed in the title "Miss World." Once goodwill exists the next problem is finding the false representation, *i.e.* would the public believe there was an association between a sponsor and F.I.F.A., where the title is used by the sponsor on relation to his products?

Where a slogan such as "Sponsor of the 1982 F.I.F.A. Soccer World Cup" is used by a company which is not a sponsor, it is submitted that such a false representation would be present. Provided that the legitimate sponsor had made use of such a title in the market place,in relation to its licensed products, passing off could be applied to restrain an unauthorised competitor from using the title. The action could be brought by both F.I.F.A. and the sponsor on the basis that they share goodwill.[69] Similar cases which have implied approval or praise which was actually given to another product or service have been held actionable as passing off. Thus where one set of goods were demonstrated on television and the defendant purported to sell his "as advertised on television," passing off was established.[70] Thus goodwill may exist in such titles as "Official Supplier" or "Official Sponsor to the Rolling Stones European Tour" so that companies who are not official suppliers or sponsors may be stopped from using such titles.

Where the title to an event is prefixed by the name of a sponsor such as "Benson and Hedges Tennis" and sufficient goodwill has been built up by the use of that title in relation to specific products (such as "Benson and Hedges Tennis T-Shirts") then it is submitted that the sponsor could stop other T-shirt companies from using the title without a licence on the basis of passing off.

In all cases, however, one must bear in mind that the authorities generally require goodwill to exist through trade in a particular product or service.[71] Thus the plaintiff failed to obtain an injunction to restrain the title of his play "Irish and Proud of it," from being used in a film unconnected with the play, since he could not establish it was his intention to make a film of it.[72]

---

[69] See the "Champagne" cases.
[70] *Copydex* v. *Noso Products* [1952] R.P.C. 38, but contrast *Cambridge University Press Ltd.* v. *University Tutorial Press* [1928] R.P.C. 335.
[71] *McCulloch* v. *Lewis A. May (Produce Distributors)* [1947] R.P.C. 58.
[72] *O'Gormann* v. *Paramount Film Service Ltd.* [1937] 2 All E.R. 113.

(2) USE OF MASCOTS, SYMBOLS, LEGENDS AND DEVICES

Passing off may be a remedy against the unauthorised use of such marks provided goodwill, false representation and damage exist. One company was able to restrain another from using "508" in relation to machines.[73] Much the same considerations apply to titles and marks except that the marks are more likely to be distinctive and therefore passing off may be easier to establish. In a recent decision of the Supreme Court of Ireland, goodwill was found to exist in three stripes used on sportswear which had received considerable exposure on television through being worn by competitive athletes. Passing off did not succeed, however, since the defendant's sportswear, which also used three stripes, had the name "O'Neill's" printed on it and the packaging. It was therefore distinguishable from the plaintiff, Adidas sportswear.[73a]

(3) NAME, IMAGE, VOICE LIKENESS

(a) *Name*

(i) *Real names.* Passing off may arise in relation to a real name. However, there are two important considerations to bear in mind. The first is that the court will be most reluctant to prevent individuals using their real surnames. Thus a professional golfer who lends his name to a new range of golf equipment would be unlikely to be able to prevent someone else of the same name doing exactly the same thing.[74] The principle does not extend to nicknames however,[75] and it is important that the defendant is acting honestly.[76]

Passing off in relation to real names has been established in a number of cases as in John Letters for Golf Club.[77] Where, however, a series of concerts was advertised as the "Richter Concerts," after the name of the conductor Herr Richter, it was held that passing off could not be established by the

---

[73] *Hymac v. Priestman Brothers* [1978] R.P.C. 495.

[73a] *Adidas v. O'Neill* [1983] F.S.R. 76, Supreme Court of Ireland.

[74] See Simonds L.J. in *Marengo v. Sunday Sketch and Daily Graphic* [1948] W.N. 92.

[75] *Biba Group v. Biba Boutique* [1980] R.P.C. 413.

[76] *Warner v. Warner* (1889) 5 T.L.R. 327.

[77] See p. 182 and contrast *Warner v. Warner* (1889) 5 T.L.R. 327, *supra.*

organisers of the original concerts against their rivals with whom the conductor had subsequently made arrangements to conduct.[78] Where the real name is that of the person who introduced the goods to the market then no monopoly will be conferred in relation to a descriptive name, such as golf clubs. The real names of professional sportsmen might be protected on the basis of the principle in *British Medical Association* v. *Marsh*.[79]

The decisions of the English courts in this context have not been followed in certain commonwealth jurisdictions. Mr. and Mrs. Henderson, which was the true married name of a couple who worked as ballroom dancers, were able to stop their name (and photograph) being used on the cover of a record of ballroom dancing music.[80]

It has become the practice in many sponsorship situations to adopt a real name which is also the name of a commercial product. There are, for example, showjumping horses bearing the name "Sony." It is unlikely that such names can be licensed exclusively to sponsors.[81] Exclusive in this context means exclusive for all race horses and not in relation to the particular horse. The names of sponsored racehorses must be registered with the Jockey Club.

(ii) *Nicknames*. Much the same principles apply to nicknames as to real names except that the courts are not concerned to protect an individual's right to use his nickname to the same extent as his real name.[82]

In what has become one of the classic cases of passing off a popular radio broadcaster "Uncle Mac" was unable to restrain the use of the name "Uncle Mac" in relation to a breakfast cereal.[83]

(iii) *Fictional names*. The English courts have been willing to recognise goodwill attaching to noms de plumes, stage and other fictional names and applied passing off to prevent their appropriation. Examples include Aunt Niomi,[84] Dr. Crock

---

[78] *Franke* v. *Chappell* (1887) 57 L.T. 141.

[79] See p. 179 above.

[80] *Henderson* v. *Radio Corporation Pty* [1969] R.P.C. 218.

[81] Subject to the possible exceptions discussed above.

[82] See *Biba Group* v. *Biba Boutique* [1980] R.P.C. 413.

[83] See *McCulloch* v. *Lewis A. May (Produce Distributors)*, above.

[84] *Landa* v. *Greenberg* [1908] T.L.R. 441.

and his Crackpots,[85] Kem,[86] Fleetwood Mac,[87] Alvin Purple,[88] and Advocaat.[89] Passing off has not yet been successfully applied to protect the licensing of a fictional name where no goodwill exists through trade in specific goods and services. The pop group ABBA could not prevent their name being used on T-shirts.[90] The Beatles were unable to stop their name being used on taped interviews[91] although damage to general reputation was pleaded but not proved. It also seems relevant to the decision that the distinctive apple device of the Beatles was not included on the record. The owners of "The Wombles" television series and books were unable to restrain the makers of Wombles Skips using the name "Wombles."[92]

(b) *Image/likeness*

(i) *Real people.* English law as discussed does not recognise a right of privacy. Where, however, the image of a real person is used in connection with a trade such as a tennis star for tennis products there seems no reason why passing off could not apply. Again, all the elements of passing off must be present.[93] In one recent South African case the courts followed very much the English approach in holding that it was not passing off to use the image of J.R. Ewing from the television series "Dallas" in connection with a restaurant. The goodwill of J.R. existed in the entertainment field.[94]

There are commonwealth authorities in which this line of cases has not been followed.[95] Thus a waterskier could

[85] *Hines* v. *Winnick* [1947] Ch. 708.
[86] *Marengo* v. *Sunday Sketch and Daily Graphic* [1948] W.N. 92.
[87] *Fleetwood Mac Promotions* v. *Davis (Clifford) Management* [1975] F.S.R. 150.
[88] *Hexagon Pty. Ltd.* v. *Australian Broadcasting Commission* [1976] R.P.C. 628, an Australian decision.
[89] *Erven Warnink* v. *Townend* [1979] A.C. 731.
[90] *Lyngstad* v. *Anabas Products* [1977] F.S.R. 62, *supra.*
[91] *Harrison and Starkey* v. *Polydor* [1977] F.S.R. 1.
[92] *Wombles* v. *Wombles Skips* [1977] R.P.C. 99.
[93] As mentioned above, note 90, Abba were unable to prevent their photograph from being reproduced on T-shirts, since they could not establish that they had goodwill themselves in the trade of their own T-shirts. *Lyngstad* v. *Anabas Products* [1977] F.S.R. 62. The Beatles failed on similar grounds: *Harrison and Starkey* v. *Polydor* [1977] F.S.R. 1.
[94] *Lorimar Productions Inc.* v. *Sterling Clothing Manufacturers (Pty.)* [1982] R.P.C. 395, Supreme Ct. of South Africa.
[95] *Henderson* v. *Radio Corporation Pty.* [1969] R.P.C 218, *supra.*

prevent a photograph showing him waterskiing from being used to advertise a waterski club.[96] It seems however that in such cases professional athletes, sportsmen and by analogy, entertainers must accept some use by the media, with commercial overtones, goes with the job.[97]

(ii) *Cartoon characters/puppets*. Although there appears to be no English authority directly in point, it should be possible to apply passing off to a cartoon or puppet just as any other distinctive product. Perhaps the nearest example is the case of *Britains* v. *Morris (M.) & Co. (London)*[98] where "Swoppetts" were ordered but inferior goods supplied. The absence of a direct United Kingdom authority may be explained by the fact that cartoon characters or puppets will often have protection as copyright works.[99]

A recent Australian case involved puppets called the Muppets taken from the television series "Sesame Street." Imitations of the Muppets were put on sale and the court found that passing off had been established. In contrast to many of the commonwealth cases already discussed, the plaintiffs were actually in the business of selling and licensing Muppet puppets. Strict quality control was maintained in any licence and the defendants' puppets were of inferior quality.[1] It seems probable that since this case would fall in line with the British authorities, the same decision would be reached here.

(iii) *Inanimate objects*. Much the same principles will apply to the use of photographs or drawings of objects, such as stately homes, football stadia, etc., as to real people.

---

[96] *Athans* v. *Canadian Adventure Camps* 80 D.L.R. (3d.) 583 (1978).
[97] See *Krouse* v. *Chrysler Canada* 12 D.L.R. (3d.) 463 (1970), Ontario High Ct.
[98] [1961] R.P.C. 217.
[99] *King Features Syndicate Inc.* v. *Kleeman (O. & M.)* [1941] 2 All E.R. 403. For copyright to apply the work must be an exact copy.
[1] *Children's Television Workshops Inc.* v. *Woolworth (N.S.W.)* [1981] R.P.C. 187.

12. Other Remedies Used to Protect Exclusive Rights

Copyright, trade marks and passing off recognise property in names, logos, titles, films, and records, etc. On the basis of such property, the sponsee is able to license, or in certain cases, assign to the sponsor rights to use such property. The practical distinction between such licences and others has already been discussed in Chapter 8 below.

It is one thing to say to a sponsor "here is my logo, it is a registered trade mark and you may use it exclusively in connection with your products" and another to purport to grant exclusive rights to use a logo when no copyright, trade mark or goodwill protected by passing off, exists. The term "exclusive," in the later example is misrepresenting the status of the logo and may amount to a misrepresentation under section 2 of the Misrepresentation Act 1967.

On the fringes of property are remedies and codes of practice which have been applied to prevent or restrict unauthorised third parties using photographs, likenesses, or making misleading statements. The basis upon which such remedies and codes have been applied is not as with copyright, trade marks and passing off, in strict acknowledgment of property rights but to redress some other injustice. Rights in property will be protected whatever the motives of the person who takes or damages it.

Injurious or malicious falsehood

The classic definition is that written or oral falsehoods will be actionable "where they are maliciously published, where they are calculated in the ordinary course of things to produce, and where they do produce, actual damage."[1] The elements of this tort are:

[1] *Ratcliffe v. Evans* [1892] 2 Q.B. 524, *per* Bowen L.J. at 527.

(a) a false statement about the plaintiff or his property;
(b) the statement must be calculated to cause the plaintiff damage;
(c) the statement must be made maliciously; and
(d) the plaintiff must show that he suffered damage as a result of the statement although the Defamation Act 1952[2] provides that special damage need not be proved where the statement is made in writing or some other permanent form and is calculated to cause pecuniary damage to the plaintiff, or where the statement relates to a profession, calling trade or business held or carried on by the plaintiff at the time of the publication.

Examples of this tort being applied include a statement about the defendant's play *Charlie Girl* to the effect that it was a "disasterous flop"[3]; writing letters to third parties claiming that goods supplied to them by a trader are in contravention of copyright or other intellectual property rights when this is not true[4]; and stating that an artist was sick and might never play again when he was merely unable to attend a concert.[5] In a sponsorship situation using a photograph of a soccer player with an accompanying statement "I always use X product" when it is known that he endorses Y product might be actionable. Statements of puff comparing one's own goods or services with those of a competitor will not be actionable unless made on the basis of an alleged defect in the competitor's goods.[6]

Defamation

Defamation has been defined as "the publication of a statement which . . . tends to lower him in the estimation of right-thinking members of society generally or tends to make them shun or avoid him."[7]

Thus the image of a famous amateur golfer[8] used in an

---

[2] Defamation Act 1952, s.3(1).
[3] *Fielding* v. *Vanity Inc.* [1967] 2 Q.B. 841.
[4] *Polydor and R.S.O. Records Inc.* v. *Harlequin Record Shops and Simons Records* [1980] F.S.R. 194.
[5] *Grappelli* v. *Block (Derek) (Holdings)* [1981] 1 W.L.R. 822.
[6] *De Beers Abrasive Products* v. *International General Electric Co. of New York* [1975] 1 W.L.R. 972.
[7] *Winfield and Jolowicz on Tort* (11th ed. 1979), p. 274, on defamation in advertisements. See also R.G. Lawson, *Advertising Law*, pp. 69–72, on which much of the following text is based.
[8] *Tolley* v. *J.S. Fry & Sons* [1931] A.C. 333.

advertisement for Frys Chocolate without the golfer's consent was held to be defamatory, the reason being that the advertisement implied that Mr. Tolly had prostituted his amateur status by receiving money for it. Defamation is unlikely to have succeeded had Mr. Tolley been a professional golfer since he would then have been permitted to receive money for the advertisement. Dafamation might apply if a trader used the image of a star or personality in an advertisement and the star was signed up exclusively to promote competitive products. The defamation here would lie in the implication or innuendo that he did not honour his contracts.

In another case a leaflet used to promote the sale of football pools stated that a particular professional footballer would give advice on football pool entries. This activity was against football association rules and was held to be defamatory.[9] In another case the head and shoulders of a professional model had been superimposed on the legs of another woman who was modelling stockings. It was held that this was defamatory since it implied that the professional model had consented to being photographed indecently.[10]

It may be defamatory to use a person's name in connection with a commercial product even where the person concerned uses that product. Thus to use a private person's name in connection with a remedy for constipation might be defamatory.[11] However, defamation was not established where a doctor's name was used in connection with a "quack" medicine.[12]

Defamation is actionable without proof of special damage where the alleged defamatory statement is concerned with a person's profession, calling trade or business.[13] In contrast to injurious falsehood, the motives of the person making the defamatory statement are not relevant to the success of the action.[14]

There is some doubt as to whether defamation can arise where the statement is made through a media not originally covered by the Defamation Act 1952. The grey areas in this

---

[9] *Rutherford* v. *Turf Publishers Ltd, The Times*, October 30, 1925.
[10] *Griffiths* v. *Bonsor Hosiery Co. Ltd. The Times*, December 10, 1935.
[11] *Mazatti* v. *Acme Products Ltd.* 4 D.L.R. 601 (1930).
[12] *Dockrell* v. *Dougall* (1889) 80 L.T. 556.
[13] Defamation Act 1952, s.2.
[14] *Ibid.* s.4.

connection are films, videos, cable television, records and tapes and skywriting.[15]

Breach of confidence

The principle behind the remedy of breach of confidence was stated in a recent Law Commission Report No. 110.[16] "He who has received information in confidence should not take unfair advantage of it." Thus where Queen Victoria had etchings made of her children and the defendant obtained copies through an employee of the queen's printer (unbeknown to the printer himself) an injunction was obtained restraining the defendant from printing a catalogue offering for sale copies of the etchings.[17] Breach of confidence bears certain similarities to copyright. Where it differs, however, is in the protection of substance rather than form. Thus copyright infringement involves making an exact copy whereas breach of confidence is not so restricted.

There are a number of conditions to satisfy before a claim for breach of confidence can be established. Where, for example, the information is already in the public domain, it is unlikely that any breach of confidence can arise, except perhaps where a person who committed the breach of confidence acquired the information before it was in the public domain. The public interest and freedom of the press are elements which weigh against treating all information as confidential. There are three main elements in establishing liability under this tort.[18]

(1) THE INFORMATION MUST BE CONFIDENTIAL

Information is perhaps a misleading term since it has been applied to photographs,[19] etchings,[20] trade secrets,[21] and

---

[15] Report of the Committee on Defamation, Cmnd. 5909 1975.
[16] Cmnd. 8388 1982, para. 6(11), and see generally Allison Coleman [1982] E.I.P.R. 73.
[17] *Prince Albert* v. *Strange* (1849) 1 Mac. & G. 25.
[18] See the judgment of Megarry J. in *Coco* v. *Clarke (A.N.) (Engineers)* [1969] R.P.C. 41 at 47.
[19] *Pollard* v. *Photographic Co.* (1889) 40 Ch.D. 345.
[20] *Prince Albert* v. *Strange* (1849) 1 Mac. & G. 25.
[21] *Seager* v. *Copydex* [1967] 1 W.L.R. 923, and *Arryll (Duchess)* v. *Argyll (Duke)* [1967] Ch. 302, details of a sentimental journey told to the Duke of Argyll.

recently to an idea for a television programme.[22] This case involved the television series called "Rock Follies," the idea for which was orally communicated to Thames Television. It was then developed into a television programme without the permission of those who conceived it. In giving judgment against Thames Television, Hirst J.[22a] identified the main elements for success in such an action as the confidential communication of an original identifiable and potentially attractive commercial idea which was capable of realisation. It was previously applied in similar circumstances in a recent Australian case to protect an idea for a television programme about millionaires with an unusual twist to it.[23]

It has been suggested by one author that the information which is protected will require at least minimal, intellectual or perhaps creative effort.[24] Mere trivial tittle-tattle will not be protected.[25] Information which is already in the public domain cannot, by its very nature, be confidential.[26] Where information to all intents and purposes appears to be confidential, there is nevertheless a balance to be maintained with legitimate access by the media and others to that information in the public interest. Thus Mrs. Khashoggi was unable to obtain an injunction to prevent details of her life being revealed by her former housekeeper.[27] In another case information obtained in confidence about the Church of Scientology, which was subsequently revealed in a book, was held to be "in the public interest."[28] Where people actively court publicity and frequently appear in the media such as sportsmen[29] or pop groups, then it is conceivable that they will be denied this remedy. Thus Gilbert O'Sullivan, Engelbert Humperdink and Tom Jones were unable to obtain an injunction to prevent their ex-public relations manager from disclosing details of their private lives.[30]

---

[22] *Fraser* v. *Thames Television Ltd.* [1983] 2 W.L.R. 917.
[22a] [1983] 2 All E.R. 101 at 122.
[23] See *General Television Corporation* v. *Talbot* (unreported); but see S. Ricketson [1980] E.I.P.R. 149.
[24] Cornish, *Intellectual Property: Patents, Copyright, Trade Marks and Allied Rights* (1981) p. 269.
[25] Megarry J. in *Coco* v. *Clark (A.N.) (Engineers)* [1969] R.P.C. 41 at 48.
[26] See p. 196 above.
[27] *Khashoggi* v. *Smith* (1980) 130 New L.J. 168.
[28] *Hubbard* v. *Vosper* [1972] 2 Q.B. 84.
[29] See *Krouse* v. *Chrysler Canada* (1970) D.L.R. (3d) 463, Ontario High Ct.
[30] *Woodward* v. *Hutchins* [1977] 1 W.L.R. 760.

(2) THE INFORMATION MUST HAVE BEEN COMMUNICATED IN
    CIRCUMSTANCES IMPORTING AN OBLIGATION OF CONFI-
    DENCE

The obligation may arise from an express or implied term
of a contract, in which case a claim for breach of contract will
also arise[31] or be implied from all the circumstances.[32] No
contractual or proprietary relationship is necessary.[33]

(3) UNAUTHORISED USE OF THAT INFORMATION AND DETRI-
    MENT TO THE PLAINTIFF

The unauthorised use of the information will usually
involve damage or detriment to the original owner. The
damage does not need to be financial[34] but it usually will be.
In the *Church of Scientology*[34a] case the consequence of the
disclosures made in the book would probably have been a
reduction in covenants and income to the church.

Breach of confidence may be relevant to the sponsorship
agreement because of the special relationship between the
sponsor and sponsee. It may be used to prevent premature
publication by unauthorised third parties of confidential
photographs, statistics, lists and other matters passed to the
sponsor by the sponsee. Once the information is in the public
domain, however the relevance ceases.

Trespass

Trespass involves interference with land or goods or the
person. If a sponsor were granted exclusive rights to take
photographs of actors performing a play or a sportsman
whilst playing a game, then trespass may be relevant in
preventing others from entering the venue where the activity
takes place. This might have particular significance in the case
of sponsored video of sports events where anyone who can
gain legitimate access to the sports ground can legally make a
recording unless the contract to enter forbids this. This
position may be contrasted with that of actors, musicians,

---

[31] See *Exchange Telegraph Co.* v. *Gregory & Co.* [1896] 1 Q.B. 147 and
   Fraser v. *Thames Television Ltd.* [1983] 2 W.L.R. 917.
[32] See *Prince Albert* v. *Strange* (1849) 1 Mac. & G. 25.
[33] *Duchess of Argyll* v. *Duke of Argyll* [1967] Ch. 302.
[34] See *Prince Albert* v. *Strange* (1849) 1 Mac. & G. 25.
[34a] *Hubbard* v. *Vosper* [1972] 2 Q.B. 84.

etc., under the Performers Protection Acts.[35] Where the video is filmed from land belonging to someone else or on common land, there can be no trespass. In one case, therefore, the plaintiff who owned a large private house was unable to prevent the defendant from flying over it and taking photographs which were offered for sale.[36] Sitting on the highway and making a sketch might be trespass against the owner of the subsoil.[37] In a recent case an injunction was awarded against the B.B.C. to prevent the broadcast of a film about the Savoy Hotel. The television equipment had been brought surreptitiously into the hotel. One of the grounds upon which the injunction was awarded was because entry with concealed cameras could amount to trespass.[38]

Nuisance

Private nuisance involves an unreasonable intereference with the use or enjoyment of land *i.e.* noise, rather than interference with the land itself. It was held not to be a nuisance to erect a stand next door to the plaintiff's racecourse and broadcast commentaries from it.[39]

Breach of contract

In one case already discussed it was held that use of a photograph without the permission of the subject amounted to breach of contract.[40] The court implied a term into the agreement which was broken when the photographer attempted to use the photograph without the permission of the subject.[41] It is unlikely that the same decision would be reached today.

Interference with contracts

This has already been discussed at p. 99.

Unlawful interference with business

This tort is mentioned only for completeness. In *ex. p. Island Records*[41] performers and record companies suffered

[35] See p. 146.
[36] *Berstein v. Skyviews and General Ltd.* [1978] Q.B. 479.
[37] *Harrison v. Duke of Rutland* [1893] 1 Q.B. 142, C.A.
[38] *Savoy Hotel plc v. British Broadcasting Corporation* (unreported).
[39] *Victoria Park Racing & Recreation Grounds Co. Ltd. v. Taylor* (1938) 58 C.L.R. 479, a decision of the High Court of Australia.
[40] *Stackemann v. Paton* [1906] 1 Ch. 774.
[41] *Ex p. Island Records Ltd.* [1978] Ch. 122.

serious damage from bootleggers. They therefore sought an injunction against the bootleggers on the basis of the Performers Protection Act 1958.[42] The injunction was granted by the Court of Appeal on the basis that "A man who is carrying on a lawful trade or calling has a right to be protected from any unlawful interference with it.;" (per Lord Denning M.R.).

The House of Lords in the Lonrho case[43] which involved the supply of oil to Southern Rhodesia has by implication overruled the Ex p. Island Records case.[44] It must be doubted therefore that such a tort does exist and if it does, whether the scope of its application is as wide as that suggested by Lord Denning in the ex. p. Island Records case.

Routh v. Webster injunction[45]

An injunction preventing the unauthorised use of a name may lie where such use exposes the owner of the name to a risk of liability. This principle was applied in the case of Routh v. Webster which involved the use of an individual's name, without his consent, as a provisional director of a joint stock company. There seems no reason why the same principle could not be extended to the unauthorised use of images. The necessity to prove a risk of liability is important and requires the risk to be tangible rather than speculative.[46] Unless there was a direct and unauthorised statement endorsing a sponsor's product, it seems unlikely that any such liability could be established.

Right of property

As already stated English law does not acknowledge any independent right of property or privacy in a name, image or likeness. Although such a right has been debated on a number of occasions,[47] it seems unlikely that any general right will be

---

[42] See p. 146.
[43] Lonrho Ltd. v. Shell Petroleum Co. Ltd. (No. 2) [1981] 3 W.L.R. 33.
[44] See R.C.A. Corp. and R.C.A. v. Pollard (1983) 9 F.S.R. 9.
[45] (1847) 10 Beav. 561.
[46] Walter v. Ashton [1902] 2 Ch. 282.
[47] See the Report of the Committee on Privacy, Cmnd. 5012 (1972).

forthcoming in the near future. Parliament has recognised the need for privacy in the area of data protection with the Data Protection Bill. This Bill covers almost any information normally held by a business, for example customer lists held on electronic machines such as computers and word processors. The bill requires persons holding such data to be registered under the Act. It is proposed that to use the data except for the purpose for which is has been registered will be a criminal offence.

False trade descriptions

The use of a statement such as "Official Supplier of the 1982 World Cup" or the inclusion of an event mascot on products re-enforces the association between the sponsor and the sponsored event or happening in the eyes of the public. Without acknowledging any property in these rights a criminal offence may be committed where the use results in a false trade description. It would be a false trade description, for example, to describe a tennis racquet "as recommended by John McEnroe" if it is not.

The legislation creating this criminal offence is the Trade Descriptions Act 1968. The object of the statute is clearly to protect the interests of the consumer. Its enforcement is in the hands of the Trading Standards Officers who are obliged by the terms of the Act to take proceedings wherever a false description has been applied.[48] Potentially it is possible to bring a private prosecution against third parties who are applying the false description to their goods or services. Private prosecutions of this type, however, are rare. The threat of criminal sanctions including fines and imprisonment, seizure of the falsely marked goods and adverse publicity should be a sufficient deterrent for the guilty party. The sponsor or sponsee should therefore report the false trade description to the local Trading Standards Office for investigation.

Where a prosecution is brought under the Act it is possible for the person aggrieved to obtain compensation from the person who applied the false description under section 35 of the Powers of Criminal Courts Act 1973, as amended by the Magistrates' Court Act 1980, s.40(1).

---

[48] Trade Descriptions Act 1968, s.26(1).

201

(1) WHAT IS A FALSE TRADE DESCRIPTION?

Essentially it is a false representation made in relation to goods and certain types of services. It is similar to misrepresentation which was discussed under the law of contract[49] but it is broader in scope. A "trade puff," for example, would not give rise to misrepresentation but it might well amount to a false trade description. A false trade description is actionable by the trading standards office and is a criminal suit. Misrepresentation is available only as between the parties to a contract and is a civil remedy. The elements required to make a false trade description actionable differ between goods and services.

(a) *Goods*

The offences in relation to goods arise where a person in the course of a trade or business applies a false trade description to goods and supplies or offers to supply goods to which a false trade description has been applied.[50] It will be seen that both the manufacturer who applies the false description to the goods and the dealer may be caught. So also may the advertising agency which prints the misleading advertisement. However, a special defence is available to the agency where it can show that the advertisement was published innocently.[51] There are four key elements to the offence. First, a trade description: the Act helps here by categorising certain statements which are made in relation to goods as trade descriptions. These include three which are likely to be relevant to sponsorship. Thus an indication that the goods have been tested by a particular person[52] or an indication that they have been approved by a particular person[53] or that they have been supplied to a particular person[54] are all potentially trade descriptions. A person in this context would include both an individual such as a tennis star or an organisation such as F.I.F.A.[55]

---

[49] See p. 59.
[50] Trade Descriptions Act 1968, s.1(1).
[51] *Ibid.* s.25.
[52] *Ibid.* s.2(1)(f).
[53] *Ibid.* s.2(1)(g).
[54] *Ibid.* s.13.
[55] Interpretation Act 1889, s.19.

Secondly, the trade description must have been applied to goods. This has a very wide meaning and would include, for example, labelling the goods, labelling the packaging, including the description in promotional leaflets, advertising or making oral statements.[56] There is one important limitation, however, which has practical relevance to sponsorship. Where the trade description or statement about goods or services is published in a newspaper, book or periodical or in any film, sound or television broadcast, it shall not be deemed to have been applied to goods or services unless it is contained in an advertisement.

Thirdly, the trade description must be false. False means to a material degree. In one case, therefore, a farmer had used some bottles which had another dairy's name marked on them. The foil cap, however, gave correct details of the origin of the milk. It was held that there was no false trade description since the words on the bottle merely described where the bottle came from, not the milk.[57]

Lastly the goods must be supplied, although not necessarily received, in the course of a trade.[58]

The following are examples of false trade descriptions in relation to goods: "Norfolk King Turkeys" which came from Denmark,[59] and "exciting leather funwear" which turned out to be plastic.[60] There has been a recent spate of prosecutions under the Trade Descriptions Act against video shops selling tapes stating that they are originals when they are, in fact, pirate copies.

(b) Services

The offence in relation to services is contained in section 14(1) of the Trade Descriptions Act 1968. This provides that certain false statements in relation to services are actionable. Actionable statements include those which imply the approval or evaluation by any person of any services. In contrast to statements in relation to goods there is an additional requirement that the statement must be made knowing that it is false or reckless, *i.e.* regardless of whether it is true or false.

---

[56] Trade Descriptions Act 1968, s.4(1) and (2).
[57] *Donnelly* v. *Rowlands* [1970] 1 W.L.R. 1600.
[58] Trade Descriptions Act 1968, s.1(1).
[59] *Beckett* v. *Kingston Bros. (Butchers)* [1970] 1 Q.B. 606.
[60] *The Times*, June 14, 1973.

False statements in relation to goods are actionable even where made innocently. Services are relevant to sponsorship since many sponsors are in the service sector, *i.e.* banks, insurance companies, building societies.

(2) TRADE DEFENCES

There are a number of statutory defences available under section 24 of the Trade Descriptions Act 1968 to those involved in proceedings under the Act. These defences are only available, however, where the person who seeks to rely upon them can prove that he took reasonable precautions and exercised due diligence. The statutory defences include: mistake, reliance upon information supplied, act or default of another person, an accident or some other cause beyond the defendant's control.

Additionally there is a special defence available to persons who have innocently published false trade descriptions.[61]

(3) APPLICATION OF THE TRADES DESCRIPTION ACT TO SPONSORSHIP

Is there a trade description applied to goods or services? Some of the more usual licences which a sponsor may acquire have already been discussed. Whether the unauthorised use by a third party can amount to a false trade description will depend upon a number of factors. False statements by third parties that their goods have been approved by or are endorsed by the sponsee will be actionable. Thus a false statement that the International Tennis Federation recommends, approves or has tested X Company's tennis balls would be a false trade description if they have not. Other phrases may create difficulties, since it must be questionable whether they actually indicate approval or endorsement. Thus "Official Sponsor of the I.T.F." or "Official Soft Drink of the World Cup" or "Official Supplier of Cameras to the World Cup" are all intended to convey the impression of approval or of endorsement but do they? In the author's view the answer must be yes. The Trade Descriptions Act refers to "direct and indirect" statements[62] as constituting a trade description. The Act also states that anything which, is not

[61] Trade Descriptions Act 1968, s.25.
[62] *Ibid.* s.2(1).

strictly speaking, a "trade description" but would be taken as indicating endorsement, etc. will, if false, be treated as a false trade description.[63]

Similar problems in finding approval arise where, for example, photographs, images, signatures or logos are used in relation to goods without any express statement that the goods are approved. The test in such cases seems to be whether or not the use of photographs and the like would be "taken for an indication" that the goods have been approved by the person. It is submitted that the man in the street would probably interpret the use of a sports celebrity's image in relation to the promotion of goods, as implying that the celebrity approved them. The same conclusion would also, it is submitted, be reached where a mascot or logo of a sports or Arts body were used on or in relation to commercial goods. Where the mascot or logo is a registered trade mark then it will be a false trade description for any unauthorised person to apply it to goods covered by the registration.[64]

The same basic principles will apply to services as have been discussed above in relation to goods. Thus if a bank stated that it was the "Official Bank appointed by the Football League" and it had not been so appointed, then a false trade description would have been made. As discussed above, there is an additional requirement with respect to statements made in relation to services and that is that they must have been made deliberately or recklessly.

Codes—miscellaneous

The Press Council Declaration of Principle of Privacy.[65] This states at paragraph 1 that "the publication of information about the private lives or concerns of individuals without their consent is only acceptable if there is a legitimate public interest overriding the right of privacy." This obviously only applies in the case of newspapers or other periodicals falling within the Press Council's terms of reference. The Council, itself, adjudicates on any complaints. One of the more notable complaints involved drawings purporting to show Miss Evonne Goolagong (now Cawley) in the nude. The *Sun*

---

[63] *Ibid.* s.3(3).
[64] *Ibid.* s.3(4).
[65] Twenty-third Press Council Report [1976] p. 150. Further declarations are made from time to time, such as that made in 1983, or the "cheque book journalism" following the Yorkshire Ripper case.

published these drawings without obtaining Miss Goolagong's consent with the result that this caused her much distress. Perhaps a civil action on the basis of nervous shock could have been brought as in *Wilkinson* v. *Downton*.[66] The complaint against the *Sun* was upheld.[67]

The British Broadcasting Corporation and Independent Broadcasting Corporation have their own complaints procedure on matters involving privacy.[68]

The British Code of Advertising Practice states in the section on the protection of privacy and exploitation of the individuals: "Advertisements should not, except in the circumstances noted below, portray or refer to any living persons, by whatever means, unless their express prior permission has been obtained." The Code also contains provisions which are designed to avoid creating the impression of an endorsement when none has been given.[69]

The British Code of Sales Promotion Practice states in section 5(2) on the protection of privacy that "Promotors should respect the reasonable right to privacy of consumers, and sales promotions should be designed and conducted in such a way as to avoid causing consumers trouble or annoyance;" and in section 5(2) that "Where the promotion may require participants to become involved in further publicity or in advertising, whether connected with the sales promotion or not, the promoters should make this clear in their promotional material. Written permission should be obtained from prizewinners where names and addresses of winners are to be used on publicity otherwise than as specified in section 6.2.4."

---

[66] [1897] 2 Q.B. 57.
[67] Twentieth Press Council Report [1973] p. 44.
[68] Where the complaint, however, relates to matters which are the subject of legal proceedings, the commission may be prevented from adjudication: *R.* v. *British Broadcasting Complaints Commission, ex p. Thames Television, The Times*, October 6, 1982.
[69] See Trade Descriptions Act 1968, s.4(7).

13. Remedies—Intellectual Property

Copyright

Remedies for infringement of copyright are available both in civil and criminal law. The scope of such remedies includes, in civil courts, relief by way of damages, injunction,[1] conversion[2] or detention. In any civil action for copyright infringement there is a presumption that copyright exists in the subject-matter of the action and that the plaintiff is the owner of the copyright.[3]

(1) DAMAGES FOR INFRINGEMENT[4]

Since copyright confers a legal monopoly on the owner and/or the licensee, it follows that where that monopoly is infringed, damage will result. A sponsor who acquires an exclusive licence to include a World Cup mark on soft drink cans will suffer a loss where the whole market is flooded with other cans bearing the same mark. His loss will be in sales. The sponsee's loss would arise where the soft drink company withholds payment of part of the agreed fee if he feels his exclusive rights are devalued. A loss might also arise where a pirate manufacturer floods the market with cheap imitations thereby destroying the goodwill attaching to the use of a particular mark. Infringement damages should be recoverable for these losses.

The court is given power to award additional damages, *i.e.*

---

[1] Copyright Act 1956, s.17(1).
[2] *Ibid.* s.18, but note criticisms of conversion damages in Green Paper, *Reform of the Law relating to Copyright, Designs and Performers Protection*, Cmnd. 8302 (1981) and in criminal courts, prosecutions.
[3] *Ibid.* s.20.
[4] *Ibid.* s.17. See Cornish, *Intellectual Property: Patents, Copyright, Trade Marks and Allied Rights* (1981), p. 369.

in excess of the actual economic loss suffered, where infringement is particularly flagrant and profitable to the defendant[5] and other relief is not available. Thus, where a photographer sold to the press photographs taken at a wedding of a man who had just been murdered, additional damages were awarded; copyright in the photograph belonged to the man's family since they had commissioned it.[6]

Where the infringement is committed by an innocent party,[7] then the only remedy available is an "account of profit." In practical terms since the infringer's motive in reproducing a copyright work will be to make a profit then an account for profit may be a satisfactory way of compensating the owner for the infringement. Indeed the copyright owner is given the opportunity of seeking this remedy in substitution of proving his damage claim against a non-innocent infringer. It is not possible to pursue both normal damages and seek an "account of profits." Account of profit, as the name implies, means that the infringer will be required to pay all the profits made from his infringement to the owner.

The burden of proving non-awareness and no reasonable grounds for suspicion under section 17(2) of the Copyright Act (above) lies upon the alleged infringer.[8]

(2) DAMAGES FOR CONVERSION[9]

The assumption is made in conversion damages that the copyright owner is also the owner of the infringing copies and, where appropriate, plates used for making them. Since the infringing copies and plates "belong" to the copyright owner, he is entitled to ask the infringer to return the infringing copies to him.[10] Whether an order is made for return of the infringing copies, is within the discretion of the

---

[5] Copyright Act 1956, s.17(3)(*a*) and (*b*).

[6] *Williams* v. *Settle* [1960] 1 W.L.R. 1072, a county court judgment upheld by the Court of Appeal; see also *Cassell & Co.* v. *Broome* [1972] A.C. 1027.

[7] Innocence defined as "not aware and had no reasonable grounds for suspecting": Copyright Act 1956, s.17(2).

[8] See the Court of Appeal judgment in *Infabrics* v. *Jaytex* [1981] 2 W.L.R. 646, not disturbed in the House of Lords reversal.

[9] Copyright Act 1956, s.18.

[10] Torts (Interference with Goods) Act 1977, s.3(2). See also *Adventure Film Productions* v. *Tully*, *The Times*, October 14, 1982 for an example of an order made to "deliver up" a film.

court. Where the infringing articles have been sold an order for delivery up will be of little relevance. Where the court does not order the return of the infringing copies to the copyright owner, damages will probably be ordered instead. Damages in conversion are not based on the economic loss suffered by the owner, but on the value of the infringing copies without regard to the cost of producing them. If the infringer produced keyrings in the shape of an event mark and sold the keyrings before being traced, damages would be based upon appropriate evidence proving the value of the keyrings. Direct sales expenses would be allowed in assessing the value.[11] Where a mark forms part only of the infringing copy such as a logo on a T-shirt, it seems that the value of the whole T-shirt and not just the mark will be relevant.[12] Conversion damages may be pursued against more than one party who deals with the infringing articles provided a separate act of infringement has occurred.[12a]

Conversion and infringement damages are cumulative in the sense that they may both be pursued simultaneously. This gives the owner the advantage of pursuing both until such time as he can see which will produce the greater sum. Double compensation for any one infringement will not, however, be awarded.[13]

Conversion can only exist, however, where there has been an infringement. No independent cause of action is created by section 18 of the Copyright Act 1956.[14] An innocent infringer will not be liable under section 18 for damages or any other pecuniary remedy, except for costs.[15] The continuation of conversion as a remedy in its present form in copyright cases is in some doubt.[16]

---

[11] *Sutherland Publishing Co. Ltd.* v. *Caxton Publishing Co. Ltd.* [1936] Ch. 323.

[12] *Infabrics* v. *Jaytex* [1981] 2 W.L.R. 646, where the House of Lords did not disturb the Court of Appeal's view that burden of proving non-awareness and no reasonable grounds for suspicion under the Copyright Act 1956, s.17(2), *supra*, lies upon the alleged infringer.

[12a] See *Rose Records* v. *Motown Record Corpn.* [1983] F.S.R. 361.

[13] *Caxton Publishing Co. Ltd.* v. *Sutherland Publishing Co. Ltd.* [1939] A.C. 178, applied in *Lewis Trusts* v. *Bamber Stores Ltd. The Times,* February 23, 1983.

[14] *Infabrics* v. *Jaytex* [1981] 2 W.L.R. 646.

[15] Copyright Act 1956, s.18(2).

[16] See *Reform of the Law relating to Copyright, Designs and Performers Protection*, Cmnd. 8302 (1981).

(3) INJUNCTIONS

The equitable remedy of granting injunctions to protect intellectual property rights is relevant to all copyright actions while the act of piracy is continuing. An injunction will enable the copyright owner to restrain the primary infringer and others from continuing to commit the infringing act. This may either be interlocutory until the trial of the action is heard, or final.

Injunctions are of two kinds, (i) negatively restrictive,[17] and (ii) positively mandatory, which includes, in effect, an Anton Piller order.[18]

This latter order enables the plaintiff to a copyright claim (or other infringement action based upon intellectual property) to apply to the high court upon an *ex parte* application for an order that permits access to the defendant's premises to inspect and remove, copy or photograph material connected with the infringement, or to deliver up infringing goods.[19] The order also usually commands the defendant to supply information which will enable his suppliers and customers to be identified.

An Anton Piller order is not a claim itself. It is an administrative litigation remedy by which the plaintiff may, on disclosure of all material facts within his knowledge,[19a] obtain evidence in support of the allegation of infringement. Before the order is made, it will be necessary for the plaintiff to show (i) an extremely strong prima facie case of infringement; (ii) serious, actual or potential damage; (iii) clear evidence of possession of incriminating documents by the defendant and (iv) the real possibility that such documents may be destroyed before an application inter partes, *i.e.* with notice to the defendant and at which the defendant can attend will be heard. The plaintiff will need to identify the specific premises to which the order is to relate.[19b] In a recent case[19c] it was held that those who were engaged in selling bootleg

---

[17] See *American Cynamid Co.* v. *Ethicon* [1975] A.C. 396.

[18] *Anton Piller K.G.* v. *Manufacturing Processes* [1976] Ch. 55.

[19] See Supreme Court Act 1981, s.72, reversing the effect of *Rank Film Distributors* v. *Video Information Centre* [1981] 2 W.L.R. 668.

[19a] *Thermax Ltd.* v. *Schot Industrial Glass* [1981] F.S.R. 289.

[19b] *Protector Alarms* v. *Maxim Alarms* [1978] F.S.R. 442.

[19c] *EMI Records Ltd.* v. *Kudhail, The Times*, June 28, 1983 where those engaged in the sale of bootleg cassettes under the name "Oak Records" had a sufficient "interest" between one another to be sued in a representative capacity.

cassettes under the trade name "Oak Records" had a sufficient identity of interest for a representative action to succeed. The confirmation by the court that a representative action will apply in these circumstances, could prove a useful development. The privilege against self-incrimination will only be available in refusing production of documents in limited circumstances.[20]

(4) CRIMINAL OFFENCES

A number of criminal offences are created by the Copyright Act.[21] Criminal sanctions should be a deterrent in discouraging piracy and one might anticipate a gradual growth of the scope of criminal remedies.[22] This growth has already evidenced itself in relation to infringing copies of sound recordings and cinematograph films by the Copyright Act 1956 (Amendment) Act 1982 and Copyright (Amendment) Act 1983. The former Act widened the scope of section 21 to make it an offence to be in possession of infringing sound recordings or cinematograph films by way of trade. The latter Act made provision for increased penalties and improved powers of search and seizure.[23]

Offences under the Act in relation to infringing copies include making for sale or hire, selling or letting for hire, exhibition in public by way of trade, importation into the United Kingdom except for private domestic use, and the performance of certain works in public being in possession of sound recordings or film by way of trade.[24] There is considerable overlap between these specific copyright provisions and civil remedies; also for conspiracy to defraud; but the copyright owner will almost always wish to proceed by way of civil action to secure injunctions and damages.[25]

Unlicensed street trading can be prohibited under local

---

[20] *Rank Film Distributors* v. *Video Information Centre* [1981] 2 W.L.R. 668, and the Supreme Court Act 1981, s.72. See also *Universal City Studios Inc.* v. *Hubbard* [1983] F.S.R. 883.

[21] Copyright Act 1956, s.21.

[22] See Cmnd. 8302 (1981), p. 50.

[23] For quantum of fines see s.75 of the Criminal Justice Act 1982. The current fine is now £1000.

[24] Copyright Act 1956, s.21(1)–(5).

[25] See *Rank Film Distributors* v. *Video Information Centre* [1981] 2 W.L.R. 668.

211

government legislation.[26] Local government officers often work alongside the police, who will ensure that the highway is not obstructed in the removal of unlicensed traders, who will often be selling pirate merchandise. The powers of the Trading Standards officers in relation to offences committed under the Trade Descriptions Act 1968 should also be considered in relation to copyright infringement. Similarly, the powers of seizure of the Commissioners of Customs and Excise regarding imports which infringe copyright might be of assistance.[26a] There has also been a noticeable growth in the development and success of industry-funded anti-piracy squads, who undertake the detective work in locating infringers, and leave prosecution to the police, under section 21 of the Copyright Act.

Trade marks

REMEDIES

The Trade Marks Act 1938 expressly states[27] that no one may take action pursuant to the Act for the infringement of an unregistered trade mark. That includes a trade mark for which an application has been made but which has not proceeded to registration. This has important consequences in the case of sponsored events. It may take one or two years before an application is actually registered and no relief on the basis of trade mark registration will be available during the period of application. It therefore requires two to three years of planning before an event takes place to ensure that money on applications is constructively spent.

The Trade Marks Act 1938, in contrast to the Copyright Act 1956, is silent in expounding in detail the statutory remedies that are available. However, the following remedies are available although the list is not intended to be exhaustive.[27a] Cross-reference should be made to the criminal offences discussed above in relation to copyright except those directly concerned with section 21:

---

[26] For example the Local Government (Miscellaneous Provisions) Act 1982 contains model licensing powers for adoption by local government. These contain street trading licensing provisions.

[26a] Copyright Act 1956, s.22.

[27] Trade Marks Act 1938, s.2.

[27a] See generally Kerly, *The Law of Trade Marks and Trade Names* (11th ed., 1983).

(a) An injunction.[28]
(b) An order for delivery up for erasure of the infringing marks or where erasure is not possible destruction of the goods themselves.[29]
(c) An enquiry as to damages or an account of profits made by the defendant from the sale of the infringing goods. These remedies are alternatives which would be available at the plaintiff's option. An account of profits, however, is generally refused where the defendant had no knowledge of the defendant's mark.[30]

Passing off

REMEDIES

The possible remedies in passing off are similar to those available in copyright infringement. Thus injunctions, interlocutory or final,[31] damages, or at the plaintiff's option, an account of profits would all be available to the plaintiff. Where the defendant acted innocently, it seems that in line with a copyright case only nominal damages will be available.[32] Similarly in the case of an account of profit the account may be limited to the time after the defendant became aware of the true facts.

Criminal sanctions also exist under the Trade Descriptions Act 1968 and cross-reference should be made to the other criminal offences discussed in relation to copyright except those directly concerned with section 21. The individual trader or sponsor would doubtless elect to claim relief under the civil remedies, in the civil courts.

---

[28] See *American Cyanamid Co.* v. *Ethicon* [1975] A.C. 396.
[29] *Dent* v. *Turpin* (1861) 2 John & H. 139.
[30] *A.G. Spalding & Bros.* v. *A.W. Gamage Ltd.* [1918] R.P.C. 101.
[31] Note the effect of the *American Cyanamid* decision.
[32] *A.G. Spalding & Bros.* v. *A.W. Gamage Ltd.* [1918] R.P.C. 101.

14. Competition Law

Getting to grips with the mass of complex legislation in this area is like trying to grasp mercury. The basic premise of competition law is that it encourages competition by outlawing certain restrictive agreements and inhibiting anti-competitive practices by firms with market power. The problem with understanding much of the legislation is that not enough time is spent with examples of what type of practices will be regarded as anti-competitive, Parliament having been content to lay down broad notions of public interest to be interpreted by the enforcement authorities. The legislation is drafted so widely that nearly every commercial practice or agreement adopted by businessmen is capable of falling within its scope, although condemnation is unlikely unless the object is to stifle competition or harm trade rivals.

Sponsorship, rather than inhibiting competition, is likely to encourage it. A key word to many sponsors is exclusivity which prima facie means that other potential sponsors are excluded from the property or services of the sponsee. Exclusivity is a red rag to a bull for the competition lawyer; however, what must be understood is that a sponsor is unlikely to invest his money in a sport, Arts or leisure project unless he knows that the same opportunities are not going to be sold to his major competitor. If they were, then this may destroy the credibility of the marketing package built around the sponsorship. For this reason exclusivity in sponsorship encourages activities that would otherwise not have taken place—an outcome which should not be regarded as anti-competitive. The four pieces of legislation which might have application to rules or contracts applying as between the sponsee and other parties are the Fair Trading Act 1973, the Competition Act 1980, the Treaty of Rome 1957 and the Restrictive Trade Practices Act 1976. The most relevant legislation is the Treaty of Rome and the Restrictive Trade Practices Act.

Examples of activities arising out of the sponsorship

relationship which could be affected by competition laws might include:

(a) a sponsee such as a National Sports Federation applying rules to its member clubs which as a condition of membership compelled them to buy all their sports equipment from the National Sports Federation. One assumes here that the National Federation has not negotiated some special discount rate for bulk supplies. However, even if this were so this need not justify the existence of such a restriction;

(b) a sponsor buying exclusive sponsorship rights to all events within a particular territory thereby preventing its competitor from using what might be a particularly suitable and attractive advertising media; and

(c) a sponsee using trade marks or copyright in a sport or Arts logo to partition markets. Thus, if the sponsee purported to grant the sponsor a right to use a logo in France on soft drink cans and another sponsor the exclusive right to use the same logo in England on soft drink cans it may not be possible to rely on trade marks rights to prevent the English sponsor exporting his soft drink cans bearing the logo into France and vice versa.

Fair Trading Act 1973

This Act permits the Director General of Fair Trading to refer "monopoly situations" for review by the Monopolies and Mergers Commission to determine whether the monopoly itself, or any practices carried on by a dominant firm operate against the public interest. A monopoly situation is deemed to exist where one firm accounts for one quarter of the market.[1]

Competition Act 1980

The Director General of Fair Trading has power to investigate any firm which he believes is carrying on a course of conduct amounting to an "anti-competitive practice."[2] Organisations with an annual turnover of less than £5 million

---

[1] Fair Trading Act 1973, s.6.
[2] *Ibid.* s.3.

are exempt, provided that their products or services account for less than 25 per cent. of the market.

Restrictive Trade Practices Act 1976 (R.T.P.A.)

There is a partial overlap between this Act and the position at common law that a contract in restraint of trade is void unless it can be shown to be reasonable, both between the parties and in the public interest. The R.T.P.A. however, tackles the problem in a different way than the common law. There is a requirement under the Act to register with the Director General of Fair Trading all agreements which include relevant restrictions accepted by two or more parties. The Director General must then refer registered agreements to the Restrictive Practices Court which will decide whether or not the restrictions are contrary to public interest. The Director General of Fair Trading does have a discretion to apply to the Secretary of State for directions,[3] where he believes the restrictions are not significant.

(1) WHO WILL BE CAUGHT BY THE ACT?

Anyone who enters into an agreement under which goods[4] or services are to be supplied[5] provided that:
  (a) both parties carry on business in the United Kingdom;
  (b) the agreement contains relevant restrictions accepted by both parties. (The parties need not accept the same relevant restriction);
  (c) restrictions cannot be disregarded under the terms of the Act[6]
  (d) the agreement is not exempt from registration.[7]

(a) *An agreement*

Contracts are clearly within the Act whether they are oral or in writing. Where a sports federation issues rules which give rise to a contract with or between[8] its members, then the

---

[3] Restrictive Trade Practices Act 1976, s.21(2).
[4] *Ibid.* s.6.
[5] *Ibid.* s.11.
[6] *Ibid.* s.9 and 18.
[7] *Ibid.* Sched. 3.
[8] See *Clarke* v. *Dunraven*, p. 92.

Act will equally apply. A term may be restrictive without being included in a contract. It is important, however, that there is some mutuality between the parties in accepting the existence of the restrictions.[9]

(b) *Between parties carrying on business in the United Kingdom for the supply of goods or services*

Agreements between a United Kingdom sponsee and a United Kingdom sponsor relating to a United Kingdom sponsored event will fall within the Act. A number of international sports federations have offices in the United Kingdom. If they license United Kingdom sponsorship rights to a United Kingdom sponsor then they will almost certainly be carrying on a business in the United Kingdom.[10]

Restrictions relating to the exclusive use of a sponsors products in a contract of employment with a professional sportsman may be caught by the legislation. This would not, it is submitted, apply to an amateur sportsman since he will not be in "business." "Carrying on business" is a question of fact in each case. The National Racing Greyhound Club was found not to be "carrying on a business in the supply of services" since its main functions were administrative/quasi judicial, *i.e.* acting as a judicial body for the discipline and conduct of greyhound racing. Had it engaged in locating sponsors for its members, then it would probably have been found to be carrying on a business for the supply of services.

Goods are distinguished from services in the Act. Many sponsorships will involve both the supply of goods and services.

(c) *Agreements containing relevant restrictions accepted by both parties*

One of the secondary issues in the Greyhound case was that the Act did not apply since any restrictions were only accepted by one party, *i.e.* the trainer. This will snatch many restrictive agreements from the jaws of the Act.

---

[9] *Fisher* v. *Director General of Fair Trading*, Kerr L.J. 1 C.R. 71 at 82. The issue in this case was whether the fact that all the trainers accepted the same restriction gave rise to an agreement between them to obey the rules of the National Greyhound Racing Association Club Ltd. As a matter of construction it was found that it did not.

[10] *Noddy Subsidiary Rights Co.* v. *I.R.C.* [1967] 1 W.L.R. 1.

A rule issued by a sports federation or club that its players must play in kit provided by a particular sponsor would at first sight seem restrictive. The same may be said of a term included in an agreement restricting the sponsee from endorsing anyone else's products. Such a restriction only applies to one party, however. It would, it is submitted, only fall within the Act where it could be successfully argued that each player had accepted the existence of the restriction between each other. On similar facts this proposition was rejected by the Court of Appeal in the Greyhound case.[11]

There is no cross-over provision for restrictions affecting goods or services. Thus although both parties need not accept the same relevant restrictions they must accept the same relevant restriction in relation to goods or services. An agreement containing relevant restrictions, one of which relates to goods accepted by one party, and the other relating to services accepted by another party would not, in the authors' view, be registrable.

Where a party is under an existing duty in law, there is no additional restriction where that duty is reflected in an agreement.[12] It has been successfully argued that owners of land do not provide services by entering into leasing agreements.[13] Such a principle might be extended by analogy to restrictions in sponsorship agreements involving licences of property, such as trade marks, copyright and goodwill.[14]

(2) CAN THE AGREEMENT OR TERMS THEREOF BE DISRE-
GARDED?

Terms which appear to be restrictive even where accepted by both parties may not be so. The Act provides that restrictions relating, for example, to quality control, standards or service or conditions of employment and certain information agreements may be disregarded for the purposes of the Act.[15] The agreement may contain other unrelated matters however and still be registrable.[16]

[11] See however, Re Austin Motor Co. Ltd. Agreements (1957) L.R. 1 R.P. at 6.
[12] Re British Waste Paper Association's Agreement [1963] 1 W.L.R. 540.
[13] Re Ravenseft Properties' Application [1978] Q.B. 52.
[14] See, however, the Restrictive Trade Practices Act 1976, Sched. 3, paras. 3, 4, 5 and 8 where exemptions are contained for certain categories of intellectual property.
[15] Ibid. s.9 and 18.
[16] Re Schweppes' Agreement [1965] 1 All E.R. 195, C.A.

(3) ARE THE AGREEMENTS EXEMPTED FROM REGISTRATION?

The exemptions are set out in the Third Schedule[17] to the Act. Again, they are immensely complex. It is difficult to see how any of them may have a great deal of relevance to sponsorship.

(4) REGISTRATION

Assuming that no exemption has been found, the agreement must be registered. Registration is made at the office of the Director General of Fair Trading.[18] No fee is payable on registration. The particulars to be furnished include the names and addresses of the parties and the whole terms of the agreement.[19] The time limit for registration is before the restrictions take effect or (if the operation of the restrictions is postponed for more than three months after the agreement is made) within three months of making the agreement.[20] If at any time after registration of an agreement it is varied or determined otherwise than by effluxion of time, particulars of the variation or determination should be furnished to the Director.[21] If the agreement is not registered on time, then restrictive terms will be void.[22] It will be unlawful for any person to give effect to such restrictions or purport to enforce them.[23] The Director General is given the power to restrain any attempted enforcement through the courts. The Act also provides that any person effected by the restriction may bring an action for breach of statutory duty.[24]

(5) POSITION OF REGISTERED AGREEMENTS

Restrictions included in registered agreements will continue to have effect. The Director General is obliged to refer registered agreements to the Restrictive Practice Court.[25] A procedure exists, however, which enables the Director

---

[17] Restrictive Trade Practices Act 1976, s.28.
[18] *Ibid.* s.23.
[19] *Ibid.* s.24(1).
[20] *Ibid.* s.24(2), Sched. 2, para. 5.
[21] *Ibid.* Sched. 2, para. 2.
[22] *Ibid.* s.35(1)(*a*).
[23] *Ibid.* s.35(1)(*b*).
[24] *Ibid.* s.35(2).
[25] *Ibid.* s.12.

General, if directed by the Secretary of State, on application by the D.G.F.T., not to refer the agreement to the Restrictive Practices Court.[26]

In January 1980 the Office of Fair Trading (O.F.T.) indicated that there were four types of restrictions which might arise in relation to sport that could not be disregarded. These included a sport trying to control the level of admission charges, obligations on clubs or players to pool income received from commercial sources, *i.e.* broadcasting, sponsorship, advertising, restrictions on clubs in negotiating for the sale of their own rights, *e.g.* broadcasting rights, and restrictions on the uses to which commercial income derived from the club could be utilised. Conversely, rules relating solely to the playing or administration of sport such as rules of the game, standard of sports equipment, etc., are not likely to be regarded as significant and referred to the court.

The following are examples of restrictions contained in agreements which were regarded as insignificant and therefore were not referred to the court: an agreement between the Fine Art Trade Guild and its members setting out terms and conditions for the authentication by the Guild of limited edition reproductions; an agreement between Dayville Limited containing restrictions, particularly concerning quality control, for the operation of ice cream parlours; restrictions contained in an agreement for operating a drain cleaning service under a franchise; and the British Code of Sales Promotion Practice and the British Code of Advertising Practice.

The Restrictive Practices Court must decide with respect to any agreement referred to it whether the restriction is contrary to the public interest.[27] There are a number of specific grounds (colloquially referred to as gateways) contained in the Act which may be used to justify restrictions as being in the public interest.[28]

Examples include the situation where removal of the restriction would ultimately deprive the consuming public of benefits or where the restriction does not restrict or discourage competition to a material degree. There is an additional requirement that the restriction must not be unreasonable, having regard to the balance of public interest.

---

[26] *Ibid.* s.21(2).
[27] *Ibid.* s.1(3).
[28] *Ibid.* s.10 for goods and s.19 for services.

If the court decides that the restrictions cannot be justified, then they will be void.[29] The court may restrain any attempted enforcement of the restrictions.[30]

About 600 service agreements have been registered since 1976. By 1981, 94 agreements had been ended, 35 have had all the restrictions removed and 86 have not been referred to the court as the restrictions were not thought to be significant.[31] The balance still remain to be considered. Of the agreements which have been filed, some include the regulation of sport such as the Lawn Tennis Association Handbook. Others have included exclusive advertising rights. Exclusive sporting television broadcast contracts are one of the most common category filed.[32] These represent a minute percentage of the total agreements entered into in the United Kingdom. Potentially, however, failure to register can have very serious consequences which is why registrability should be closely examined before agreements are concluded which contain restrictions. The possibility of a precautionary registration or advice from the O.F.T. might be considered.

There are provisions for ensuring that the court may withhold consideration of an agreement if it is being dealt with by the EEC.[33]

EEC competition law

INTELLECTUAL PROPERTY AND ARTICLE 85

Great Britain is a member of the European Economic Community. The Treaty of Rome is the Community Charter which contains regulations which are intended to have the effect of breaking down national frontiers to create a Common Market. The national laws of the member countries on the other hand recognise and seek to protect intellectual property in the form of copyright, trade marks and goodwill. The way in which this protection is achieved is through conferring a legal monopoly in a market. Therein lies the conflict between the Treaty of Rome breaking down "bar-

---

[29] *Ibid.* s.2(1).
[30] *Ibid.* s.2(2).
[31] *Ibid.* s.21(2).
[32] Note the powers given under the Broadcasting Act 1981.
[33] Restrictive Trade Practices Act 1976, s.5.

riers" and intellectual property rights erecting or, at least, protecting them.

The Treaty of Rome attempts to strike a balance between these two conflicting principles. Economic and technological investment may be encouraged by the legitimate protection of market monopolies. The balance is an uneasy one.

(a) *The balance between free movement of goods and recognition of intellectual property*

The Treaty of Rome does not interfere with the existence of intellectual property rights. Indeed Article 222 of the Treaty states "this Treaty shall in no way prejudice the rules in Member States governing the system of property ownership." The distinction is drawn between the existence of these rights and their exercise. It is only the exercise of intellectual property rights which can infringe the EEC Competition rules.

Article 85 is the main provision in the Treaty which defines circumstances where the exercise of intellectual property rights may potentially infringe the Treaty. Article 85 has three paragraphs to be read in conjunction with Council Regulation 17/62 which implemented it. Paragraph 1 of Article 85 contains the basic prohibition against restraints on competition. Paragraph 2 states that an agreement which infringes Article 85(1) will be "automatically void." Paragraph 3 enables the commission to declare Article 85(1) inapplicable to an agreement provided that it meets certain criteria.[34]

Article 85 states:

> "The following shall be prohibited as incompatible with the common market: all agreements between undertakings, decisions by associations of undertakings and concerted practices which may affect trade between member states and which have as their object or effect the prevention, restriction or distortion of competition within the common market."

The two circumstances likely to have application to sponsorship are the licensing of intellectual property agreements which limit or control production, markets, technical devel-

---

[34] The Treaty of Rome, Art. 9(1) of reg. 17/62 gives the commission sole power to declare Art. 85(1) inapplicable under Art. 85(3) subject only to review of its decision by the Court of Justice.

opments or investments[35] and agreements which share markets or sources of supply.[36]

(b) *Exemptions and negative clearance*

If an agreement appears to infringe Article 85(1) it may yet be exempted by the commission because it falls within a block exemption[37] or on an individual exemption given by the commission after an agreement has been duly notified to it by one of the parties.

An exemption under Article 85(3) should be distinguished from a negative clearance.[38] In the case of an exemption the commission is asked to state that notwithstanding that the agreement may infringe Article 85(1), it should be exempted. Negative clearance, on the other hand, is a statement by the Commission (which is open to challenge by domestic courts) that as a matter of interpretation the agreement does not infringe Article 85(1).

Fortunately, both an individual exemption and negative clearance are applied for in the alternative on the same form. Little thought need therefore be given to the merits of pursuing one ground at the expense of the others.[39]

(c) *When will Article 85(1) bite?*

For Article 85(1) to apply the licence agreement must be between economically independent undertakings and not between members of the same group of companies. Another category of exempted agreements is that which is set out in the Notice on Agreements of Minor Importance.[40] This notice confirmed that agreements which have a minimal effect upon the market were not caught by the prohibition in Article 85(1). The *de minimus* test has two conditions both of which must be satisfied:

    (i) the products do not represent in a substantial part of

---

[35] *Ibid.* Art. 85, para. 1(b).

[36] *Ibid.* Art. 85, para. 1(c). Note the recent decision stated in Nungessor K.G.'s Kirt Eisle V, etc., Commission No. 258178 to the effect that an open exclusive licence agreement was not necessarily contrary to Art. 8.

[37] The Treaty of Rome, Art. 87.

[38] *Ibid.* Art. 2.

[39] See Form A1B of Commission Regulations 27 of May 3, 1962 (O.J. 1962 1118: O.J. 1959–1962 132).

[40] Commission Notice of December 19, 1977 (O.J. 1977 C.313/3).

the common market more than 5 per cent. of the total market for such products, and

    (ii) the aggregate annual turnover of the participating undertakings does not exceed E.C.V. (Units of account) 50 million (this is currently £28,500,000).

(d) *Licensing of sponsorship rights and the Treaty of Rome.*

(i) *Parallel imports from other EEC countries: Trade Marks.*[41] Once goods have been sold in one member state then they may be lawfully sold by a licensed third party anywhere within the EEC. Suppose a sponsor is licensed to use as a mascot which has been registered as a trade mark in Italy on T-shirts, neither the sponsor nor the sponsee could use the trade mark rights to prevent a French T-shirt licensee importing T-shirts bearing the same mascot into Italy.

This situation arises from a series of cases commencing with Grundig Consten,[42] and the Commission concept of "exhaustion of rights." This concept is based upon Articles 30–34 which command the progressive abolition of restrictions on imports or exports and Article 36 which recognises that restrictions may nevertheless exist to protect intellectual property provided they are not used as a means of arbitrary discrimination or disguised restriction between member states. See however the recent decision of *Industrie Diensten Groep* v. *Beele.*[43] The rights will be exhausted even where the goods are marketed in a state where no intellectual property rights exist.[44]

Where a trade mark is owned by different companies, it would seem logical that one owner should be able to prevent the other from selling in their respective territories. In most circumstances this will be so. Where, however, the trade mark has a common origin, *i.e.* it was originally owned by the same person, then the *HAG* case[45] is authority that trade mark rights cannot be used to prevent imports by the other into the

---

[41] Note the Commission's proposals relating to the harmonization of EEC trade marks laws: see [1982] J.B.L. 70.

[42] *Établissements Consten Sarl and Grundig-Verkaufs-GmbH* v. *Commission of the European Economic Community* [1966] E.C.R. 299.

[43] Case 6/81 [1982] 3 C.M.L.R. 102.

[44] *Merck & Co. Inc.* v. *Stephar B.V.* case 187/80 [1981] E.C.R. 2063, This was a patent case which, by analogy, should apply to trade marks and copyright. See also Case No. 16/74 *Centrafarm B.V.* v. *Sterling Drug Inc.* [1976] 1 C.M.L.R. 1.

[45] Case 192/73 *Van Zuylen Frères* v. *Hag A.G.* [1974] E.C.R. 731.

territories occupied by either of the two owners. This case has been much criticised.

Where the two trade marks are similar but no common ownership ever existed, then the respective owners may prevent imports into their territories by relying upon their trade mark registration within those territories.[46]

Trade mark rights may be enforced to stop parallel imports where the imported products are of different or inferior quality.[47]

(ii) *Parallel imports from other EEC countries: Copyright.* The first judgment relating to exhaustion of copyright was the Deutsche Grammaphon case.[48]

The judgment was developed in the case of *Musik-Vertrieb Membran GmbH* v. *Gema*.[49] Copyright falls under the concept of industrial and commercial property in Article 36 especially when exploited commercially in the form of licences capable of affecting distribution in the various Member States of goods incorporating protected literary or artistic work. The rules on parallel imports which apply to other forms of intellectual property apply equally to copyright.

The situation in relation to services rather than goods in which copyright may exist is similar to that applying to goods.[50] In *Coditel S.A.* v. *Cine Vog Films S.A.*[51] the copyright owners of a French film granted certain exclusive rights to a Belgium distributor and other rights to a German channel. It was held by the Court of Justice of the European communities that the mere fact that the proprietor of a film had granted an exclusive right to one distributor did not necessarily give rise to an agreement, decision on concerted practice prohibited by Article 85. Where the effect is substantially to restrict the distribution of films or disturb competition in the film market then it may infringe Article 85. The issue however, remains to be decided by the courts. This case has relevance to sponsorship and exclusive licences

---

[46] Case 119/75 *Terrapin (Overseas) Ltd.* v. *Terranova Industrie C.A. Kapferer & Co.* [1976] E.C.R. 1039.

[47] Case 3/78 *Centrafarm B.V.* v. *American Home Products Corp.*, [1978] 2 C.M.L.R. 63.

[48] See p. 224, n.42.

[49] Cases 55 and 57/80 [1981] F.S.R. 433.

[50] Art. 59 contains similar language to Arts. 30–36.

[51] Case 262/81 (No. 2) [1983] F.S.R. 148.

involving intellectual property to the sponsor, *e.g.* exclusive use of copyright material such as videos, records, logos, etc., by one sponsor. In the majority of sponsorship situations, however, it is probably correct to say that if these rights were not offered on an exclusive basis, the sponsor would be unlikely to undertake the sponsorship in the first place.

(iii) *Parallel imports from outside the EEC.* Intellectual property rights arising from trade marks or copyright may be used to prevent parallel imports from outside the EEC. Thus E.M.I. were able to prevent the import of records from America bearing the Columbia trade mark.[52]

(iv) *Unlicensed merchandise.* In most circumstances the inability of the owners and licensees of trade marks or other categories of intellectual property to prevent parallel imports from other EEC countries only affects legitimate licensees. Intellectual property rights may always be exercised to prevent companies who pirate the marks, *i.e.* use them without a licence.

The proper purpose of a trade mark has been recognised by the European Court of Justice[53] as protecting the owner against competitors wishing to take advantage of the reputation by selling products illegally bearing the owner's trade mark.

ARTICLE 85 AND SPONSORSHIP AGREEMENTS GENERALLY

The above paragraphs have considered the position in relation to trade marks and copyright (by analogy goodwill protected through passing off insofar as it might be relied upon to protect exclusive rights should be treated in a similar way). Unlike copyright and trade marks, however, passing off is not recognised through international convention as a generally applicable remedy.[54] Design copyright is within the definition of property defined in Article 222. In the authors' view these are the most likely circumstances in which a sponsor or sponsee will be affected by the Treaty of Rome.

[52] *E.M.I.* v. *C.B.S. United Kingdom* [1976] E.C.R. 811 Cases 51, 86 & 96/75. See also *Polydor and R.S.O. Records Inc.* v. *Harlequin Record Shops and Simon Records* [1980] F.S.R. 194.
[53] Case 3/78 *Centrefarm B.V. Rotterdam* v. *American Home Products Corp., New York* [1978] 2 C.M.L.R. 63.
[54] See *British Leyland* v. *Armstrong Patents Co.* [1983] F.S.R. 50.

As already discussed[55] a sponsorship object or licence must generally exist as property to be granted on an exclusive basis. Purported exclusive licences which do not exist in relation to property are open to challenge without reliance upon the Treaty of Rome or other competition legislation. The Treaty of Rome might apply to exclusive rights which do not necessarily involve intellectual property.[56] If a sponsee such as an organising committee of an event offers exclusive advertising services to one sponsor such as the display of stadium boards at a venue, then one could argue that prima facie this falls within Article 85. Since the sponsor is unlikely to invest in the sponsorship in the first place without exclusivity and as long as there are other sports events at which the sponsor's competitors can acquire advertising services it seems, in the authors' view, highly improbable that this activity would be construed as offending the Treaty of Rome.

Whether or not the sponsorship involves intellectual property, certain clauses should be avoided in exclusive licence agreements unless their existence can be justified. These include:

   (a) Export bans.[57]

   (b) No challenge clauses, where, for example, the sponsor is obliged to refrain from challenging the validity of the right which has been licensed to him.[58]

   (c) Non-competition clauses which oblige the sponsor to refrain from competing in any way with the sponsee.

ARTICLE 86(1) OF THE TREATY OF ROME

Article 86 seeks to ensure that the objectives of the Common Market are met and that trade and competition therein are not distorted by unreasonable exploitation of market power. It might apply, for example, in circumstances where one particular sporting body abused its position to extract artificially inflated financial terms from its sponsors, or one company registers a trade mark in a member state which the applicant knows is being used by a competitor in another member state.[59]

[55] See Chap. 8.
[56] See p. 118.
[57] See *Re Stemra* [1983] 3 C.M.L.R. 494.
[58] See, for example, *A.O.I.P.* v. *Beyrand* [1976] 1 C.M.L.R. 14.
[59] *Oy Airam A.B.* v. *Osram GmbH* [1983] F.L.R. 108.

NATIONAL LAW

The scope of Articles 85 and 86[60] is relevant to national law as well as to the decisions of the Commission and European Court of Justice. In *Belgische Radio & T.V.* v. *S.A.B.A.M.*[61] the European Court of Justice confirmed that Articles 85 and 86 created individual rights which it is the duty of the national courts to implement. In *Coditel S.A.* v. *Cine Vog Films S.A.* it was suggested that it was for the national courts to determine whether the object of an exclusive film distribution agreement was to prevent, restrict or distort competition. The English High Court recently made such a decision in relation to United Kingdom design copyright.[62]

Articles 85 and 86 have most frequently been raised as defences to infringement actions.[63] The Court of Appeal has, however, recently confirmed that an interim injunction could be issued to restrain the Milk Marketing Board from abusing its dominant position under Article 86.[64]

---

[60] See pp. 222 and 227.
[61] Case No. 127/73 [1974] E.C.R. 313.
[62] *British Leyland Motor Corp.,* v. *Armstrong Patents Co.* [1983] F.S.R. 50.
[63] But it will not always be successfully pleaded: see *British Leyland Motor Corp.* v. *Armstrong Patents Co.* [1983] F.S.R. 50.
[64] *Garden Cottage Foods Ltd.* v. *Milk Marketing Board* [1982] 3 W.L.R. 514.

15. Sponsorship Controls

Sponsorship in its current form is a modern marketing technique. Its growth has undoubtedly been aided by the communications and media boom from the late fifties onwards. The most relevant controls relating specifically to sponsorship are concerned with broadcasting.

STATUTORY CONTROLS

Theatre

The Theatres Act 1968 abolished censorship of plays.[1] The Act replaced censorship, however, with criminal liability similar to that arising under the Obscene Publications Acts. Liability attaches under the Theatres Act 1968 where it can be established that the performance of a play is obscene.[2]

Films and videos

Film censorship is achieved in an indirect way by the requirement for a licence to be issued broadly wherever a film is to be exhibited to the public or shown in private for commercial gain.[3] The licensing authority will be the Greater London Council for London or relevant district council for other areas. The terms of the licence will usually be those recommended by the Home Office. The Home Office Model Licence contains a provision that no film may be shown unless it has received a certificate from the British Board of Film Censors. There is also a provision in the model

---

[1] Theatres Act 1968, s.1(1).
[2] *Ibid.* s.2(1) and see licensing controls.
[3] See the Cinematograph (Amendment) Act 1982.

conditions giving the Licensing Authority the ability to object to advertisements outside cinemas.[4]

In each case the specific terms of the licence will require examination, however, on the basis of the model conditions the licensing authority would seem able to object to the sponsors advertisements both inside and outside a cinema. A sponsored film shown at a cinema and certain other premises would require a certificate from the British Board of Film Censors. The scope of the original Cinematograph Acts of 1909 and 1952 respectively have been extended by the Cinematograph (Amendment) Act 1982. This Act applies to all exhibitions of moving pictures except live broadcasts by the B.B.C. or I.B.A.[5]

Films and videos are also subject to the provisions of the Obscene Publications Act 1964 which is discussed later.

Broadcasts

Broadcasting[6] in the United Kingdom is controlled by the government. That includes: broadcasting by public television on the commercial[6a] and non-commercial[7] networks; information technology services such as Ceefax and Oracle; upleg to point to point satellites and broadcasting to direct broadcasting satellites; radio, both non-commercial-radios 1, 2, 3 and 4 and local radio, *e.g.* Radio London and commercial *e.g.* Capital radio. Only the United Kingdom position is considered here. The control of broadcasting is exercised via the Wireless Telegraphy Act 1949, the British Telecommunications Act 1981, the Broadcasting Act 1981 and B.B.C. Royal Charter and Licence. An overview of how this complex situation operates is thus.

The Wireless Telegraphy Act 1949 essentially requires anyone who wishes to establish or use a station for wireless telegraphy to obtain a licence.[8] Wireless telegraphy is defined

---

[4] See Bailey, Harris and Jones, *Civil Liberties—Cases and Materials* Butterworths (1980) p. 23.

[5] Cinematograph (Amendment) Act 1982, s.1, or distribution by a system licensed by the Secretary of State under the Post Office Act 1969, s.89.

[6] See *Independent Television Companies Association* v. *Performing Rights Society Ltd.* (1983) I.M.L. 40 for a discussion of the meaning of "broadcasting."

[6a] I.T.V. and other I.B.A. Franchises and Channel 4.

[7] B.B.C.1 and B.B.C.2.

[8] Wireless Telegraphy Act 1949, s.1.

in section 19 of the Act and covers the emission or receiving of signals which are not transmitted on any material substance, *i.e.* they are broadcast and not received, diffused or transmitted via cable. The issuing authority for a licence under the Wireless Telegraphy Act is now the Secretary of State for the Home Office.[9]

The licence takes the form either of an agreement between the B.B.C. and Secretary of State for the Home Department for the B.B.C. or the Broadcasting Act 1981 for the I.B.A. The Broadcasting Act 1981 confirms the continued existence of the I.B.A. through to December 31, 1996.[10] The B.B.C. licence is separate from its incorporation document, the latter being a Royal Charter. The B.B.C.'s Royal Charter continues until December 31, 1996.[11]

Taking the Broadcasting Act 1981 and B.B.C. Royal Charter and Licence together, at the present time the B.B.C. and I.B.A. operate a monopoly of public service broadcasting in the United Kingdom. The government lays down various overriding principles in both the Broadcasting Act 1981 and in the B.B.C. licence to carry a range of programmes and sound broadcasts. The range to be covered includes education and entertainment. The programmes and sound broadcasts are also required to achieve a high standard of quality.[12] Other terms of the licences prevent the broadcast of programmes which offend against taste or decency.[13] The Secretary of State has reserved a discretion in the case of both B.B.C. and I.B.A. broadcasts to compel either or both to refrain from making any particular broadcast.[14]

The services of both the I.B.A. and B.B.C. operate on a national, regional and in the case of radio, local basis. The I.B.A. awards franchises to regional contractors such as central or southern who supply the programmes. The I.B.A. itself does not supply any. The B.B.C. orginates its programming not only via London but also through its Network

---

[9] This responsibility was transferred from the Minister of Posts and Telecommunications in 1974.
[10] Broadcasting Act 1981, s.2(1).
[11] The terms of the B.B.C. licence and Royal Charter are published in the B.B.C. annual report and handbook.
[12] Broadcasting Act 1981, s.2(1) and the resolution of the Board of Governors of the British Broadcasting Corporation, dated January 8, 1981.
[13] *Ibid.* s.4(1)(a).
[14] *Ibid.* s.29(3) and the B.B.C. Licence, s.13(4).

Production Centres. The B.B.C.'s English Television Service is organised into eight regions. Both B.B.C. and I.B.A. services operate in a way like the National Electricity grid. Programming is "plugged" into the grid from the different regions.

(1) THE B.B.C. AND SPONSORSHIP

Section 12 of the B.B.C. Licence states: "The Corporation shall not without the prior approval of the Secretary of State . . . send or emit . . . any sponsored programme."

Sponsored programme is defined as "any matter which is provided at the expense of any sponsor . . . for the purpose of being broadcast for general reception and is the subject of a broadcast announcement mentioning the sponsor or his goods or services."[15]

On a literal interpretation this precludes the B.B.C. from broadcasting a programme the production of which has been financed by the sponsor *and* which contains mention of the sponsors goods or services. It does not preclude the B.B.C. from showing a sponsored sport, Arts or leisure events since the sponsorship funds have gone to financing the event and not the production of the programme.

The concern of the B.B.C. is impartiality. If sponsorship finance goes towards the production of the programme then there must be a possibility that the contents of the programme will not be impartial. It might be assumed, for example, that a film financed by an oil company dealing with pollution might not treat the facts objectively. The interpretation of the licence by the B.B.C. has in the authors' view followed this approach. Whatever the terms of the licence the B.B.C. has the ultimate decision to accept or decline the broadcast at least before it commits itself to the broadcasting contract. This places it in a strong bargaining position to impose limitations on recognition given to sponsors of sports and other events. In any case the B.B.C.'s contract will be with the event organiser and not the sponsor directly. The maintenance of broadcasting integrity of the B.B.C. and sponsored programmes was discussed at length in the report of committee on the *Future of Broadcasting*.[16] One conclusion of the report which

---

[15] B.B.C. Licence, s.1.

[16] The Report of the Committee on the Future of Broadcasting. Cmnd. 6753 (1977) para. 10.18.

has not been fully adopted was that Channel 4 should be permitted to broadcast sponsored programmes.

In 1981 the then Deputy Managing Director of the B.B.C. Mr. Bill Cotton, prepared a report on sponsorship and B.B.C. television. In broad terms that report accepted that it was in the interests of the public that the B.B.C. should broadcast certain sponsored events. It recognised that most sports events depend upon support from sponsors.[17] The most comprehensive document which gives guidance to B.B.C. policy on sponsorship is the B.B.C. and Advertising Guidelines last issued in December 1982. This document covers all forms of indirect advertising and not just sponsorship. Some of the rules concerning indirect advertising may have relevance to sponsorship although they are not discussed here. Internally the B.B.C. issues an orange card to its programme staff also giving guidance on sponsorship. Based upon these documents and with the B.B.C.'s kind response to the authors' enquiries, the following appears to the authors to be the practice of the B.B.C. as at August 1983. Since policies are subject to change, it is suggested that the following be regarded as guidance only.[18]

(a) *Sponsored programmes in contrast to sponsored events*

The B.B.C. will not broadcast sponsored programmes. It may and in most cases will broadcast events which are sponsored. The B.B.C. understands sponsored events to be events attended by the public which owe their existence to the money put in by sponsors. One must also interpret this to include events which owe their existence partly to sponsors. One should anticipate that the B.B.C. will seek to include restrictions or limitations in the broadcast contract. These restrictions will attempt to prevent the credit and advertising given to the sponsor from the interfering with the enjoyment of the programme from a viewer's standpoint. The B.B.C. has engaged in co-productions, for example, David Attenborough's "Life on Earth" in association with the United States publisher Time Life. It is submitted that the line between

[17] Approximately 75 per cent. of sports events broadcast on television are sponsored. The number of concerts and artistic events which are sponsored is also increasing.
[18] The European Sports Sponsorship Code, discussed at p. 256 *ante*, recommended that domestic broadcasters should produce public guidelines.

co-production and sponsorship can be a difficult one to draw. The distinction suggested by the B.B.C. however, is that co-production is funding provided by a co-producer in exchange for broadcasting the programme, whereas funds provided by a sponsor secure recognition during the broadcast of the sponsor's goods or services. The B.B.C. will exercise its judgment on grounds of editorial and programme content in each case and balance those against the public interest in showing the programme.

(b) *Broadcasting sponsored events*

Advertising: perimeter boards. The B.B.C. acknowledges in its advertising guidelines the distinction made at p. 14 of this book that perimeter advertising need not necessarily be linked to sponsorship although it might be. The rules affecting perimeter advertising which is not connected with sponsorship are that political statements are banned, as are the advertising of individual brands of cigarettes. The B.B.C. will not permit advertising to be placed between the camera and the action, and in sporting events, the rules of the European Broadcasting Union should be considered. Many stadia where events are broadcast include continuous perimeter advertising which will be shown. In contrast, the basic rule for sponsored sports events (assuming that they are not subject to E.B.U. rules, *supra*) is two advertising boards or banners within view of the main camera.

The identification given on the boards or banners will at the B.B.C.'s discretion, either be the name of the sponsor associated with the particular event, or the registered title of the sponsored organisation. As with perimeter advertising, placing of the boards or banners is important and they must not come between the viewer and the action. Advertising boards are unlikely to arise at sponsored Arts events and it is unclear what policy the B.B.C. would adopt to boards being displayed at an event, such as a pop concert.

Clothing, vehicles and other trappings. The B.B.C. will not normally allow sponsors' identification on clothing where it is sufficiently prominent to interfere with the viewers enjoyment of the action. The rigidity of the approach was illustrated by the refusal of the B.B.C. to broadcast the Alan Minter/Tony Sibson fight because Minter appeared in the ring with a sponsor's name printed prominently on the side of his shorts. This attitude was further demonstrated by paragraph 32.4 of August 1, 1981 contract between the B.B.C. and Football League which prohibited any identification on a players tracksuit except: the club emblem, the manufacturer's logo and the name of the club, which must be within certain dimensions. This situation has now changed in relation to football as shirt advertising is permitted. There can be little doubt that this will lead to relaxation in relation to other sports. Complex issues arise where the name of a large corporation is synonymous with the manufacturer of a range of clothing. The KIM logo which was owned by an Italian leisureware firm is a similar logo to that used to promote a brand of cigarettes. Again identification or clothing is unlikely to apply in relation to Arts or leisure events and B.B.C. policy in that respect is therefore unclear.

A similar policy to that operated by the B.B.C. in relation to clothing seems to apply to sponsor identification on cars, horses, trailers, blankets, finishing tape, etc. Sponsor identification is therefore permitted for example on racing cars and the finishing tape of the London Marathon.

Prizes/presentations. The B.B.C. will broadcast the presentation of a prize at the end of a sponsored event. The Marley Pro-Celebrity Golf Tournament on B.B.C.2 involved a senior official of the sponsoring company 'presenting the winners with a prize, etc., at the end of the competition. The B.B.C. will seek to limit mention of the sponsor in the prize-giving sequence to a minimum, *i.e.* once. It is thought that this would apply equally to Arts or leisure events, such as a sponsor of the Miss World competition.

Verbal credits during the broadcast. The general rule is that these should be limited to a maximum of two verbal credits for the sponsor in a programme. Where, however, an event is known by its sponsored title such as "Milk Cup" or "Cornhill Tests," then it will be difficult to avoid giving credits. Similar problems arise with horses which are called after sponsors such as "Sony." There are even athletes these days who have changed their names to that of a sponsor. This policy should apply in relation to both Arts and leisure events.

Credits in the Radio Times. The rule here is one mention for the name of one sponsor in the main programme guide

235

and a single mention in any associated article. It might be observed that whereas recognition of the sponsor's name in the title to sponsored sports events occurs frequently, the same recognition does not appear to have been given to sponsors of Arts and leisure events.

On screen credits. On screen credits are given in limited circumstances to timing and computer companies where their equipment is being used at sporting events. The general rule is one credit which should be agreed in advance with the B.B.C. Credit for Benson and Hedges' part funding of the Society of West End Theatre Awards in 1982 was given after the programme. This should apply to sports, Arts and leisure.

Brand names. It seems general policy never to give recognition to a sponsors brand or product name unless it has become synonymous with the name of the company, *e.g.* Coca-Cola. This should apply to sport, Arts and leisure.

Acknowledgment for co-sponsors. B.B.C. policy favours only one sponsor receiving credit for a sponsored event. This will not necessarily prevent more than one sponsor displaying boards or banners or similar identification at a sponsored event but it is unlikely that the B.B.C. would give verbal or on screen credits to more than one sponsor.

Reporting and reviewing sponsored events. Current policy appears to be reflected in the News and Current Affairs Index dated October 1980: "The inclusion of references to commercial sponsors of events is justified if . . . the sponsorship is of such an order that omitting to mention it would be to omit significant journalistic detail as well as being unfair to the sponsor." This policy should apply without distinction to sport, Arts and leisure.

Tobacco advertising. This is subject to a code of practice insofar as sponsorship of particular sports and advertising individual tobacco brands are concerned. The B.B.C. will comply with this code, which is discussed at p. 255.

(c) *B.B.C. Radio*

The scope of the B.B.C.'s licence covers radio as well as television, hence the policy outlined above will apply to both.

Although the expansion of television via cable, and satellite broadcasting has received wide publicity, a gradual expansion of radio services has been taking place over the last decade. In 1980 the Home Office published a report specifically concerning local radio. Although the government has not to date shown any relaxation on its sponsorship regulations insofar as they effect local radio, there must be scope for change in this area. Sponsorship of broadcasts on a local basis might assist funding.[19] It is to be noted in this context that the 1982 B.B.C. advertising guidelines, whilst confirming that local radio broadcasts are to comply generally with the guidelines, acknowledge that finance from sources which generally concern themselves with the welfare of the community might be considered.

(d) *B.B.C. and direct broadcasting by satellite*

On March 4, 1982[20] the government following the Home Office Report on Direct Broadcasting by Satellite (D.B.S.), gave approval, in principle to the B.B.C. operating two D.B.S. channels. One would be on a subscription basis, which would broadcast feature films, major sporting, cultural and other events and the other would show a selection of the best programmes from around the world. One might suggest that the licence given to the B.B.C. for operating the D.B.S. service could permit greater scope for sponsored programmes. However, since the first two channels will be operated by the B.B.C. the satellite broadcasts will be subject to the general B.B.C. regulations discussed above unless they are amended.

The B.B.C. has an operating subsidiary called B.B.C. Enterprises which engages in commercial projects. This company is subject to certain rules relating to sponsorship.[21]

(e) *Teletext*

The B.B.C. teletext service, Ceefax, is subject to the general terms of the licence.

---

[19] See *Home Office Local Radio Working Party*, Third Report (1980), para. 7.30.

[20] See H.C. Deb. Vol. 19, ser. 70, col. 414.

[21] Broadcasting Act 1981, s.8(7).

(2) THE I.B.A.

The Broadcasting Act 1981 states in section 8(6) that " . . . nothing shall be included in any programmes broadcast by the authority which states, suggests or implies . . . that any part of any programme broadcast by the Authority which is not an advertisement has been supplied or suggested by any advertiser; and, except as an advertisement, nothing shall be included in any programme broadcast by the authority which could reasonably be supposed to have been included in the programme in return for payment or other valuable consideration to the relevant programme contractor or the Authority."

There are qualifications to this general rule which may have some relevance to sponsorship.[21a] These are: (i) items designed to give publicity to the needs or objects of a charitable or benevolent organisation; (ii) reviews of literary, artistic or other publications or productions including current entertainments; (iii) items consisting of factual portrayals of doings, happenings, places or things being items which, in the opinion of the authority, are proper for inclusion by reason of their intrinsic interest or instructiveness and do not comprise an undue element of advertisement; and (iv) announcements of the place of any performance included in the programme and acknowledgments.

Taking the general rule and qualifications together, their effect is similar to the restrictions contained in the B.B.C. licence except sponsored programmes are not specifically excluded. The terms of the Act are infringed when the programme is used as a means of promoting the sponsor or his products.

The Broadcasting Act 1981 provides that the I.B.A. shall prepare a code for guidance on the interpretation to be placed on certain parts of the Act in addition to a Code of Advertising Practice.[22] With the advent of Channel 4 the I.B.A. issued a press release[23] entitled "Programmes funded by non-broadcasters." The Broadcasting Act 1981 permitted the I.B.A. to operate Channel 4 following the Annan Report. Although the Annan Report seemed to recommend a more liberal approach be adopted to sponsored programmes by Channel 4, this has not altogether been reflected in the Act.

[21a] *Ibid.*
[22] *Ibid.* s.5(1).
[23] January 15, 1982.

Channel 4 is, under the terms of the Act, required "to encourage innovation and experiment in the form and content of programmes."[24] That is the only difference which applies to its programme in contrast to that of the other I.B.A. programme contractors. The clause outlined above[25] which, as a general policy, outlaws sponsored programmes applies to Channel 4 in the same way as the other contractors. It is not a new clause either, since it goes back to the 1973 Act.

(a) *Sponsored programmes*

The press release on programmes funded by non-broadcasters which in the authors' view might include sponsors, may be summarised as follows. This applies to all I.B.A. television programmes and not just Channel 4.

   (i) The content of the programme is the responsibility of the broadcaster.

  (ii) On screen credits to any non-broadcaster who funds or part funds a programme will only be given with the I.B.A.'s approval.

 (iii) Such credits or other forms of acknowledgment will only be considered by the I.B.A. where the programme consists of factual portrayals of doings, happenings, places or things. This is the distinction which the B.B.C. licence fails to put into words. This may permit financing or part financing of the broadcast of artistic, sporting, leisure or entertainment events. Since the subject matter is purely factual, even if it were the intention of the funder/sponsor to influence the contents of the programme, it would prove difficult, to achieve. A series of nature programmes sponsored by Shell could hardly be objectionable unless, of course, they dealt with the effect of pollution on wildlife. Such events exist independently of the broadcast itself. This will not permit funding of news or current affairs.

 (iv) Credits or acknowledgments where permitted may appear at the beginning or end of the programme. The wording must be approved by the I.B.A. Restrictions may be imposed on the amount of publicity which the funder gives to the programme.

  (v) The funder of a programme who receives a credit or

---

[24] Broadcasting Act 1981, s.11(1)(*c*).
[25] *Ibid.* para. 8(6).

acknowledgment will not be permitted to purchase advertising air time during or around transmissions of the programme. (There is a further provision in Schedule 2 to the Act in rules for advertisements which require any advertisement to be clearly distinguishable from the rest of the programme.)

Further guidelines on sponsored programmes are given in the I.B.A. Television Programme Guidelines.[26] It is understood that those are to be revised in one or two minor respects which will not effect the text that follows. It is understood that the principle change will be the incorporation of the press release discussed above directly in the guidelines. These may be summarised as follows.

Programmes which are financed or part financed by sponsorship and originate outside the United Kingdom, such as the United States, may be broadcast subject to the omission of the sponsors message or credits. Such programmes must also satisfy the requirements of section 8(6) of the Act.[27]

No special arrangements may be made with the sponsor of such programme whose credit has been deleted for purchase of advertising airtime, etc., to coincide with the broadcast.

The names of sponsored plays, books, films, records and sporting events may be mentioned in reviews (and presumably as news items).

(b) *Coverage of sponsored events*

The I.B.A. recognises, as does the B.B.C. the public interest in showing most sponsored events. Detailed guidelines have been prepared. These are annexed in full in Appendix VI.[28]

(c) *I.B.A. radio*

Although many of the specific guidelines given by the I.B.A. relate to television broadcasts, the basic rules expressed in the Act, *i.e.* section 8(6), apply equally to radio broadcasts.

---

[26] [1979] Revised edition, s.11.
[27] See p. 239 above.
[28] See p. 315 below.

(d) *Advertisements*

Advertisements included before, during or after programmes are regulated by section 8 of and Schedule 2 to the Act
together with a code which has been issued.[29]

(e) *Teletext*

The I.B.A. is authorised to appoint teletext contractors.
The general restrictions on sponsorship contained in section
8(6) of the Act do not apply to teletext services such as
Oracle. The Broadcasting Act 1981 makes separate provision
for the regulation of such programmes[30] by the I.B.A. A code
entitled "The I.B.A. Code for Teletext Transmissions" has
been issued. This code prohibits sponsorship. There is a
proviso, however, which states that the prohibition shall not
extend to a matter included in a teletext transmission which is
not an advertisement and which is similar to those items listed
as (i), (ii) or (iii) at p. 238 above.[31]

(3) CABLE TELEVISION

Cable television has existed for a number of years in areas
where it was impossible to receive a signal by way of a direct
broadcast. The signal would be broadcast to the nearest
receiver and relayed from there by cable. There have also been
a number of community experiments involving television and
sound signals transmitted via cable. Such experiments have
included advertising but sponsorship of programmes has not
been permitted. Control of advertising has usually been
achieved by adoption of the I.B.A. Code of Advertising
Standards and Practice.

Two pilot subscription cable television services have been
operating under licence since the end of 1981. The terms of
the licence state that "the licensee shall ensure that no
advertisement or sponsored programme material is included
in the programme distributed." "Sponsored Programme
Material" means "any matter which is provided at the
expense of the sponsor (that is any person other than the
licensee and performers) for the purpose of being broadcast

[29] The I.B.A. Code of Advertising Standards and Practice.
[30] Broadcasting Act 1981, s.15.
[31] Part A (v).

and is subject to a broadcast announcement mentioning the sponsor or his goods or services."

The government has recently issued a White Paper on its plans to permit the development of the cable industry[32] following the Hunt Inquiry[33] which in turn followed the Report of the Information Technology Advisory Panel and Broadcasting Policy.[34] The White Paper outlines a number of proposals for the future of cable television in the United Kingdom to enable its expansion. A new statutory cable authority is to be set up to award franchises and exercise a degree of oversight on the services provided. The services would include both programme and interactive services, with provision for D.B.S. channels. Sponsorship, with appropriate safeguards, will be permitted so as to contribute to finance. Advertising will be controlled by a code of practice to be drawn up by the new cable authority. The cable franchises should not be able to acquire exclusive rights to important events of national interest which are protected under section 30 of the Broadcasting Act 1981. (At the present time the scope of this Act applies only to broadcasting.) Pay per view will also be permitted subject to the public broadcasting channels' interests, regarding events they have customarily broadcast being protected.

At the present time, anyone wishing to operate a cable system in the United Kingdom, except British Telecom, requires a licence from the Secretary of State for Industry, or British Telecom. under section 15(1) of the British Telecommunications Act 1981, and a programme licence from the Home Secretary under section 89 of the Post Office Act 1969. The recently published Telecommunications Bill contains both provisions for licences to be issued to cable operators and creates offences where cable programme services are provided without licences.

(4) THE EUROPEAN BROADCASTING UNION

Although the scope of this book is primarily concerned with the United Kingdom situation, one cannot ignore the

---

[32] *The Development of Cable Systems and Services*, Cmnd. 8866 (1983).

[33] Report of the enquiry into cable expansion in broadcasting policy, Cmnd. 8679 (1982).

[34] *Ibid.*

European Broadcasting Union in any question involving broadcasts of sponsored events, particularly sports events.

The European Broadcasting Union was established in Torquay, England in 1950. The E.B.U. is a non-governmental association of organisations which operate broadcasting services. The organisation is governed by Swiss Law and is non-commercial and non-political.

Its main objectives are to support the interests of its members in every activity, to cater for each country's growing need for news, education and entertainment, to seek common solutions to legal and technical problems and to develop the exchange of television and radio programmes.[35]

Part of the role of the E.B.U. involves the negotiation of agreements for televising events on behalf of its members such as the B.B.C. The E.B.U. is usually invited by the host broadcaster to negotiate on its behalf only in the case of major events such as the First World Championships in athletics. In other cases it may take a more passive role in offering advice.

Eurovision, which is a system for exchanging programmes between E.B.U. members without charge during a limited period of time, is operated by the E.B.U.

The E.B.U. has prepared a recommendation for offers of Eurovision transmissions involving sponsorship. A copy of this recommendation is contained in Appendix II.[36] The E.B.U. has also prepared specific recommendations for advertising at sports events, which are set out in Appendix II.[37]

A similar system to that operated by the E.B.U. is operated in the Eastern Block by O.I.R.T.

(5) CENSORSHIP

Both the B.B.C. and I.B.A. are subject to controls designed to ensure that nothing broadcast offends good taste, decency or is otherwise offensive to public feeling.[38] The courts will reluctantly interfere with the judgment of the B.B.C./I.B.A. on such matters.[39]

---

[35] See *E.B.U. Handbook*, p. 4.
[36] See below, p. 300.
[37] See below, p. 302.
[38] Broadcasting Act 1981, ss.4 and 5.
[39] *Att.-Gen., ex rel. McWhirter* v. *Independent Broadcasting Authority* [1973] Q.B. 629.

Books, videos, photographs and similar matter

Section 2(1) of the Obscene Publications Act 1959 as amended by the section 1(1) of Obscene Publications Act 1964 states that " . . . any person who, whether for gain or not, publishes an obscene article or who has an obscene article for publication for gain (whether gain to himself or gain to another) shall be liable."

This Act covers books, records, videos, photographs, paintings and sculptures etc. There is a defence in the case of the public good on the grounds that publication is in the interests of science, literature, art or learning.[40] Publication would include displaying an obscene painting at an art gallery.[41] Publication does not include exhibition in cinemas or television or sound broadcasts.[42]

The Indecent Displays (Control) Act 1981 now regulates the public display of indecent matter. The Act makes it an offence to cause or permit an indecent display to take place.[43] The offence is committed where the material in question is visible from a public place. The Act clearly covers photographs, advertisements, book covers, boxed videos, etc. The Act does not apply to matters broadcast by the I.B.A. or B.B.C. or to a programme transmitted via cable or to the performance of a play or to the exhibition of a film at licensed or exempted premises, nor does it apply to a display at an art gallery or museum provided that it is not visible by the public from outside.[44]

Planning controls[45]

There are a number of statutory provisions dealing with both the erection and display of advertisements. These are the Town and Country Planning (Control of Advertisements) Regulations[46] as amended by the Town and Country Planning Act 1971,[47] as amended by the Local Government and

---

[40] Obscene Publications Act 1959, s.4(1).
[41] *Ibid.* s.1(3)(*b*).
[42] *Ibid.* proviso to s.1(3)(*b*).
[43] Indecent Displays (Control) Act 1981, s.1(1).
[44] *Ibid.* s.1(4)(*b*).
[45] See generally *Encyclopedia of Planning Law and Practice*, para. 1–111.
[46] (S.I. 1969 No. 1532)
[47] ss.63,64 and 109, pursuant to s.292 and Sched. 24, of which the above instruments are saved.

Planning (Amendment) Act 1981. Advertisements, even where they constitute a development within the meaning of the Town and Country Planning Act 1971, will not require planning permission as opposed to consent for their display provided they fall within the Advertisement Regulations.[48] Enforcement of controls made under the Act may be by removal of advertisements or fines.[49]

The term advertisement is given a broad definition and includes hoardings, signs, models, etc. The Advertising Regulations apply to the display of an advertisement on land or buildings. The Advertising Regulations exclude certain types of advertisements from falling within the terms of the regulations and thereby requiring consent provided they do not arise within a special control area.[50] These are:

(a) advertisements on enclosed land. Land is not regarded as enclosed where the advertisement is clearly visible from outside the enclosure. Sports grounds would probably fall within this exception;

(b) advertisements displayed inside buildings[50a];

(c) advertisements displayed on or inside a vehicle;

(d) an advertisement incorporated in and forming part of the fabric of a building; and

(e) advertisements displayed on an article for sale or packaging thereof.

Where an advertisement is not within these exceptions then the express consent of the local authority will be necessary for its display. There is a further class of advertisements[51] where consent is deemed to have been given. These are of minor consequence and include such matters as "for sale" signs outside houses and professional name plates.

Fly posting for a sponsored event would, in the authors' view, require consent under the Advertising Regulations.

The local authority or G.L.C. as appropriate, is given special powers to regulate advertisements positioned near trunk roads.[51a]

---

[48] Town and Country Planning Act 1971, s.64. But note that advertisements on land may give rise to an additional rates liability.
[49] £200 fine under the Town and Country Planning Act 1971, as amended.
[50] (S.I. 1969 No. 1532) reg. 3.
[50a] But note reg. 12.
[51] *Ibid*. Pt. III.
[51a] *Ibid*. reg. 18(1)(c).

Aerial advertising

The Civil Aviation Act 1982 prohibits aircraft from emitting or displaying an advertisement or other communication which is audible or visible from the ground.[52] The Civil Aviation (Aerial Advertising) Regulations 1971[53] provides for certain exceptions to the general prohibition on aerial advertising. These include marks for example which enable the type of aircraft to be identified, and include the mark of the owner, demise charterer or operator.[54] There is a general exemption from the regulations for balloons of less than one metre in linear dimensions. There has recently been some debate on relaxing these regulations particularly with respect to aerial balloons.

Licensing

(1) LONDON[55]

The G.L.C. is given authority to issue licences which broadly arise in circumstances which involve public entertainment of some description. Thus a licence will be required wherever public music and dancing takes place (including nude posing and entertainment booking offices), public boxing and wrestling, theatres, cinemas and cinematograph exhibitions, private places of entertainment and exhibitions at Alexandra Palace, Central Hall Westminster, Earls Court, Olympia and the Royal Festival Hall.[56]

The licensing of private places of entertainment may arise where the G.L.C. or boroughs adopt the terms of the Private Places of Entertainment (Licensing) Act 1967. General

---

[52] Civil Aviation Act 1982, s.82. This section repealed section 7 of the Civil Aviation (Licensing) Act 1960, pursuant to which the Civil Aviation (Aerial Advertising) Regulations (S.I. 1971 No. 1968) of 1971 were made. This subordinate legislation remains in effect by virtue of the Interpretation Act 1978, s.17(2)(b).

[53] (S.I. 1971 No. 1968).

[54] Civil Aviation (Aerial Advertising) Regulations 1971, reg. 4(1)(c).

[55] See Halsbury's Laws of England (4th ed.), Vol. 29, para., 112.

[56] The G.L.C.'s authority for these purposes arises under a number of different enactments; see Halsbury's Laws of England (4th ed.) Vol. 29, para. 112. The G.L.C. also issues rules of management in relation to all places of public entertainment licensed by the G.L.C. These give specific guidance on the matters to be complied with, where a licence is given. Copies are obtainable from the G.L.C., publication No. 7168, 1242–8.

conditions may be imposed by the G.L.C. in relation to the conduct of entertainments which are provided.[57]

Safety certificates under the Safety of Sports Grounds Act 1975 are required in the case of any sports stadium which has accommodation for more than 10,000 spectators.[58] The G.L.C. is also the Fire Authority for issuing fire certificates under the Fire Precautions Act 1971 and the "Litter Authority" under the Litter Act 1983.

In addition the G.L.C. is the highway authority for all metropolitan roads, the London Borough Council and the Common Council of the City of London being the authorities for all highways within the boroughs and city respectively. Where road closures or other interference with the highway is necessary due to sponsored events such as the London Marathon or sponsored road races, special consideration must be given to questions of obstruction or interference with the Highways under the Highways Act 1980.[59] The powers of the Chief Officer of Police for prescribing the route of processions under section 3 of the Public Order Act 1936[60] should also be taken into account. This power arises broadly where the procession may involve the risk of public disorder. The Road Traffic Act might also require consideration in particular cases. For example, cycle racing is forbidden on a public road.[61]

Sponsored events which involve the use of crown land or the royal parks, will be dealt with by the Secretary of State for the Environment. The control of other London parks and open spaces is within the jurisdiction of the G.L.C., the London Borough Councils and the Common Council of the City of London. The powers enjoyed include the right to charge admission to certain open spaces.

(2) OTHER AREAS

Control of licensing for events or exhibitions outside London which may involve sponsorship will be in the hands

---

[57] The London Government Act 1963 and the Greater London Council (General Powers) Act 1978.
[58] Safety of Sports Grounds Act 1975, s.1.
[59] Highways Act 1980, s.130.
[60] See *Cawley* v. *Frost* [1976] 1 W.L.R. 1207 for the scope of the Act in relation to public premises.
[61] Road Traffic Act 1972, s.21.

of local government.[62] One may generalise insofar as the majority of local authorities will control many public events through requiring a licence to be issued. Such provisions are likely to effect the use of roads, parks and similar public places.

The authority to issue entertainment licences has recently been transferred from local licensing justices to district councils in England and Wales.[62] These relate to public music and dance, or other public entertainment of a similar kind[63] and public contests, exhibitions, displays of boxing, wrestling, judo, karate or any similar sport.[64] The local authority will have responsibility for issuing safety certificates at large sports grounds under the Safety of Sports Grounds Act 1975. In some cases, it will own the venue where sponsored events take place.[65] Control of the use of national parks is also a responsibility of the local authority.

The sale of intoxicating liquor whether within or outside London will require a licence. New legislation has recently been introduced[65a] which should make it easier for a club or other organization which is not conducted for private gain to obtain a licence to sell intoxicating liquor.

Sunday performances

The Sunday Observance Act 1780, s.3, makes it an offence to advertise or cause to be advertised any public entertainment or amusement for which people have to pay for admission and which takes place on a Sunday. This Act may inhibit the advertising of a sponsored event but will not prevent the event from being held. The Act does not apply to theatres or cinemas where a play or film is shown on licensing premises. Similar exceptions exist in relation to museums, galleries, etc. Further restrictions apply by virtue of the Sunday Observance Acts 1625 to 1780 and the Sunday Entertainments Act 1932. The 1625 Act prohibits an assembly or meeting of persons for sport and similar pastimes outside

[62] See the Local Government (Miscellaneous Provisions) Act 1982.
[63] *Ibid.* s.1(2) and see *Lidster* v. *Owen* [1983] 1 W.L.R. 516 for the application of the Public Health Acts (Amendment) Act 1890 regarding "public order" considerations in the renewal of a licence.
[64] *Ibid.* s.2(2).
[65] See *Buckingham* v. *Shackleton* [1981] 79 L.G.R. 484, D.C. Where a local authority paid athletes certain expenses in relation to a sponsored event.
[65a] Licensing (Occasional Permissions) Act 1983 (c.24).

their parish. It is not unlawful to assemble to play sport on a Sunday within the parish. The 1932 Act prevents the imposition of penalties arising in relation to certain activities such as musical entertainment where these have been licensed. The Sunday performances legislation has inhibited the growth rather than prevented the development of Sunday sport, entertainment and leisure.

Lotteries and amusements

The Lotteries and Amusement Act 1976 provides that all lotteries except those specifically exempted by the Act are illegal.[66] The exemptions include small lotteries which are incidental to an exempt entertainment, such as bazaars, fetes, sports events and private lotteries.[67] To qualify for these exemptions the entire proceeds of the lottery must be devoted to the objects of the qualifying organisation which conducts the lottery or advertises the scheme. It is recommended that legal advice should be sought before the scheme is undertaken if it is thought that an exemption applies. What comprises a lottery is not defined in the Act. This has resulted in a number of judges giving their own views on what is meant by the legislation.

The key elements which emerge from such views on what comprises a lottery are that there must be: (i) a distribution of prizes; (ii) the distribution must be by lot and chance and therefore not based upon the exercise of skill or judgment; and (iii) consideration must have been given by the participant to enter the lottery.

(1) PRIZES

Although there must be a prize, it need not be provided directly by the promotors. It would make no difference, for example, if each participant in a lottery agreed to send £1·00 directly to the winner rather than leave that to the promotors.[68]

(2) LOT OR CHANCE—ABSENCE OF SKILL

Where the prize is awarded on the basis of skill exhibited by the participant and not merely by pulling a lucky number

[66] s.1 except those which constitute gaming.
[67] s.3 and s.4.
[68] *Atkinson* v. *Murrell* [1973] A.C. 289.

from a hat, it will not be a lottery. It is important, of course, that selection by the judges or promotors is based upon the skill shown. A lottery will still exist if the participant is required to demonstrate skill but the selection by the judges is arbitrary.[69]

The degree of skill required to avoid the creation of a lottery need not be high but some real skill must exist. Thus forecasting the outcome of a horse race or football match was found to require sufficient skill[70] as did predicting the number of births and deaths in London in a week.[71] In contrast, determining when one match from a box ignited with the different coloured flame did not require sufficient skill.[72] Similarly, a promotion which involved purchasing a jar of coffee and rubbing out three out of ten dots did not require sufficient skill. The competition was won if the three dots spelt out the word "win."[73]

(3) GRATUITOUS ENTRY

A lottery will involve payment of money or other consideration by the participant. If no money or other consideration is given, then no lottery can exist. In the case of *Whitebread & Co.* v. *Bell* customers were given envelopes when they entered Whitbread pubs. The envelopes were the entries to a competition. There was no requirement or condition that the person entering the pub should buy a drink. It was held that such a competition could not be a lottery.[74]

This position was recently affirmed by the House of Lords in the case of *Imperial Tobacco Ltd.* v. *Att.-Gen.*[75] However, this case may be clearly distinguished from *Whitbread & Co.* v. *Bell* as the participant had to purchase a packet of cigarettes before being entitled to enter the competition.

---

[69] *Blyth* v. *Hulton & Co. Ltd.* (1968) 72 J.P. 401.
[70] *Caminada* v. *Hulton* (1891) 60 L.J.M.C. 116, *Moore* v. *Elphick* [1945] 2 All E.R. 155.
[71] *Hall* v. *Cox* [1899] 1 Q.B. 198.
[72] *Andren* v. *Stubbings, The Times,* October 16, 1924.
[73] *Police* v. *Nestlé Co. (N.Z.) Ltd.* [1970] N.Z.L.R. 416.
[74] [1970] 2 Q.B. 547.
[75] [1980] A.C. 718.

(4) AMUSEMENTS WITH PRIZES

A block exemption exists with respect to an amusement with prizes notwithstanding that it may also be a lottery where it takes place during any exempt entertainment, *i.e.* a bazaar, sale of work, fête, dinner, dance, sporting or athletic event or other entertainment of a similar character.[76] To qualify for the exemption, however, the proceeds must not be used for private gain, and the amusement with prizes shall not be the only inducement for persons to attend the exempt entertainment.[77] Further exemptions exist with respect to licensed premises.[78]

Prize competitions

It is unlawful to conduct in or through any newspaper or in connection with any trade or business or the sale of any article to the public, any competition in which prizes are offered for the forecast of: (i) future events; (ii) past events, the results of which are not yet ascertained or generally known: and (iii) any other competitions which do not depend to a substantial degree upon the exercise of skill.[79]

Many sponsors may wish to promote their products in association with events which they sponsor. Competitions are often organised for this purpose. It is therefore important to be aware of the extent of these provisions.

The Act only bites where a competition in the common sense meaning of the word exists. Cards inserted into cigarette packets which gave the opportunity to purchasers of the cigarettes to receive spot cash prizes, were found not to be competitions. Had the purchaser been asked to complete a series of questions, then that would have been different.[80]

Where the competition does depend to a substantial degree upon skill (the test is not substantial skill) then it will not fall within (iii) above. Thus a competition in which the participants were asked to match nine pictures with places in the United Kingdom was found to depend to a substantial degree upon skill.[81]

[76] Lotteries and Amusements Act 1976, s.3(1).
[77] *Ibid.* s.15(4).
[78] *Ibid.* s.16(1).
[79] See Lotteries and Amusements Act 1976, s.14.
[80] See *Imperial Tobacco Ltd.* v. *Att.-Gen.* [1980] A.C. 718.
[81] *Witty* v. *World Services Ltd.* [1936] Ch. 303.

Medicines

There are a number of restrictions which apply to advertising medicinal products. Thus no advertisement of medicinal products may be issued to the public where the advertisement relates to the treatment of a number of human ailments.[82] These ailments include tuberculosis, cancer, and diabetes. Similarly, no advertisement may be issued in connection with a contraceptive which suggests that is is a highly reliable method of birth control. There are exceptions.[83]

Food and drugs

Various powers exist for the appropriate ministry to issue orders and make regulations concerning advertisements for food and drugs which are intended for sale to humans.[84]

Statutory control of advertisements in general

Only one or two of the most likely applicable statutory regulations regarding advertisements have been included here. An excellent summary of the relevant statutes is contained in Appendix L to the British Code of Advertising Practice.[85]

NON-STATUTORY CONTROLS

Tort

There are a number of specific torts which may limit the exercise of rights or licences acquired by the sponsor.

---

[82] Medicines Act 1968 and Medicines (Labelling and Advertising to the Public) Regulations 1978 (S.I. 1978 No. 41).

[83] Medicines (Labelling and Advertising to the Public) Regulations 1978 (S.I. 1978 No. 41).

[84] See the Food and Drugs Act 1955 and the Weights and Measures Act 1963, and also the Agricultural Marketing Act 1983.

[85] (6th ed. 1979.) Such legislation appears to be increasing all the time. See, for example, *Jenkins* v. *Lombard North Central plc, The Times*, August 11, 1983, where use of a logo on the side of a car was held not be to be an advertisement under the Consumer Credit (Advertisement) Regulations (S.I. 1980 No. 54).

(1) TRESPASS TO LAND AND GOODS

The use of land without the authority of the owner or some other person empowered to authorise its use, will amount to trespass. Many sponsored events will involve the use of land, either to stage the event or to erect stadium boards or banners. It is important, therefore, to secure proper consent for its use.

Trespass arises from either entering or remaining on land belonging to another or placing an object or protuberance upon it.[86] Land for this purpose will include buildings and other permanent objects on the site. The erection of a stadium advertising board at a venue without permission would clearly amount to trespass.[87] Similarly a sign which encroached only partly on someone's land would nevertheless be a trespass.[88]

Trespass to goods involves the unlawful interference with goods rather than land. The offence is now regulated by the Torts (Interference with Goods) Act 1977. In one case[89] it was found to be trespass to goods to change tyres exhibited on a car at a motor show.

(2) NUISANCE

Nuisance falls into three main categories: public, private and statutory. All three categories have potential application to a sponsorship situation particularly where a large outdoor event is being sponsored.

A statutory nuisance covers those acts or omissions which have become a criminal offence by statute. For example, the Public Health Act 1936 empowers local authorities to prosecute anti-social behaviour amounting to a nuisance.

Of more relevance to sponsorship is a public nuisance. This has been defined as an act or omission which materially affects the reasonable comfort and convenience of the life of a class of Her Majesty's subjects.[90] In one case, for example, a large sponsored rock festival was organised at a park with very few facilities. It was shown that a previous concert

---

[86] *Salmond and Heuston on the Law of Torts* (18th ed. 1981).
[87] See *Gifford v. Dent* (1926) 71 S.J. 83.
[88] *Kelsen v. Imperial Tobacco Co.* [1957] 2 Q.B. 334.
[89] *G.W.K. Ltd.* v. *Dunlop Rubber Co. Ltd.* [1926] 42 T.L.R. 376.
[90] *Att.-Gen.* v. *P.Y.A. Quarries* [1957] 2 Q.B. 169.

organised for the defendants resulted in nude bathing, excessive noise and traffic congestion. An injunction was issued restraining the concert from taking place.[91] Another case involved an injunction restricting the frequency of competitions and the noise levels of boats at a motor boat and water ski club.[92] Two further cases involved the owners of houses near football grounds which were used occasionally for speedway racing, securing injunctions to prevent excessive noise.[93] In another case, an illuminated sign depicting Father Christmas placed outside a shop attracted a large crowd which prevented access to other shops. This was held to amount to a public nuisance.[94]

A private nuisance involves interference of some description with the enjoyment of land. Thus where one neighbour erected boards on his own property which had the effect of preventing advertisements on the other neighbour's wall from being seen, that amounted to an actionable private nuisance.[95]

Contract

Controls may exist in relation to the use of land or other proprietary matters to be acquired in a sponsorship situation through contract. The owner of a sports ground on which stadium advertising boards are to be erected may not be in a position to grant such rights in view of a covenant in his lease. In one case, for example, the erection of advertisements on a wall were found to be in breach of a covenant not to allow any act which would disturb the lessor.[96] In such a case whether or not the activity in question is in breach of covenant will be a matter of construction.

Similar covenants have involved an undertaking in the case of a theatre not to assign, demise or otherwise part with any estate or interest therein. An exclusive licence was granted to use and sell advertising space on the theatre. It was held that there had been no breach of covenant since all that had been granted was a permission to use space for advertising. That

---

[91] *Att.-Gen. (Ontario)* v. *Orange Productions Ltd.* [1971] D.L.R. 21 at 257.
[92] *Kennaway* v. *Thompson* [1981] Q.B. 88.
[93] *Att.-Gen.* v. *Hastings Corpn.* (1950) 94 S.J. 225 and *Stretch* v. *Romford Football Club* [1971] 113 S.J. 741.
[94] *Burnstein* v. *Gamages Ltd., The Times,* December 10, 1930.
[95] *Cobb* v. *Saxby* [1914] 3 K.B. 822.
[96] *Heard* v. *Stuart* [1907] T.L.R. 164.

was held not to amount to an assignment, demise or otherwise parting with possession.[97]

Prior assignments or grants of rights by venue owners will obviously affect the ability of the sponsee to grant sponsorship rights. Such prior rights may relate to almost any matter.

Tobacco

A voluntary agreement was first entered into between Her Majesty's government, the Tobacco Advisory Council, on behalf of United Kingdom tobacco manufacturers and the cigarette importer members of Imported Tobacco Products Advisory Council in 1977. The spirit of that agreement acknowledged the substantial contribution made by the tobacco industry to United Kingdom sporting events via sponsorship. At the same time, the Code attempted to protect those who might be particularly vulnerable in associating cigarettes with health.

The Code was last revised in 1982 and announced by Mr. Neil MacFarlane, Minister for Sport, on March 3, 1982.[98] Some of its more interesting features include the requirement that the tobacco companies will support non-televised minor and amateur activities, the requirement to consult with the Minister for Sport on any proposal to sponsor a sport not previously sponsored by the industry, a ban on sponsoring sports in which the participants are less than 18 years of age, an expenditure ceiling, and inclusion of government health warnings on static promotional signs. The scope of this voluntary Code is limited exclusively to sport. It does not effect Arts or leisure activities.

An entirely separate code known as the "Cigarette Code" exists in parallel to the voluntary agreement on Sports sponsorship. The code is a result of discussions between the Department of Health and Social Security (on behalf of the United Kingdom Health departments), the manufacturers and importers of cigarettes (represented by the Tobacco Advisory Council and the Imported Tobacco Products Advisory Council) and the Advertising Standards Authority. However, there were aspects of the agreement to which the A.S.A. are not parties, such as the inclusion of the Govern-

---

[97] *Daly* v. *Edwardes* [1901] T.L.R. 115.
[98] See the Department of Employment Press Notice.

ment health warnings and the prohibition of cigarette advertising on video cassettes and in satellite broadcasts. Although the code does not apply to advertising by tobacco companies in relation to events they sponsor (even Arts and leisure events) it may nevertheless have indirect relevance to sponsorship.[99] The code applies to advertising in general and is not, as with the voluntary agreement on sponsorship, restricted to sport. It provides, for example, that cigarette companies should not include personal testimonials by well known persons.[1]

A Private Member's Bill called the Tobacco Products (Control of Advertising, Sponsorship and Sales Promotion) was recently presented to the House of Commons by Laurie Pavitt M.P. If adopted, this bill would have given the Minister wide powers to make orders and regulations relating to sponsorship by tobacco companies.

In certain EEC countries such as France, regulation of tobacco advertising has already been taken further than voluntary codes. In one case, for example,[2] "Philip Morris," which is a brand name for cigarettes, was incorporated in the title of a charitable foundation, "The Philip Morris Foundation for the Cinema." The Foundation would give assistance in distributing films, in return for which the name of the Foundation was to be prominently displayed on posters. This was held to be unlawful advertising of a brand name.

The European Sports Sponsorship Code

The third Conference of European Ministers responsible for sport was held in 1981. Resolutions passed at the conference based upon the notion that it would be to the benefit of sport and the general public to set out in a generally accepted and supplementary voluntary code regulations for sponsorship in sport. The Council of Europe has produced a Code which falls into two parts, the first being "Introduction and Explanatory Memorandum" and the second the "Guiding Principles."

---

[99] British Code of Advertising Practice, App. H, para. 1(7).

[1] *Ibid.* App. H, r. 2, 9.

[2] *Procureur de la Republique* v. *François Pierre Benveniste* [1981] C.C.C. 505.

(1) THE INTRODUCTION

The introduction to the "guiding principles" identifies the organisations involved with sponsorship from the participants to the governments concerned with the social consequences. It makes the point that sponsorship is a "partnership" between sport and commerce. It recognises the desire to achieve a balance in the partnership between the sponsor's interest and that of the governing bodies of sport to ensure that it is not overcommercialised. Considerable emphasis is placed on the contribution that the media should play in making the sponsorship work.

(2) THE GUIDING PRINCIPLES

The guiding principles comprise a number of specific points all of which have already been made throughout the text of this book. Certain points, however, are so important that they are repeated here:

"(iii) Parties should conclude written agreements specifying:
(a) The duration of the agreement.
(b) All undertakings by the sponsor.
(c) All concessions to the sponsor by the sponsored.
(d) All publicity and advertising arrangements between the two parties.
(e) An obligation to consult on any use to be made of the agreement outside it's immediate scope."[3]

"(iv) Before entering into the arrangements referred to under (iii) d above the sponsored [sponsee] should consult with the representatives of the mass media (broadcasting and newspaper organisations) likely to be interested in reporting a sports event in order to reach an agreement on advertising deriving from the arrangements and, in particular, its treatment by television bearing in mind such organisations' editorial independence."[4]

"(v) The mass media, national television organisations particularly, are invited to draw up, in collaboration with national sports bodies, and publish as soon as possible a detailed Code of Practice concerning the transmission of

---

[3] The European Sports Sponsorship Code, r. 3(iii).
[4] *Ibid*. r. 3(iv).

advertising material at sporting events, so that uniform national criteria can, wherever possible, be adopted for all sports in each country . . . ."

Other codes of practice dealing with advertising or sales promotion

(1) INDEPENDENT· BROADCASTING AUTHORITY CODE OF ADVERTISING STANDARDS AND PRACTICE

This Code applies to the broadcasting of commercials and radio advertisements. The Code is made pursuant to section 9 of the Broadcasting Act 1981 and supplements the general principles relating to advertisements which are included in Schedule 2 to the Act. The general principles form part of the Act but the Code does not. The Code is similar in its language to the British Code of Advertising Practice discussed next. The Code covers the content of advertisements.

(2) BRITISH CODE OF ADVERTISING PRACTICE (B.C.A.P.)

The Code binds the advertiser, advertising agency and media owner but the principal responsibility for observing its terms is with the advertiser. The Code consists of a number of rules which reflect the principles of "good advertising" as they apply to areas such as charity, children and cosmetics. The three existing principles of good advertising are stated at the beginning of the Code. These are:

"All advertisements should be legal, decent, honest and truthful."

"All advertisements should be prepared with a sense of responsibility both to the consumer and to society."

"All advertisements should conform to the principles of fair competition as generally accepted in business."

Most parts of the Code are applicable to advertisements linked to a sponsorship,[5] for example, an advertisement containing a false or misleading endorsement or testimonial.[6] Where testimonials or endorsements are used the advertiser

---

[5] But note B.C.A.P. App. M, r.1(7), stating that the Code does not apply to advertising at events sponsored by tobacco companies.
[6] B.C.A.P., para. 4(7).

must be careful not to give the impression of independent approval where none has been given. The advertiser should also be able to substantiate claims made. Permission needs to be obtained where the advertisement features real people. It is beyond the scope of this book to examine the Code in depth, however, both the sponsor and the sponsee should be aware of its existence.

The Code applies to all advertisements including those shown in the cinema, except: broadcasting advertisements, advertisements in media published outside the United Kingdom, advertisements for medicine advertised to the medical profession and certain types of mail order advertisements.

The ultimate authority having responsibility for enforcement of the Code is the Advertising Standard Authority. This authority investigates complaints made by the public and also monitors and investigates of its own volition advertisements which may be in breach of the Code.

The Code only applies to an advertisement which is defined as a "paid for communication addressed to the public or a section of it, the purpose of which is to influence opinions or behaviour of those to whom it is addressed."[7] Where the Sponsor, as part of his sponsorship package receives a page of advertising in the programme of an event then it is submitted that these rules will apply. Where however he receives credit by the media in referring to an event as, for example, "Embassy World Snooker Championships," then this will not be subject to these rules.

(3) BRITISH CODE OF SALES PROMOTIONS PRACTICE (B.C.S.P.P.)

The scope of the B.C.S.P.P. as its title suggests, is sales promotion. The Code is administered in the same manner as the B.C.A.P., the ultimate authority with responsibility for the Code being the Advertising Standards Authority. The particular areas covered by the Code include premium offers, personality promotions, prize promotions, etc. Like the B.C.A.P. it does not deal with sponsorship but its relevance is where the sponsor chooses to promote his sponsorship in some manner contemplated by the Code.

The Code starts off with certain enshrining principles. These are:

[7] *Ibid.* s.1.

"(1) All sales promotions should be legal and conform to the principles of fair competition as generally accepted in the business . . .

(2) In particular, so far as the consumer is concerned the terms of any offer should be equitable, its presentation should be clear and honest, and its administration should be swift and efficient."

The general rules of conduct stated in the Code include protection of privacy[8] and ensuring that publicity and promotional material is not misleading.[9] Specific rules concern free offers, prize and charity linked promotions.

Arts Council guidelines

The guidelines are issued to organisations as a condition of receiving subsidy. They require supported organisations to acknowledge appropriately their Arts Council subsidy in all their promotional material.

In relation to sponsorship they require client organisations to ensure that the importance of the Arts Council's contribution is also clearly ascertained from all publicity material. In particular display advertising which features the name(s) of commercial sponsors should also appropriately acknowledge Arts Council subsistence. Acknowledgement of the element of Arts Council support given for a whole year's work of a client should not be overwhelmed by that accredited to business sponsorship for a particular event.

Sports Council guidelines

Where the Sports Council provides funds for facilities, then the recipient will be required to acknowledge that the facilities have been grant-aided by the Sports Council. It is understood that where the Sports Council provides funds for a sports event, then a similar acknowledgment will be required for the Sports Council's contribution.

[8] B.C.S.P.P., para. 5.2.
[9] *Ibid.* para. 5.5.

16. Tax, VAT, Hope and Charity

INTRODUCTION

At the time of writing there is no specific sponsorship tax ruling existing in the United Kingdom based on the traditional tax sources. These are parliamentary, judicial, H.M. Treasury, Board of Inland Revenue and H.M. Customs and Excise.

Sponsorship's existence, however, has been acknowledged by H.M. Customs and Excise VAT Leaflet No. 701/5/81[1] for VAT purposes, and also by a joint H.M. Treasury-Inland Revenue Memorandum for general tax purposes prepared in January 1981 as part of H.M. Treasury evidence for the House of Commons Committee on Education, Science and Arts. With the consent of both Government Departments, it has been reproduced in Appendix III[2] as a current statement of "the position on sponsorship and gifts under present taxation arrangements," to cite its own preamble.

Furthermore, as Lord Goodman testified in his evidence to the House of Commons Committee from his position as a former Chairman of the Arts Council and as the present Chairman of A.B.S.A., on April 1, 1981: "There is some recognition needed of the Inland Revenue . . . . The Inland Revenue have been enormously helpful to us, *i.e.* A.B.S.A. . . . If a company has any doubt, therefore, Somerset House has instructed the Inspectors of Taxes that they should advise whether that doubt is real or not."[3] For company of course, read the other legal identifiable persona. This acknowledgment contrasts sharply with the less generous impression given to an Anglo-American seminar on the same theme a year earlier in 1980 and republished in 1981.[4]

The aim of this chapter is to create within its own

---

[1] Reproduced in respect of sponsorship rights at p. 290 below.
[2] See Appendix III below at p. 304.
[3] Eighth Report from the Education, Science and Arts Committee on the Public and Private Funding of the Arts, Session 1980–81 (1982; H.C. 49–II) pp. 291–292.
[4] British American Arts Association, *Tax Policy and Private Support for the Arts in the United States, Canada and Great Britain* (1981) at p. 72.

self-imposed limits a clear and concise compass through the annually changing statutory and juridical territories as they relate to sponsorship. Indeed, since this chapter was initiated, tax laws have not remained static. The Revenue published proposals on December 29, 1982 for fundamental changes in double taxation arrangements which may be introduced during the mid-1980s. Throughout the preparation of this chapter during 1983, Parliament, tax tribunals, and the Courts have all legislated extensively in areas which affect it, with built-in indications of further inevitable developments for the future; and the Government gave notice in 1983 of preparations for a new Consolidating Bill which it is hoped will be ready for introduction early in the Parliamentary Session 1987/88.[5]

Generally, therefore, for the subject-matter of this chapter, as with sponsorship generally, known legal principles have to be applied to identifiable sponsorship situations and vice versa. This chapter aims to set out the legal principles which govern sponsorship arrangements in the field of tax, VAT and charities, but it should be remembered that a book can never be an adequate substitute for legal advice.

TAXATION DIFFERENCES FROM OTHER LEGAL AREAS

Before examining the joint Treasury-Revenue Memorandum certain crucial differences between taxation and other United Kingdom legal categories should be emphasised. This is partly because of the fragmented nature and numbers of so many different revenue sources, jurisdictions, interpretations and personnel concerned with the function of the United Kingdom tax system. It is necessary therefore, to identify these differences briefly.

Acceptable tax law sources in addition to Parliament and the courts exist in Inland Revenue and Customs and Excise Practice Notes, and accountancy methods approved by the courts for tracing and tracking solutions to particular tax problems.

Tax law today is operated, practised and implemented by an ever increasing army of accountants, inspectors of taxes, customs and excise officers, charity commissioners, general and special tax commissioners and VAT commissioners,

---

[5] H.C. Deb., Vol. 46, col. 140 (July 20, 1983).

alongside the traditional legal battalions of Parliamentary draftsmen, judges, barristers, solicitors and taxpayers.

Tax laws initiate from political considerations more than any other democratically inspired legislation. Indeed, the first ever[6] Income Tax Acts originated from the need to raise revenue to finance the Napoleonic Wars.

Tax disputes require energetic and often expensive pursuit from the inspectors of taxes and customs and excise officers, via the appropriate commissioners' tribunals, single High Court Revenue List Judge, and Court of Appeal up to the House of Lords. Yet sufficient financial resources need to exist to challenge revenue rulings in the courts. This is not the fault of the Inland Revenue or H.M. Customs and Excise. It is inherent in the preparation and conduct of adversarial litigation; and in appropriate circumstances the Revenue, on its own initiative, or at the Courts' requests, will bear the costs of litigation to clarify any uncertain or developing area. So far no legal aid exists to assist any citizen in preparing and presenting at the initial tax or VAT tribunal hearings the crucial factual evidence on which so many later legal pronouncements will be based. Legal aid may be available to those who qualify under the appropriate means tests for appeals to the higher courts, but often when it is too late to affect the vitally important conclusions of the commissioners about the evidence.[7]

Tax litigation and the inevitable costs burden is liable to produce an imbalance between the bottomless purse of the Revenue and Customs and Excise disputant and the limited resources of the taxpayer. Even a national body of the Football Association's size, not eligible for legal aid, felt obliged to enlist the financial support of the Sports Council and of the Central Council of Physical Recreation. This was to pursue through the Court of Appeal and the House of Lords its ultimately successful challenge to the Revenue opposition to the Charity Commissioners' registration of its Youth Trust Deed in 1980.[8] The Bar Council and the Law Society in 1976 backed to the later stages in the Court of Appeal a barrister's successful attempt to overturn a single High Court judge precedent of 1926 that law books expenditure was deductible expenditure as "intellectual"

---

[6] 38 Geo. III, c. 16 and 39 Geo III, c. 13.

[7] The crucial importance of the finality of commissioners' factual findings which will not be overturned lightly was recently re-emphasised by the House of Lords in *Cole Brothers* v. *Phillips* [1982] S.T.C. 301.

[8] *I.R.C.* v. *McMullen* [1981] A.C. 1.

plant[9]; and the Bar Council also supported to the House of Lords the lady barrister who challenged the Inspector of Taxes and the General Commissioners for disallowing her claim to deduct as an allowable professional expense her obligatory dark court clothes. Her personal preference was for lighter coloured clothes. Although one High Court Judge, three Court of Appeal Judges and one Law Lord (five in all) favoured the taxpayer, the majority of four Law Lords had the last word in favour of the Revenue; and they have created a Pandora's Box for future uncertainty about clothing allowances, not confined to lady barristers, when rejecting her claim under the duality principle dealt with below.[10]

The tax laws in these examples cited above would have remained unchanged if the interests beyond the litigants' personal taxes had not been backed by group assistance. Tax laws touch the hem of the largest communal interests, with the financial dice loaded against the taxpayer because of the expense involved in litigation under the adversarial system. The present Master of the Rolls, Sir John Donaldson, as Donaldson L.J. before he succeeded Lord Denning, crystallised the position clearly (but incompletely in respect of contrasting financial resources) when he observed in *I.R.C.* v. *Garving*[11]:

> "There is a certain fascination in being one of the referees of a match between a well-advised taxpayer and the equally well-advised Commissioners of Inland Revenue conducted under the rules which govern tax avoidance. These rules are complex, the moves are sophisticated and the stakes are high."

Rules relating to the taxation of sponsorship monies have not yet been individually formulated to create an exclusively identifiable area for this particular match in which tax avoidance is permissible but tax evasion is not. Other countries have different sanctions for penalising the latter concept.[12] In the United Kingdom sanctions are statutorily laid down by Parliament. For sponsorship the starting point with any recognised rules is the "present tax arrangements"

---

[9] *Munby* v. *Furlong* [1977] Ch. 359 at 369.
[10] *Mallalieu* v. *Drummond* [1983] S.T.C. 665.
[11] [1980] S.T.C. 298 at 313.
[12] International Bar Association, *I.B.A.: Tax Avoidance, Tax Evasion* (1982).

(P.T.A.) set out in the joint Treasury-Revenue Memorandum which we will now turn to in detail.

H.M. Treasury and Inland Revenue Memorandum

The H.M. Treasury Memorandum, prepared in conjunction with the Inland Revenue is entitled, "Taxation in the context of private sponsorship and of gifts of art objects to public and private institutions".

The Memorandum assumes in the reader a basic awareness of the conceptual framework for United Kingdom taxation based upon its six Schedules A–F, and that the taxation of corporation income and expenditure is determined according to recognised income tax principles. Also, for purposes of corporation tax, assessments are made by the rules applicable to income under the same income tax Schedules and the statutory Cases rules under them.

Other assumptions in the reader are that the courts which interpret the law accept accountancy principles for distinguishing between revenue and capital items, and as to the structure and operation of the United Kingdom charity system, with its underlying qualifications for tax reliefs.

These assumptions will require consideration in their appropriate context below. Although the Memorandum explains that it was "provided for the Education, Science and Arts Committee [of the House of Commons] in connection with its enquiry into the public and private funding of the Arts," its contents are applicable to every sphere of sponsorship, including the whole spectrum of sport, Arts and leisure.

The structure of sub-headings which are set out in this first authoritative United Kingdom taxation guideline on sponsorship is summarised below from its sequence as follows.

Private sponsorship

  (i) Covenanted payments;
  (ii) Business expenses.

Gifts

Capital transfer tax (C.T.T.) and capital gains tax (C.G.T.).
  (a) Outline of the taxes;
  (b) General exemption for gifts;
  (c) Detailed provisions affecting gifts of works of art.

Other capital tax reliefs for the Arts

  (i) Conditional exemptions
 (ii) Maintenance funds.
(iii) Acceptance in lieu and private treaty sales.

Heritage tax reliefs

Gifts for national purposes in lieu of tax debts

Because understanding of the P.T.A., under its sub-heading "Private Sponsorship" for item "(ii) Business expenses" requires less technical procedural details than are necessary for the charity law item "(i) Covenanted payments," we have reversed this sequence. We begin with the relatively more straightforward method of how, to cite the Memorandum, "A payment in sponsorship of the Arts [ergo, of sport, and leisure, too] may qualify for tax relief in one of two ways," *i.e.* "business expenses."

Business expenses—qualification for tax relief

1. The Memorandum summarises in convenient form what tax practitioners will readily identify as the accepted arrangements under the provisions of section 130(*a*) of the Income and Corporation Taxes Act 1970. This section will be found in Appendix IV. The underlying theme for Schedule D sponsors (without the extra refinement for Schedule E sponsees to which we refer later) is the "wholly and exclusively" test summarised in the memorandum thus:

> "A sponsorship payment will normally be a deductible expense in computing business profits for tax purposes if it is of a revenue nature (*i.e.* not a capital payment) and is incurred wholly and exclusively for the purpose of the trade."

The two qualifications of "a revenue nature" and "wholly and exclusively for the purpose of the trade" are further explained in the Memorandum by way of summarising the judicial and revenue constructions of the statutory provisions contained in section 130(a)–(u) inclusive thus:

> "The first condition means that no deduction is allowable for any lump sum donation towards, for example,

the building or modernisation of a theatre or the purchase of a work of art,"

i.e. emphasising the revenue contrast with capital payment.

"The second condition means that the business purpose—generally advertising—must be the sole purpose for which the payment is made."

This emphasises and affirms the "wholly and exclusively" test.

The sentence:

"The expenditure will not be admissible if it is incurred for a dual purpose—*e.g.* both promoting a business and promoting a charitable or benevolent object."

in the Memorandum, is followed by a final paragraph under this section, which provides a thread with the "Covenanted payments" qualification for tax relief and charitable sources. It will be dealt with finally under this category of "Business expenses." To understand the theme underlying this relief in the P.T.A. requires a glance at the section and the traditional judicial attitudes towards it in the reported cases.

Section 130(*a*) of the Income and Corporation Taxes Act 1970 (hereinafter called I.C.T.A.) succeeds earlier legislation which contains the formula "wholly and exclusively." The P.T.A. Memorandum clearly contemplates this section, which would apply to companies, clubs, organisations and individuals who are not employed. Employees, or for tax purposes, "the holder of an office or employment" under section 189 of I.C.T.A. contains an additional element, *i.e.* "wholly, exclusively and necessarily." Subject to this important addition of the words "and necessarily," the interpretations of "wholly and exclusively" are applied without distinction to all income earners, and thereby sponsors and sponsees. Sponsors would primarily be concerned with section 130. The statutory charge to tax under which section 130 operates and controls "wholly and exclusively" is formally "Case I or Case II of Schedule D." The statutory details which identify these Cases and Schedule are set out in sections 108 and 109 of I.C.T.A. which we have included in Appendix V. These key words of section 130 have been interpreted judicially and administratively in a functional manner summarised below, controlled by the P.T.A. explanation of "a revenue nature." How advertising came in from the cold, to be enshrined as it now is, within the P.T.A. Memorandum's second condition cited above for qualification as a deductible business expense, illustrates how tax law changes down the years.

Section 130 specifies in its material part at the outset:

> "Subject to the provisions of the Tax Acts, in computing the amount of the profits or gains to be charged under Case I or Case II of Schedule D, no sum shall be deducted in respect of
> (a) any disbursements or expenses, not being money wholly and exclusively laid out or expended for the purposes of the trade, profession or vocation."

We do not here elaborate on the last three categories of trade, profession or vocation which are subject to considerable judicial construction, but for present purposes may be regarded as self-explanatory. In 1880 the famous brewers, then trading as Watney & Co. claimed to deduct certain expenses in ascertaining their net profits under a Schedule D similarly worded to that which exists today.[13] Those expenses comprised certain large premiums and fixed rents paid to purchase leases of licensed public premises to promote or increase sales of beer after it had been processed and produced. On appeal against the Special Commissioners rejection of the claim, the High Court doubted whether advertisement or promotional costs after production expenditure could be allowed for computing net taxable profits without Parliamentary or Court of Appeal authority.[14]

Nearly 50 years later in 1928 that concept of advertising expenditure, albeit by way of analogy and illustration, was accepted by the single and Court of Appeal judges. They considered a claim by an asphalting company concerning a written guarantee. It was made with the hope of obtaining a contract associated with the Wembley British Empire Exhibition at the time when the famous Stadium was being constructed. The guarantee failed to clinch the deal but it was enforced for payment. The appeal judges overruled the single judge and restored the General Commissioners' conclusion that the expense was "wholly and exclusively" allowable.[15]

---

[13] (16 & 17 Vict. c. 34.)

[14] *Watney* v. *Musgrave* (1880) I.T.C. 272 at 277.

[15] Equivalent to s. 130(1) under r.3(*a*) to cases 1 or 2 under Sched. D to the Income Tax Act 1918 (8 & 9 Geo. V, c. 40). See *Morley* v. *Lawford & Co.* [1928] 14 T.C. 229 at 237, 244.

Of equal importance to the verdict on that Wembley case was the Court of Appeal's citation from an earlier House of Lords ruling[16] by the then Master of the Rolls, Lord Hanworth[17]

> " . . . 'no degree of ingenuity can frame a formula so precise and comprehensive as to solve at sight all the cases that may arise' . . . .You cannot find a formula which will consider the question off-hand. The difficulty is illustrated by the number of cases which have been decided on the one side and on the other."

On the disallowance side, a decision in 1982 turned the century's wheel of history full circle when Watney & Co's successors as Watney Combe Reid & Co. also came to court. They failed to prove as deductible expenses certain *ex gratia* payments to tenants of tied houses in return for giving up their tenancies. The payments were made on *income* account. No new asset was obtained, and the preservation of goodwill with continuing tenants was intended after hostile and widely publicised reactions to earlier terminations of other tied tenancies. Nevertheless, the Revenue claimed successfully that the payments were of a *capital* nature for a group of companies' management programme. Thus they were not made "wholly" and "exclusively" for trading purposes.[18]

Since tax is concerned with public issues, in areas which could overlap with sponsorship, two contrasting examples may be seen. In the 1950s a famous sugar firm launched a nation-wide anti-nationalisation campaign to preserve the company from losing its business and to preserve its assets and also the industry. On the oral and documentary evidence the House of Lords upheld the Special Commissioners' finding that these expenses qualified for relief.[19] Subsequently, a brewery company's apportioned share of trade expenses for a Sunday opening crusading campaign was allowed for revenue expenditure as one of its methods for carrying on business.[20] On the other side of this line expenses were disallowed later to a company's contributions to a trade association whose objects were wider than business trading.[21]

---

[16] *Per* Loreburn L.C. in *Strong & Co.* v. *Woodfield* [1966] A.C. 488 at 452.
[17] [1928] 14 T.C. 229 at 240.
[18] *Watney Combe Reid & Co. Ltd.* v. *Pike* [1982] S.T.C. 733.
[19] *Morgan* v. *Tate & Lyle* [1955] A.C. 21.
[20] *Cooper* v. *Rhymney Breweries* [1965] 44 T.C. 509.
[21] *Joseph Thompson & Sons* v. *Chamberlain* [1962] 40 T.C. 657.

So, too, were printing costs for a political objective not associated with the company's trade.[22] Also disallowed for an overconscientious concern, which was *ultra vires* certain statutory objects, were disbursements undoubtedly for the benefit of the racing industry in general but beyond the trading totalisator operation of the Racecourse Betting Control Board.[23] By contrast, the Jockey Club changed the Rules of Racing to permit company ownership and thereby sponsorship through the advertising of animals in training and thus complement the long-standing sponsorship of famous races. Such a domestic change by a private Club did not affect the revenue and Parliamentary statutory rules. If the "wholly and exclusively" test is satisfied, then the sponsorship qualifies for tax relief. Each claim will turn, of course, on its own facts.

The P.T.A. Memorandum clearly contemplates allowable business expenses for sponsors. Sponsorship income for the non-charitable recipient-sponsee will usually be treated as trading income for tax purposes; and the same rules of "wholly and exclusively" will apply except for the emoluments of "the holder of any office of employment" under section 189 and Schedule E. The extra element already identified here of "necessarily" has been as fruitful of case law as the wider recognised and accepted test itself. Two examples suffice here to illuminate the distinction. The Bank Manager who joined a club for furtherance of custom under the encouragement of his employers was disallowed the expense under the necessarily rule[24]; the company director who used a club as a substitute for hotel accommodation qualified.[25]

Each case turns on its own facts, as indeed, does the distinction whether the taxpayer is categorised either as self-employed under Schedule D or as holder of an office under Schedule E. Dame Lilian Braithwaite was a distinguished actress with many different contracts for various acting services in the United Kingdom and overseas. She argued that although resident in the United Kingdom, her overseas contracts for which she need not pay tax under a separate group of contracts brought her into an office holder category. The Court held in 1931 that she was carrying on her

[22] *Bearland* v. *Kramat Pulai* [1953] 1 W.L.R. 1332.
[23] Today the Horserace Totalisator Board. See *Racehorse Betting Control Board* v. *Young* [1959] 1 W.L.R. 813.
[24] *Brown* v. *Bullock* [1961] 40 T.C. 1.
[25] *Utitz* v. *Elwood* [1965] 42 T.C. 482.

profession on two continents simultaneously, and was taxable cumulatively under Schedule D.[26] Fifty years later in the 1980s a more sophisticated arrangement would include the company service or partnership agreement structure to develop or exploit personal talents as illustrated in the David Frost case,[27] subject to double taxation arrangements which at the date of publication are subject in turn to the Inland Revenue December 20, 1982 proposals; and subject also to the House of Lords' re-appraisal of tax planning schemes on the basis of looking beyond the legal nature to the overall intention behind any transaction. This began in 1981 with the well-known *Ramsay*[28] decision, and at the time of completing this chapter the issue is en route from the Court of Appeal to the House of Lords again in the anxiously awaited case of *Furniss* v. *Dawson.*[29]

A different application of the *capital* payment principle from the "wholly and exclusively" test which does qualify for tax relief under Schedule E occurred when amateur Rugby *Union* players surrendered their amateur status to become Rugby *League* professionals. Their respective signing-on fees under the Rugby Football League Bye-laws were held to be an allowable once and for all "*capital* sum in consideraton" for loss of status, and not an *income* emolument.[30] Finally, in *Duff* v. *Williamson*[31] a doctor's research scholarship sum equivalent to (but not identified as) a sponsorship arrangement was held by Special Commissioners to be outside the taxable category under which it was assessed. On appeal by the Revenue it was held to have been received by the taxpayer in the terms of a contract and thereby a normal incident of his profession. The issue was more fundamental than expenses. It went back to the issue of taxable or not. For "wholly and exclusively," however, the following general elements are extractable from the cases for an allowable claim:

(a) it must be a revenue as distinct from a capital item of expenditure: an accountancy practice issue, see citations above;

(b) it must have been incurred for business purposes;

---

[26] *Davies* v. *Braithwaite* [1931] 18 T.C. 198.
[27] *Newstead* v. *Frost* [1980] 1 W.L.R. 135.
[28] *W.T. Ramsay Ltd.* v. *I.R.C.* [1981] S.T.C. 174.
[29] [1983] S.T.C. 549.
[30] *Jarrold* v. *Boustead* [1964] 41 T.C. 701.
[31] [1973] 49 T.C. 1.

(c) it must have been incurred for profits of the business to be allowed as deductible from them;

(d) it must be lawful and not *ultra vires*; and

(e) it must have been incurred only for business and not dual purposes.[32]

This last element prohibiting duality is expressed as the second condition in the P.T.A. Memorandum limiting the normal deductibility of business expenses. It also leads into the whole concept of charities and covenanted payments, with which it overlaps.

The dual purpose problem is linked to statute, judgments and concessions. Section 130(*b*) of the I.C.T.A. prohibits payments which are "distinct from the purposes of the trade, profession or vocation." For sponsors it was exemplified by two post-First World War hospital subscriptions by the company Bourne & Hollingsworth for employees of that former well-known drapery store. The Revenue by concession acceded to a £50 subscription; but challenged a £1,000 subscription on the basis that it stemmed from philanthropic motives and not for profit-earning purposes, even though the profit-earning employees personally and the company ultimately benefited.[33] A re-alignment of the evidence in the light of today's social climate, of workers' welfare as vital for economic health, could now produce a different result, just as the decision in the same period of *Daphne* v. *Shaw*[34] which rejected law books as a deductible expense for plant was reversed 50 years later in *Munby* v. *Furlong*.[35]

Duality for sponsees is illustrated by a part-time guitarist and a clergyman. In *Prince* v. *Mapp*[36] an operation on a finger to enable a guitarist to continue to play professionally and to continue to pursue his hobby of playing was disallowed under this head; but a clergyman who spent £105 on a bespoke funeral cloak to protect him from the rain during rural funeral services on wet days persuaded General Commissioners with proof by photographic evidence of its necessity for work as required by his Bishop: on facts[37] which

---

[32] See the present tax arrangements (P.T.A.) in Appendix III below, pp. 305–306.

[33] *Bourne & Hollingsworth* v. *Ogden* [1929] 14 T.C. 344.

[34] [1926] 11 T.C. 256.

[35] [1977] 1 Ch. 359.

[36] [1970] 46 T.C. 169.

[37] *Re The Rev. Ivo Morshead, The Times*, January 8, 1983, p. 3 (unreported).

were distinguishable from the circumstances in the case of *Mallalieu* v. *Drummond*,[37a] involving the female barrister and her claim for the expense of dark court clothes. Coincidentally, this decision followed closely the High Court allowance of an appeal on principle by the Revenue from a different General Commissioners' conclusion that £134 spent by a vicar on a slide projector for "visual sermons" was not "necessary" for performing his duties.[38] Both decisions are unlikely to be subject to appeals.

Clerical conflicts with the Revenue in the past have not been unknown. Before the First World War they went all the way up to the House of Lords for the decision that the parson's Easter offerings were subject to tax.[39] The offerings were attributed to the office of employment as distinct from the personal esteem in which the vicar was held. Thus they contrast with sportsmen's benefits from public subscriptions which are never subject to tax.[40]

The pathways down which the acceptable outlets for section 130 allowances are now recognised open up a permutation of highways and bye-ways not contemplated in the P.T.A. Memorandum. This is almost inevitable and understandable; because every tax situation and circumstance must be tailored to the individual taxpayer, whether individual, club or other unincorporated organisation, company or charity. Before identifying these possible and potential areas the following should always be borne in mind:

(a) the almost daily litigation and contemplated legislative changes;

(b) the appropriate facts;

(c) the attitude and response of the appropriate tax inspector;

(d) the financial necessity, capacity and will to pursue a claim all the way through the tribunal hierarchy already apparent from this chapter.

Those highways and bye-ways down which the section 130 allowances could travel and intersect may be summarised into eight headings which we look at below.

[37a] [1983] S.T.C. 665. See p. 264, n. 10.

[38] *White (Inspector of Taxes)* v. *Higginbottom* [1983] S.T.C. 143.

[39] *Blakiston* v. *Cooper* [1909] S.T.C. 347.

[40] See generally *Seymour* v. *Reed* [1927] 11 T.C. 554 at 645. *Moore* v. *Griffiths* [1972] 48 T.C. 338.

(1) PAYMENTS OF ESTEEM OR BENEFITS

For sponsors within section 130 of I.C.T.A. and for sponsees generally, payments of a non-contractual and unsolicited kind are usually allowed; but not if "stamped with the character of a trading receipt", as when a company trading as an ice rink was funded by a single donation from an associated curling· club,[41] and a professional jockey by a grateful winning owner.[42] Contract and even discretionary receipts are disallowed.[43]

(2) PAYMENTS IN KIND OR FRINGE BENEFITS

The problems of "boot money" income in amateur sport directed public attention during 1982 to what could be a breach of sporting governing body (*i.e.* Rugby Football Union) regulations although, as indicated above, a once-and-for all signing fee for a change of status from amateurism to professionalism would be held at present to be an allowable capital sum and not a taxable emolument as income. Such benefits are, however, validly apportionable in value for tax purposes. An employee provided with a suit was held assessable on the second-hand value.[44] The test for tax liability is whether it is capable of being converted into money or to pecuniary account.[45]

(3) LOSSES

Sponsors rather than sponsees will be affected by trading losses but allowances can be available to sponsees in respect of employment: any loss must arise from a trade or business being undertaken on a commercial business for profit-earning purposes. Depending upon the appropriate taxpayer's individual circumstances, relief is available under the I.C.T.A. in four different situations, thus:

    (a) through set-off against other income in the appropriate year of assessment;

---

[41] *I.R.C.* v. *Falkirk Ice Rink* [1975] S.T.C. 434.
[42] *Wing* v. *O'Connell* [1927] I.R. 84.
[43] See in addition to p. 273 above, *Davis* v. *Harrison* [1927] 11 T.C. 707 (soccer) and *Moorhouse* v. *Dooland* [1955] Ch. 284 (cricket).
[44] *Wilkins* v. *Rogerson* [1935] 19 T.C. 174.
[45] *Tennant* v. *Smith* [1892] 3 T.C. 158.

(b) by carry-forward against subsequent profits;
(c) by carry-back of losses in early years of trade; and
(d) on discontinuance terminating trade.

(4) INTELLECTUAL PROPERTY ALLOWANCES

Alphabetically they would appear under the heads of copyright, know-how, patents and trade mark. In the present context they are dealt with in ascending order of complexity.

(a) Patent fees and expenses are specifically provided for by section 132 of the I.C.T.A.

(b) Registration or the renewal of registration of a trade mark is allowed under section 132 of the I.C.T.A.

(c) Copyright: purchase expenses are not specifically provided for by statute, but subject to accountancy practice, they would either be an allowable trading expense, or, in the light of the *Munby* v. *Furlong* case concept of extending "plant" to "the intellectual storehouse" (*per* Lord Denning), allowable as a capital allowance item.

(d) Know-how has been subjected to statutory definition and litigation decisions varying in complexity. As is the case with industrial information or techniques, every situation will depend upon its own circumstances. The form of purchase will frequently be very relevant and should be framed within the appropriate tax structure. The document which represents the starting-point for any transaction is often the crucial evidence so far as tax liability is concerned.

(5) INVESTMENT

The border lines between investment and trade will require identification before resolving the question whether allowable tax relief is available..

(6) DOUBLE TAXATION

Company residence will be reviewed under proposed legislation contained in the Inland Revenue's publication of December 20, 1982 entitled *"Taxation of International Business."*

(7) OVERSEAS ENTERTAINMENT EXPENSES

Overseas customers may be entertained as an allowable expense but domestic customers may not. These statutory provisions[46] raise an important issue for future hopes in respect of sponsee developments. This exists because as is specified in the P.T.A. Memorandum for *sponsor's* expenses: "no deduction is allowable for any lump sum donation towards for example, the building or modernisation of a theatre, or the purchase of a work of art." This may well be changed by the courts or legislation in the foreseeable future because of the progressive developments indicated below.

(8) POSSIBLE LEGISLATIVE CHANGES AND FURTHER LITIGATION

With the development of sponsored company boxes and their ambience at entertainment arenas, the difference between overseas and domestic customers must be accepted, subject to the reasonability of claims. Furthermore, at present the disallowance of sponsors' contributions to buildings or modernisation must be recognised, too. What should not be overlooked however, is the shift in emphasis by the courts to capital allowances for plant which has been developing imperceptibly and was checked in the Burnley Football Club company's one quarter of a million pounds grandstand case.[47] The following situations have all qualified: moveable office partitions,[48] swimming pools for use on a caravan site,[49] grain silos,[50] and law books[51]; and more recently, by the House of Lords, lighting and decor in entertainment premises,[52] and, by the High Court, a building society's window display decoration screens.[53] The Burnley case failed, but what has escaped the notice of traditional commentators are four crucial elements in the earlier stages:

    (a) the distinguished Special Commissioners presided over by the then Presiding Commissioner, the late H.H. Monroe, Q.C., together with his associate Commis-

---

[46] I.C.T.A. 1970, s.411.
[47] *Brown* v. *Burnley Football and Athletic Co. Ltd.* [1980] S.T.C. 424.
[48] *Jarrold* v. *John Good & Sons* [1963] 40 T.C. 681.
[49] *Cooke* v. *Beach Station Caravans* [1974] 49 T.C. 514.
[50] *Schofield* v. *R & H Hall* [1974] 49 T.C. 538.
[51] *Munby* v. *Furlong* [1977] 1 Ch. 359.
[52] *I.R.C.* v. *Scottish & Newcastle Breweries* [1982] S.T.C. 296.
[53] *Leeds Permanent Building Society* v. *Proctor* [1982] S.T.C. 821.

sioner, Mr. R.H. Widdows, found as a fact that the new Burnley football club grandstand qualified for a repair allowance, although it was disallowed under the head of plant;

(b) the single High Court judge disagreed with this finding of fact and overruled the Special Commissioners;

(c) no higher appeal was lodged in the manner which ultimately succeeded with F.A. Youth Trust charity appeals via the Court of Appeal to the House of Lords;

(d) although evidence was tendered from the football company's architect that he advised the new stand because of the unsafe condition of its predecessors, no evidence was required under the Safety of Sports Grounds Act 1975. This safety statute was not enforceable at the date of the Burnley assessment, and also not applicable at that time were the present retrospective effects of section 40 of the Finance Act 1978, upon section 49 of the Finance (No. 2) Act 1975. These treat for capital allowance purposes certain expenditure on buildings as being on plant (unless a deduction could be obtained elsewhere) to which the safety statute applies.

Finally, in the appropriate circumstances it is conceivable that claims could exist for a capital allowance in respect of user as a sports industrial building,[54] or for an investment allowance under the new Government Business Expansion Scheme,[55] with which the two Finance Acts of 1983 replaced the earlier Business Start-up Scheme. Any or all of these allowances could justify legitimately arguable claims to be made in the right circumstances for the progressive experiments and initiatives which are rapidly emerging throughout the growth leisure industry for artificial playing surfaces, multi-user all purpose covered sports stadia, arenas and theatre complexes, and leisure/recreation centres generally. Thus on different evidence and in similar circumstances, and in the light of the line of the developing decisions cited above, sponsees on the right set of facts with the right financial support should be prepared for a re-play of the *Burnley* case to establish that in the right situation "the building or modernisation of" an entertainment centre could qualify for tax relief. If that and all else fails, then Parliament should be

[54] Capital Allowances Act 1968, s.10; Finance (No. 2) Act 1975, s.49.
[55] Finance Act 1983, s.26, Sched.5; Finance (No. 2) Act 1983, s.5, Sched. 2.

lobbied to change the law in the community's interest, which happened with the successful campaign to abolish entertainment tax.[56]

There is one final business expense outside the section 130 of the I.C.T.A. and P.T.A. Memorandum ambit which leads back to the mixed business charity sphere; and that is expenditure on scientific and educational research. If it falls within a recurring revenue nature then it qualifies under section 90 of the Capital Allowances Act 1968. If it is of a capital nature then it qualifies under the same statute for a special capital allowance.

The Revenue concession granted as long ago as the *Bourne & Hollingsworth* decision is epitomised in the last paragraph of the P.T.A. Memorandum under the head of "Business Expenses." Structured negatively it concludes with the recognised categories of communal benefits designating charitable status:

"Apart from the generally 'wholly and exclusively' test for business expenses there is a special tax rule which disallows gifts in computing business profits. From 1980–81 a gift to charity which would otherwise be allowable will not be disallowed by the rule about business entertaining and gifts. This replaces in part the existing extra-statutory concession which continues to apply to gifts which are reasonably small in relation to the donor's business, satisfy the wholly and exclusively rule and are made to a local body established for educational, cultural, religious, recreational or benevolent purposes."[57]

These last words lead logically and naturally to the second principal head of covenanted payments found in the P.T.A. Memorandum.

Covenanted payments—qualification for tax relief

Here the P.T.A. Memorandum is comprehensive if set against a background which presupposes a built-in knowledge of United Kingdom charitable status. It points out as evidence before an investigation into *Public and Private*

---

[56] A.P. Herbert (later Sir Alan), *No Fine on Fun* (1957).
[57] See P.T.A. Memorandum, Appendix III.

Funding of the Arts; that "Many of the bodies which promote activities in the field of the arts are established charities."

The world of sport was not covered by the inquiries' terms of reference or directly by its evidence. For a mixture of reasons mentioned hereafter sport has been slower than the Arts in alerting itself and those affected by it to the undoubted tax relief advantages of charitable status. These comprise relief partly or wholly derived from the effects of (alphabetically): capital gains tax; capital transfer tax; corporation tax; development land tax; income tax and local authority rating tax.[58] These reliefs are not limited to Sport, Arts or Leisure, but for present purposes and the P.T.A. Memorandum this chapter is concerned with those topics alone.

Consistent with tax law generally, there is an amalgam of statutory, judicial and administrative sources which must be recognised. Statute, judicial interpretation, Charity Commission registration, Inland Revenue option to object, and public interest, all interact between and on each other. Legislatively the origins are contained in the celebrated statute passed in the reign of Elizabeth 1 in 1601.[59] These were refined judicially by Lord MacNaghten in the no less celebrated case of *The Commissioners for special purposes of the Income Tax* v. *Pemsel*[60]; then partly codified, and clumsily so, by Parliament in the little-used Recreational Charities Act 1958, and followed by the Charities Act in 1960, with its built-in powers of registration by the Charity Commissioners and objection to such registration by the Inland Revenue.

For nearly a century the yardstick or measure of qualification for valid charitable status has been Lord MacNaghten's four principal divisions in *Pemsel's Case* of trusts for
  (a) relief of poverty,
  (b) advancement of education,
  (c) advancement of religion, and
  (d) other purposes beneficial to the community.
Those heads identify the substantive foundation. The F.A. Youth Trust Deed case illuminates the procedural

---

[58] Rates from non-charitable sources comprise a form of local authority taxation which cannot be ignored when completing sponsorship deals affecting, for example, rate paying occupiers on whose land perimeter advertising boards are sited.

[59] 43 Eliz. 1, c. 4.

[60] [1891] A.C. 531.

framework.[61] The Deed was registered by the Charity Commissioners in 1972. The Inland Revenue lodged objections to it. They were upheld by Walton, J.[62]; confirmed by a majority of two to one in the Court of Appeal in 1979,[63] but ultimately reversed unanimously by the House of Lords in 1980. Thus three judges supported the Revenue, six the Charity Commissioners and the F.A.; but without funding from the Sports Council and the Central Council of Physical Recreation, the law would have remained as it was before Walton J. adjudicated.[64] Indeed, the New South Wales Equity Court in *Kearins* v. *Kearins*[65] during 1957, an authority not cited in any of the F.A. Youth Trust arguments or judgments, had followed the Aldenham School decision[66] and accepted a bequest to Sydney University Rugby Club as being validly charitable. Thus to an extent the law depends upon which courts are invited by litigants to rule upon it, which in turn depends upon those who can afford litigation.

The P.T.A. Memorandum explains in the following manner, broken down into sub-paragraphs for ease of presentation, how the *covenanted payments* arrangements are recognised through the Revenue's eyes. For the sake of clarity we have sub-divided the Revenue's statement into its application first, to companies and secondly to individuals.

(1) COMPANIES

(i) "An annual payment by a company to such a charity (*i.e.* an established charity registered by the Charity Commissioners) under an irrevocable disposition or covenant covering a period of more than 3 years (up to 5th April 1980 the period was more than 6 years) is deductible in computing total profits for corporation tax purposes."

The source of this arrangement is section 248 of the I.C.T.A. as amended by section 55(3) of the Finance Act 1980.

---

[61] *I.R.C.* v. *McMullen* [1981] A.C. 1.
[62] [1978] 1 W.L.R. 664.
[63] [1979] 1 W.L.R. 130.
[64] *i.e.* against extending education to limited age groups in physical education and upholding a First World War decision about a fives court at Aldenham School *Re Mariette* [1915] 2 Ch. 284.
[65] (1957) S.R. 286 (N.S.W.).
[66] *Re Mariette, supra.*

> (ii) "The company makes the covenanted payments under deduction of tax but the charity claims repayment of the tax deducted from the Inland Revenue."

Thus the company's payments will be a charge on income and thereby deductible by the company in computing its liability to corporation tax. The company deducts tax at the basic rate, hands it over to the Inland Revenue, from whom the charity claims the refund. Close companies which comprise many private family companies are specifically provided for and warned about their special position in the subsequent paragraph of the P.T.A. Memorandum.

(2) INDIVIDUALS

> (i) "A similar payment by an individual qualifies for income tax relief at the basic rate of income tax and the relief is effectively obtained by the taxpayer deducting tax at the basic rate and retaining it when he makes the payment."

The individual donor personally saves no tax in the manner permitted to a trading company, but the charity obtains the benefit and in substance receives the gross amount which would have been paid without deduction by the taxpayer. Practical requirements by the Revenue of evidence of payment and deduction of tax and other formalities are inevitable aspects of the mechanism, for which professional individual advice is presumed to exist by the P.T.A. Memorandum.

> (ii) "From 1981–82 onwards income tax relief at the higher rates and for the investment income surcharge is allowed to individuals in respect of charitable covenants, subject to a ceiling relief for payments of [£5,000] per annum.[67] In order to pass on this relief to the charities themselves covenantors will need to increase their net giving since tax will continue to be deductible at the basic rate only from the annual payments. Relief at the higher rates and for the investment income surcharge is given to the covenantor."

[67] The figure for exemption of covenanted payments from excess tax liability has been increased to £5,000 from £3,000 by the Finance Act 1983, s.23.

This concession leaves the private donor at a disadvantage compared to a company's computation of liability; and the House of Commons Select Committee in its October 1982 Report after citing evidence of limited individual covenanting recommended that "Donations from individuals to non-profit arts organisations up to 10 per cent. of pre-tax income should be tax-deductible on an annual basis."[68] Not surprisingly the Goodman Committee on Charity Law and Voluntary Organisation in 1976 concluded similarly, even "up to a possible maximum of [individuals] total incomes."[69]

(3) CLOSE COMPANIES

Finally, under the P.T.A. Memorandum dealing with covenanted payments, its concluding paragraph covers the "close company" which affects the majority of private companies, controlled by five or fewer participators or participators who are directors. The Goodman Committee acknowledged the problem[70] because of the tax liability created by covenanted donations being regarded as distributions to shareholders "thereby attracting taxation at higher rates." It was recitified by section 56(4) of the Finance Act 1980, which added section 457(1A) to the I.C.T.A.[71] Significantly, the Memorandum's paragraph ends with an acknowledgment to the controlling aspect of company tax allowances, whether for a close company or otherwise: "where a covenanted payment is made wholly and exclusively for the purpose of the company's trade, no such apportionment is made," *i.e.* it will be treated under a section 130 I.C.T.A. expenditure. Shorn of this concluding reference to the section 130 situation, the close company P.T.A. statement falls into two separate sentences (with our own sub-divisions) thus:

> (i) "covenanted payments qualify for relief from corporation tax; but for years up to 1980–81 inclusive [*i.e.* prior to the Finance Act 1980 amendment, cited above] if the payments were deducted in arriving at the company's distributable income, relief from income tax

---

[68] Eighth Report from the Education, Science and Arts Committee on the Public and Private Funding of the Arts Session 1981–1982 (1982; H.C. 49–II), para. 59, p. cxxviii.

[69] Report of the Goodman Committee, para. 123, p. 54.

[70] *Ibid.* para. 125, p. 55.

[71] With effect from April 6, 1981, as specified in the P.T.A. Memorandum.

was restricted to the basic rate by apportioning the gross amount of the payments amongst the company's participators and charging them to tax at the excess (if any) of their personal tax rates over the basic rate."

This was the position causing concern to the Goodman Committee. The consequences of reform are summarised in the P.T.A. Memorandum thus:

(ii) "As a consequence of the allowance of relief at the higher rates and the investment income surcharge from 1981–82, covenanted sums paid by close companies to charities from 6 April 1981 will cease to be apportioned to a participator if the amount to be apportioned to that participator added to amounts of other charitable covenants, made personally or apportioned from other close companies, does not exceed £5,000."[72]

The significance of this particular relief in manner contemplated by the Goodman Committee Report is not for enabling charities to recover more than basic tax rates. The emphasis is encouragement to private close company covenantors to make greater contributions with no additional costs to themselves. Here as with every stage of sponsorship tax issues, individual advice is anticipated.

The remainder of the P.T.A. Memorandum covers the permutations of tax reliefs for gifts which were prepared for the enquiry entitled, *Public and Private Funding of the Arts.* As they relate to more limited (but no less important cultural) areas than business expenses and covenanted payments are generally recognised to cover, they have been reproduced for their authoritative sources and authenticity verbatim in Appendix III without detailed comment here. Cumulatively they contributed to many of the 77 trenchant Recommendations summarised in the House of Commons Select Committee's October 1982 Report,[73] which incorporated its earlier Interim Reports' proposals on tax and VAT issues. As we shall see in the VAT section below,[74] one beneficial result has occurred already at the National Heritage VAT level. Another has been H.M. Treasury's July 1983 publication, concurrent with a shorter one from the Office of

---

[72] This sum was increased to £5,000 from £3,000 by the Finance Act 1983, s.23.
[73] Eighth Report, *supra.* Vol. 1, pp. cxxiv–cxxix. See below, p. 306–309.
[74] See below, p. 286.

Arts and Libraries on *Capital Taxation and the National Heritage*.

Treasury transactions with donors of gifts in lieu of tax debts create a Government subsidy rather than a sponsorship situation. How to balance the proportion of tax to be commuted has sustained a continuing debate before, during and since the preparation of this chapter between successive Governments, the House of Commons Committee, and all interested parties, which may never end.[75]

CHARITY COMPANY FORMATION

One final area of charitable tax relief is not covered by the P.T.A. Memorandum, namely the creation of a company for charitable sponsorship activities, subject to satisfying the tests for charitable trading under section 360(1)(*e*) of the I.C.T.A. These create tax relief only if the profits are applied solely to the purpose of the charity and either

(i) the trade is exercised in the course of the actual carrying out of one of the primary purposes of the charity, or

(ii) the work in connection with the trade is mainly carried out by beneficiaries of the charity.

The company's structure would be formed by the charity holding shares in the company through its trustees or nominees. The company would covenant to pay the charity sums equal to its profits, and such payments would be charges on income and therefore be deductible. Two contrasting examples from Glasgow illustrate the application of this course.

A music festival's admission profits were attributed to the "trade" which was carried on mainly by the beneficiaries of the charity, the choir competitors.[76] Profits of an annual sports meeting not limited to an age group which, if it had been, would have qualified for a conventional education bracket, were not exempt.[77] Even the progressive approach of the House of Lords to physical education in the *F.A. Youth Trust Deed Case* would probably not have saved this particular fund. Sport as such is not charitable; nor is art or any other generic concept. Within one of the four heads of

---

[75] See the letter from Mr. Hugh Leggatt, Honorary Secretary of *Heritage in Danger*, in the *Daily Telegraph*, September 6, 1983.

[76] *I.R.C.* v. *Glasgow Musical Festival Association* [1926] 11 T.C. 154.

[77] *I.R.C.* v. *Glasgow (City) Police Athletic Association* [1953] 34 T.C. 76.

poverty, education, religion or general communal good, a start can be made. If an organisation such as the police or any other equivalent Athletic Association were to "hive off" its activities into a sub-structure acceptable within the recognised categories, then relief would be available. In the end, the Charity Commissioners guidance, subject always to no Revenue objection, would be the ultimate practical safeguard.

Conclusions on Tax

Without over-elaborating the procedural and costs elements which underline the mechanics for operating the United Kingdom tax laws in relation to sponsorship, what may be identified as a *leitmotiv* is the application of Maitland's reminder of Maine's celebrated dictum: "The substantive law of the realm is secreted in the interstices of procedure." Without the spiral of litigation levels, the law would be left as regulated by Parliament. The position of VAT is no less complex; but time has not yet allowed or created in respect of VAT the same degree of legal undergrowth which blocks and hinders the paths of taxpayers and, indeed, of tax gatherers, too.

Value Added Tax

INTRODUCTORY

Value Added Tax, known as VAT, became part of Britain's statute law on April 1, 1973. It is innovative in that those responsible for paying the tax have to act as their own assessors to some extent, rather than having that aspect of their work done completely by tax inspectors. Politically, it was introduced to harmonise Britain's indirect taxes with other members of the European Economic Community. Historically, it was introduced to replace the old purchase and selective employment taxes. Administratively, it creates problems of cost effective labour. Pragmatically, and practically it is here to stay unless and until in relation to the areas of Arts, sport and leisure it can be made to follow its predecessors of entertainment tax and purchase tax and disappear entirely. Indeed, an Interim (Third) Report from the House of Commons Committee recommended progressive modification and ultimate exemption by 1985 of VAT on "all cultural services which are in the public interest."[78] The initial Government response to that Interim Report was to reject it, on grounds of difficulties of definition and preferential reliance on "direct assistance in the form of grants,"[79] and, by inference to recreation as well as to the Arts sector for public funded bounty and benefit.

There was a similar initial resistance to the campaigns which ultimately achieved abolition of the old entertainment and purchase taxes on the Arts and recreation; but an encouraging early response to that Interim (Third) Report's Recommendation has already appeared during the preparation of this chapter with the Value Added Tax (Works of Arts, Etc.) Order 1983,[79a] which came into operation on May 31, 1983. Subsequently it has been absorbed into the sixth Schedule[79b] to the consolidating Value Added Tax Act, 1983, which came into force on October 26, 1983. The effect of this legislation has been to exempt from VAT those cultural objects such as manuscripts, paintings and properties, which are accepted in satisfaction of other capital tax debts or sold by private treaty (under what are known as the much criticised douceur arrangements) to those national bodies such as the National Gallery and the British Museum, all of which are listed in Annex 1 to the P.T.A. Memorandum and set out formally in paragraph 12 of the sixth Schedule to the Finance Act, 1975.[80] It does *NOT* cover other disposals of works of art, etc., which are distinguishable from those to national heritage bodies. These continue to be taxable under normal VAT business transaction requirements.

VAT AND SPONSORSHIP

(a) *Registrable business services*

VAT applies to all services supplied by businesses which are registrable. The turnover level for registration is reviewed annually. Since this chapter began it has been increased from the amount of £15,000 under the Finance Act 1982 to £18,000 during 1983. If there is no business activity there is no supply of services. Sponsorship is a commercial business arrange-

---

[78] [1981; H.C. 239].
[79] See [1982] B.T.R. 962. For definition difficulties, see T.S. Eliot, *Notes Towards the Definition of Culture* (1948).
[79a] (S.I. 1983 No. 809).
[79b] Group II, Sched. 6.
[80] See Appendix III, p. 309 below.

ment comprising a payment for services supplied by the sponsee. Thereby it creates a potentially taxable supply. Whether or not VAT has to be charged, and with what effect if it is applicable, depends on the VAT status of both the sponsor and the sponsored recipient beneficiary (sponsee) and the true nature of the business deal.

Three recent cases contrast the applicability or non-applicability of VAT to essentially recreational situations.

A highly technical legal decision[81] in the High Court confirmed an assessment by Commissioners of Customs and Excise, upheld by a VAT tribunal, that a time-sharing holiday cottage agreement for one week in each year over a period of 80 years did not comprise a zero-rated supply. It did not satisfy the real property test of "a tenancy for a term exceeding 21 years"[82] and therefore the land-owner appellants were assessable, as providing a supply of services, for value-added tax at the standard rate. In an earlier finding a landowner had granted sporting rights to shoot to friends and relatives, who, in turn, would pay a fee for such rights. A supply of services undoubtedly was admitted by the landowner. The Customs and Excise contended that the business of supplying shooting rights was being carried on. Evidence was tendered before the VAT tribunal by the taxpayer and his accountant with documents and accounts. The tribunal found as a fact first that no advertisements sought guns or, save for one exception, a letting of the shoot; and secondly that the invitees were as already stated *i.e.* friends and relatives, and thus no business supply of services existed. The High Court confirmed the tribunal's finding and dismissed the Customs and Excise appeal. Sporting supplies without the key business element therefore did not require registration and VAT.[83]

Finally, prior to both of these High Court decisions, a VAT Tribunal upheld an appeal against the assessment of the Commissioners of Customs and Excise of a recreational bowling club. It operated and was affiliated to the national governing bodies under its two separate sections, indoors and general: the English Indoor Bowling Association [EIBA] and the English Bowling Association [EBA]. They were assessed

---

[81] *Cottage Holiday Associates Ltd.* v. *Customs & Excise Commissioners* [1983] S.T.C. 278.

[82] Construed from the definition section Finance Act 1972, s.46(1) and item 1 of group 8, Sched. 4, as amended by the Finance Act 1977, para. 19 of Sched. 6.

[83] *Customs and Excise Commissioners* v. *Lord Fisher* [1981] S.T.C. 238.

together as an entity. Each separately had an insufficient level of turnover to justify mandatory registration. The Tribunal upheld their contentions that *neither* was liable to register for VAT purposes.[84]

The application of VAT to sponsorship business supplies must differentiate between the sponsor, the sponsee and any sponsoring agency, and also in relation to United Kingdom and overseas services.

(b) *Sponsor*

(i) *Non-registered.* Even if, contrary to the usual expectations, a sponsor is itself or himself not registered for VAT because the amount of its or his own taxable supplies is below the registration threshold of £18,000 then the sponsor nevertheless will be obliged to pay VAT tax on any supplies provided by any registered sponsee under a sponsor-deal. At present the amount is 15 per cent. In such circumstances no reclaim by the non-registered sponsor will be available. Usually this will occur with a relatively small or exempted supplying sponsor.

(ii) *Registered.* If the sponsor is registered for VAT, then the sponsoring company or individual will be able to treat VAT payment charged on the sponsorship fee as an input and offset this against the sponsor's own VAT output paid by customers or traders to the sponsor on the sponsor's own supplies, or alternatively reclaim it from the Customs and Excise. The VAT in these circumstances does not enter the profit and loss account, acting in effect as a posting box for the Customs and Excise, and passing it on to the sponsored beneficiary.

(iii) *Apportionments and partial exemptions.* Exempt or partially exempt potential business sponsors include banks, bookmakers, building societies, insurance companies and certain property companies. Partial exemption entitles the supplier to apportion between taxable and exempt supplies; but the sponsee's if registered to charge VAT remains. Any percentage amount which the sponsor cannot apportion

---

[84] *A.G. Hayhoe* (*On behalf of Watchet Bowling Club and Watchet Indoor Bowling Club*) v. *Customs and Excise Commissioners*, VAT Tribunal ref. LON/80/341, January 13, 1981 (unreported).

against its or his own taxable supplies will have to be provided or borne personally.

(c) *Sponsee*

Three situations potentionally arise.

(i) *Non-registered.* The non-registered sponsee whose sponsored monies do not bring the sponsorship payment within the present £18,000 registration threshold does not charge VAT on the sponsorship payment involved in the transaction.

(ii) *Non-registered until sponsored payments.* If the sponsorship payment will bring the sponsored beneficiary into the VAT area then the sponsored recipient should register and VAT tax of 15 per cent. should be added. If it is not added in this circumstance the sponsored beneficiary will be obliged to account to Customs and Excise for the VAT tax and the sponsored payment will be reduced accordingly, *i.e.* the sponsored payment will be deemed to include VAT at the current rate.

(iii) *Registered.* When the sponsee registered before the sponsorship deal is arranged, then disclosure should be made at the earliest stage of negotiations to enable the VAT payment to be incorporated in the final agreed amount for payment.

(iv) *Agents, clubs, unincorporated associations, charities and overseas.* Third party interventions from agencies or other entrepeneurs does not affect the basic VAT liability between sponsor and sponsee. Theatrical agents illustrate the Customs & Excise acknowledgment of specialised practices. Those who contract with artistes for an agreed period and fee known as a Nett Act or Nett Deal can refer to a special VAT leaflet No. 710/1/83 explaining briefly how they should account for VAT.

The agent or third party's position if liable to VAT as a supplier of business services is accountable for VAT on commission received from either party. The same position applies to a Club or other unincorporated association providing taxable supplies to an amount above the registrable limits, with recognition of the possible advantages, if appropriate, from sectional divisions within a club, as illustrated by the indoor and general recreational bowling citation above.[84a]

Charities have not yet succeeded in their understandable campaign for general relief from VAT. Certain specific reliefs relate to disabled, medical, poverty and youth club services. Their VAT position should be checked and investigated before any sponsorship deal with such sources is concluded.

Overseas trading generally is not subject to VAT but at the time of writing a twelfth EEC Directive is contemplating altering this. The crucial test is where the services are supplied. The location of the supplier is the crucial test, and this neutral description is chosen here deliberately. Practising and academic lawyers know the practical and difficult distinctions between residence and domicile, and for this purpose where the balance of activity exists. Again, ascertainment of the true position is essential. Thus, the Celtic Football Club in Glasgow successfully appealed to the Scottish Court of Session that business entertainment expenses of hotel accommodation for overseas matches and club officials should be allowed as recoverable input tax. They were obligatory under the European Cup rules of UEFA.[85]

(v) *Conclusion.* H.M. Customs and Excise VAT Leaflet No. 701/5/81 provides specific guidance in an Annex[86] to it in respect of Sponsorship rights as follows (with our own restructuring and numbering):

> "The tax value for the supply of sponsorship rights includes:
> (1) not only the money received from the sponsor but also
> (2) (a) any payments made by the sponsor to third parties in respect of the expenses of staging a competition or event and
> (b) and the value of any prizes given to the team competitors taking part under the terms of the sponsorship agreement."

If any doubts exist about the extent of the VAT liability or issue then the local H.M. Customs and Excise offices should

---

[84a] See p. 288, n.84.
[85] *Celtic Football & Athletic Co. Ltd.* v. *Customs & Excise Commissioners* [1983] S.T.C. 420.
[86] See H.M. Customs and Excise VAT leaflet, No. 701/5/81, Annex, p. 10.

be consulted for such guidance as the absence of any judicial decision allows. The three examples cited at the outset here indicate the potential areas for differences of interpretation which could arise. They will inevitably be expanded as the sponsorship explosion will dominate for ever the future worlds of sport, Arts and leisure.

Appendix I

A: Short form precedent of sponsorship contract

To Bethersden P.T.A.
[Address]

Dear Sirs,

I have summarised below the basic terms and conditions which apply to Sponsorship by our company, X Co. Ltd. (hereinafter X Co.) of the Arts Exhibition which you the Bethersden Parent Teachers Association (hereinafter P.T.A.) are holding at Bethersden Village Hall on July 21, 1984 (hereinafter the Exhibition).

Please sign both copies of this letter in the space indicated below in acknowledgement of our agreement and return one copy to us. You should retain the second copy for your own files.

(1) In consideration of X. Co. paying the P.T.A £500 the P.T.A. has agreed that X Co. shall have the following rights in relation to the Exhibition:

  (a) the Exhibition shall be called the *X Co. Art Exhibition* and the P.T.A. shall refer to the Exhibition by this title;

  (b) X Co. shall have the right to erect a banner in the entrance area of the Exhibition containing its name and welcoming the public to the Exhibition;

  (c) X Co. shall receive a credit in the Exhibition catalogue as sponsor of the Exhibition;

  (d) X Co. shall have the right to host at its cost a private preview at the Exhibition on July 22, 1984 at which employees and guests of X Co. may attend;

  (e) the Chairman of X Co. shall present the prizes at the end of the Exhibition

(2) It is understood that no other commercial organization shall acquire any sponsorship rights from the P.T.A. in relation to the Exhibition.

(3) The £500 shall be payable as to £250 on receipt by X Co. of the copy of this letter duly signed by the P.T.A. and £250 on the day following closure of the Exhibition whereupon this agreement shall terminate.

Yours sincerely

....

for and on behalf
of X Co.

accepted for
and on behalf
of the P.T.A.

B: Long form precedent of sponsorship contract

This Agreement is made the   day of   1984 by and between

X Company Limited, a Company incorporated in accordance with the laws of England with its registered office situated at The Mall, Kensington (hereinafter called Company), and

the Organizing Committee of the English Marathon, an unincorporated Association whose address is 3, The Hove, Worthing (hereinafter called Org. Comm.) who have duly empowered (its president) in accordance with its constitution to execute this agreement in its name and on its behalf, and

whereas Org. Comm. are responsible for holding the 1983 English Marathon on the 12 June 1984 at Bethersden Kent (hereinafter The Marathon), and

whereas Org. Comm. owns various valuable commercial rights and licences in relation to the Marathon, and

whereas Company wishes to promote its name and products in association with the Marathon by acquiring a defined package of rights and licenses (hereinafter called the Main Sponsor Package),

now therefore it has been agreed:

293

1. *Grant*

1. (1)   Org. Comm. hereby grants to Company the rights and licences listed below in relation to the Marathon for the promotion of Widgets (hereinafter called Company Products). The said rights and licences may be exercised worldwide by Company and shall, unless otherwise stated, be exclusive to Company in that Org. Comm. undertakes not to grant any of the rights and licenses which comprise the Main Sponsor Package to companies or other entities engaged in the manufacture or sale of Widgets except Company.

1. (2)   The rights and licences which comprise the Main Sponsor Package granted hereunder for the inclusive consideration specified in paragraph 5 hereof are as follows:

1. (2) 1.   the right to display a banner bearing the name of Company and or representations of Company Products to be positioned over the finish line of the Marathon;

1. (2) 2.   a royalty free licence to use the official commercial symbol of the Marathon (hereinafter called the Mark) on Company Products, stationery and in promotional or advertising campaigns reasonably related thereto. Copies of the Mark will be supplied to Company as soon as possible;

1. (2) 3.   one full page of advertising for Company Products in the official Marathon programme and official results publication;

1. (2) 4.   the right to display Company Products at the trade exhibition at the Marathon;

1. (2) 5.   the right to present a trophy at an official ceremony or other suitable occasion to be known as the "Co. Trophy" to the male Marathon winner;

1. (2) 6.   guaranteed entry to the Marathon for at least 5 Company employees or their nominees;

1. (2) 7.   the right and licence to use the title "Official Supplier of Widgets" to the Marathon;

1. (2) 8.   hospitality facilities for executives of Company and their V.I.P. guests at the Marathon together with access to 5 V.I.P. seats in the finish area of the Marathon.

2. Restrictions on Company

The rights and licences granted herein must be exercised subject to any consents, permissions or approvals required herein and in accordance with the rules and regulations applicable to the Marathon, including without limitation, those of the broadcasting authorities the Org. Comm. or its governing sports and federations, the advertising standards and laws of the countries in which any of said rights and licences may be exercised. Company shall be responsible for complying with these matters and therefore it is understood that Company shall exercise the rights and licences granted herein at its sole risk. Org. Comm. shall supply Company with details of such rules and regulations where they become known to Org. Comm. from time to time.

3. Company undertakings

3. (1)   Company agrees to make available on loan Company Products in sufficient quantities to satisfy the normal requirements of the Org. Comm. on the day of the Marathon. The said Company Products shall be installed in the finish area at the Marathon and shall be available for use by the Press, V.I.P.s and officials attending the Marathon.

3. (2)   Company agrees to assist Org. Comm. in controlling and protecting the ownership and goodwill in, or attaching to, the Mark and other proprietary rights licensed herein by undertaking: (a) to reproduce the appropriate Trade Mark or Coyright notice as advised in writing by Org. Comm. wherever a usage takes place; (b) to provide samples and artwork related to any usage or intended usage when requested in writing by Org. Comm.; (c) to report to Org. Comm. any unauthorised use of these rights that comes to its attention; (d) to co-operate fully and at its expense in any prudent action taken against unauthorised or pirate users; and (e) to use the Mark only on Company Products of equivalent standards of quality to those previously approved by Org. Comm.

3. (3)   In order to protect exclusivity of other companies who may acquire rights and licenses in relation to

the Marathon, Company undertakes that it shall not knowingly engage in joint promotions utilising the Mark or other rights licensed herein with any third parties (other than its own subsidiaries), without the prior written approval of Org. Comm.

4. *Org. Comm. obligations*

4. (1) Org. Comm. shall work with Company to develop at company's cost a guidance manual. The said manual shall provide full information such as data and statistics on the Marathon with suggestions on how the Company can obtain maximum use of the rights and licenses acquired herein.

4. (2) Org. Comm. undertakes to use its best efforts to maximise exposure of the Marathon and involvement of Company therein through television and other media and to keep Company advised from time to time of the progress thereof. To this end Org. Comm. shall ensure that all material within its control including press releases and handouts includes proper credits for Company as the main sponsor of the Marathon where appropriate. Further, Org. Comm. shall use its best efforts to encourage the media to give proper credits to Company as the main sponsor of the Marathon.

4. (3) Org. Comm. undertakes to use its best endeavours to prevent any obstructions being placed in front of Company banners.

4. (4) Org. Comm. shall nominate a member of its Executive as a liaison officer to co-ordinate the involvement of Company in the Marathon.

5. *Consideration*

In consideration of the rights and licences granted herein Company shall pay Org. Comm. the sum of £50,000 and provide Company Products, where appropriate under Paragraph 1. (2) 7. and 3. (1) hereof. Payment shall be made to following account at:

National Westminster Bank Ltd,
Bethersden Branch.

Account Name: England Marathon
Account No: 371
in accordance with the following schedule:

On signature	12,500
April 1	12,500
May 1	12,500
June 1	12,500

The financial consideration expressed herein excludes VAT, withholding or remittance taxes and therefore such taxes should they become due under applicable regulations shall be the responsibility of Company.

6. *Term*

This Agreement may only be terminated in the event: (a) that either Org. Comm. or Company enter into a composition or arrangement with their creditors, have a receiver extended in accordance with paragraph 8.

7. *Termination*

This Agreement may only be terminated in the event: (a) that either Org. Comm. or Company enter into a composition or arrangement with their creditors, have a receiver appointed or pass any resolution for winding up or a court order is made to that effect; (b) at election of Org. Comm. where Company fails to remedy a material breach of a term of this Agreement within 45 days of receipt of a written notice requiring said breach to be remedied; (c) at election of Company where Org. Comm. fails to remedy a material breach of this agreement within 45 days of receipt of written notice requiring the said breach to be remedied. Any such notice should be served at the respective addresses specified above. On expiry or termination all rights and licences shall revert forthwith to Org. Comm. and Company shall cease all and any use of the rights and licences granted herein.

8. *Option*

Org. Comm. hereby grants to Company the first right of refusal to acquire a main sponsorship package similar to the Main Sponsor Package in relation to any 1985 England marathon that Org. Comm. holds. Company shall have a period of 30 days in which to accept or decline the terms proposed by Org. Comm. for the involvement of Company in the said Marathon.

9. *Cancellation of the Marathon*

In the unlikely event that the Marathon or substantial parts thereof do not take place in 1984 for any reason beyond the control of Company then Org. Comm. and Company shall negotiate in good faith with a view to mutually agreeing upon an equitable reduction in the Consideration payable hereunder. Such reduction shall take into account the value received by Company from the exercise of all the rights and licences granted hereunder. If the parties fail to reach agreement then the matter shall be referred to arbitration in accordance with the Arbitration Act 1950 or any substitution thereof then in force. In no event shall Org. Comm. be obliged to return to Company more than the aggregate consideration payable by Company under the terms hereof less a 10 per cent allowance for administrative charges incurred by Org. Comm. in relation to the said Marathon.

10. *Assignment*

No assignment of this Agreement in whole or part shall take place without the written consent of both parties.

11. *Severability*

Should any term of this agreement be considered void or voidable under any applicable law then such term shall be severed or amended in such a manner so as to render the remainder of this agreement valid and enforceable unless the whole commercial object is thereby frustrated.

12. *Confidentiality*

Org. Comm. and Company agree to keep the financial contents of this agreement secret and confidential and no disclosure thereof may be made without the written consent of both parties.

13. *Entire understanding*

This Agreement contains the entire understanding between the parties and may not be varied orally.

14. *Proper law*

The interpretation, construction, validity and performance

of this Agreement shall be governed in all respects by English law.

Signed.....................
For and on behalf of
X Company Ltd.

Signed.....................
For and on behalf of
The Organizing Committee.

Appendix II

A: European Broadcasting Union (Regulations)

Recommendation concerning offers for Eurovision transmission involving sponsorship

The Administrative Council,

considering that some of the member organizations participating in Eurovision are not entitled, under their governing laws or statutes, to transmit sponsored programmes,

noting that sponsorship of sports and other events is steadily increasing, both in quantity and in intensity of advertising for the sponsor,

bearing in mind that, under their governing laws or statutes, most member organizations participating in Eurovision are obliged either to keep advertising separate from the rest of programming, or to exclude any advertising whatsoever from their programmes,

recognizing that potential relaying organizations need the greatest possible protection against transmitting unforeseen credits, advertisements, etc., which otherwise they would have objected to,

considering that the best way of affording such protection is by requesting the offering broadcasting organization to include in its offer the fullest possible information on any credits, advertisements, etc., which may be seen or heard during the course of the transmission.

recommends that whenever making an offer for Eurovision transmission involving some form of sponsorship or related practice, member organizations should include in their offer to the Geneva Permanent Services complete, detailed information, to the best of their ability, on any credits or other references to the sponsor or a similar outside party, or on any other manifestations of advertising referring to the sponsor or similar outside party, which may be seen or heard during the course of the transmission (for the purposes of this recom-

mendation all hereinafter referred to as "sponsorship"). Such information should in particular contain the following points:
1. Sponsored *programmes*
1.1 The specific *appearance* of the credits or references to the sponsor (e.g. "credit . . . ", "in collaboration with . . . ", "with kind support of . . . ", and the like; references to the sponsor's role, attitude, activities, products or services, etc. during the course of the programme; appearance of the sponsor's name or trademark on advertising panels, banners, etc.);
1.2 The *form* of the credits or references to the sponsor (sound or visual?);
1.3 The *timing* of the credits or references to the sponsor (e.g. immediately before or after the actual programme, any time within the course of the programme);
1.4 Only where applicable, the express *prohibition* for relaying organizations to *black out*, where technically possible, the credits or references to the sponsor. (Consequently, where no such indication is given, each relaying organization is entitled to black out, subject to national laws and rules of its respective country.)
2. Sponsored *events*
2.1 the specific *appearance* of the credits or references to the sponsor (e.g. "credit . . . ", "in collaboration with . . . ", "kindly sponsored by . . . ", and the like; references to the sponsor's role, attitude, activities, products or services etc. during the course of the event; appearance of the sponsor's name or trademark on advertising panels, banners, participants' clothes or equipment, etc.);
2.2 the *form* of the credits or references to the sponsor (sound or visual?);
2.3 the *timing* of the credits or references to the sponsor (e.g. immediately before or after the event, during the intermission, at no fixed points during the course of the event);
2.4 the *official name of the event and of the prize*, if any (e.g. "Harvey's Piano Competition", "Coca Cola Cup", "Colgate Masters' Grand Prix", etc.);
2.5 the *names of participants* which include some form of advertising (e.g. "The Marlboro Singers", a "Campari" football team, a horse named "Stuyvesant", etc.);
2.6 only where applicable, the express *prohibition* for relaying organizations to *black out*, where technically possible, the credits or references to the sponsor, to give the *event* and/or the *prize* and/or *participants* whose name includes

some form of advertising *a designation of their own.* (Consequently, where no such indication is given, each relaying organization is entitled to black out or give designations of its own, subject to national laws and rules of its respective country.)

2.7 As regards sponsored *sports* events, in addition to the information required under 2.1 to 2.6 above, the offering organization shall also indicate to what extent and in which particular respect, if at all, the *EBU principles on advertising* at venues for internationally televised sports events (Legal Collection No. 425.6) have not been complied with by the organizer of the event.

Sports events

ADVERTISING IN INTERNATIONAL TRANSMISSIONS

The Administrative Council decided to recommend active and supplementary active members to apply the following principles on advertising at the venues for internationally televised sports events and to request those members which are unable to apply the said principles to notify the Secretary General in writing without delay (Administrative Council decision of 10 December 1976; for comments, see circular SG 51 of 23 February 1977 and the Authentic interpretation forming item 425.7):

PRINCIPLES ON ADVERTISING AT VENUES FOR INTER-NATIONALLY TELEVISED SPORTS EVENTS

Active member organizations are recommended, where they originate an international television transmission of a sports event, to refuse to accept advertising which fails to comply with the principles set out below, which represent a minimum. Derogations from these principles should be allowed only exceptionally, in special cases, for reasons which are considered absolutely imperative by the said member organizations which will inform the Permanent Services of such derogations as promptly as possible.

1) Advertisements must not affect the quality of coverage or interfere with a complete and aesthetically satisfying view of the event for the television audience, for example by being placed on two or more tiers positioned in camera range.

2) Advertisements must not be positioned between the camera and the action.

3) The colours used for advertising must not adversely affect the television picture, and the use of fluorescent colours is banned. Luminous advertisements are likewise banned.

4) Advertisements must be placed on permanent supports forming an integral part of the venue and no occasional installations are allowed. This prohibition applies *mutatis mutandis* to cases where the event is staged at a venue without permanent installations.

Advertising on mobile supports such as banners, pennants, etc. is prohibited.

5) The size of the panels and of the advertisements must remain within limits compatible with a picture of the sports event entirely visible on the television screen from all angles.

6) No advertising may be made in sound during the transmissions.

7) Advertising must not infringe the national rules of the country where the sports event is staged.

8) Advertising must not be in a script which is not in use in the country where the sports event is staged. Advertising copy in a language other than the national language of the country where the event is staged is prohibited.

9) Advertising on clothing, equipment and the playing surface where the event is staged is prohibited in principle and will be allowed only where it has become customary for the type of sports event in question.

Appendix III: H.M. Treasury[1] Memorandum: Taxation in the Context of Private Sponsorship and of Gifts of Art Objects to Public and Private Institutions

Note by HM Treasury

1. This memorandum is provided for the Education, Science and Arts Committee in connection with its enquiry into the public and private funding of the arts. It sets out the position on sponsorship and gifts under present taxation arrangements and has been prepared in conjunction with the Inland Revenue.

PRIVATE SPONSORSHIP

Income and Corporation Taxes

2. A payment in sponsorship of the arts may qualify for tax relief in one of two ways:

> (i) *Covenanted payments.* Many of the bodies which promote activities in the field of the arts are established charities. An annual payment by a company to such a charity under an irrevocable disposition or covenant covering a period of more than 3 years (up to 5 April 1980 the period was more than 6 years) is deductible in computing total profits for corporation tax purposes. The company makes the covenanted payments under deduction of income tax but the charity claims repayment of the tax deducted from the Inland Revenue. A similar payment by an individual qualifies for income tax relief at the basic rate of income tax and the relief is effectively obtained by the taxpayer deducting tax at the basic rate and retaining it when he makes the payment. From 1981–82 onwards income tax relief

[1] Submitted to the Education, Science and Arts Committee of the House of Commons appointed under S.O. No. 86A: Eighth Report (1982; H.C. 49–II).

at the higher rates and for the investment income surcharge is allowed to individuals in respect of charitable covenants, subject to a ceiling relief on payments of £3,000 per annum.[2] In order to pass on this relief to the charities themselves covenantors will need to increase their net giving since tax will continue to be deductible at the *basic* rate only from the annual payments. Relief at the higher rates and for the investment income surcharge is given to the covenantor.

Where the company is a "close company" (broadly, a company controlled by 5 or fewer participators) covenanted payments qualify for relief from corporation tax; but for years up to 1980–81 inclusive, if the payments were deducted in arriving at the company's distributable income, relief from income tax was restricted to the basic rate by apportioning the gross amount of the payments amongst the company's participators and charging them to tax at the excess (if any) of their personal tax rates over the basic rate. As a consequence of the allowance of relief at the higher rates and the investment income surcharge from 1981–82, covenanted sums paid by close companies to charities from 6 April 1981 will cease to be apportioned to a participator if the amount to be apportioned to that participator added to amounts of other charitable covenants, made personally or apportioned from other close companies, does not exceed £3,000.[3] However, where a convenanted payment is made wholly and exclusively for the purposes of the company's trade, no such apportionment is made.

(ii) *Business expenses.* A sponsorship payment will normally be a deductible expense in computing business profits for tax purposes if it is of a revenue nature (i.e. not a capital payment) and is incurred wholly and exlusively for the purpose of the trade. The first condition means that no deduction is allowable for any lump sum donation towards, for

---

[2] Increased as from April 6, 1983 to £5,000 by the Finance Act 1983, s.23(1).

[3] Further increased as from April 6, 1983 by £5,000 by the Finance Act 1983, s.23(2).

example, the building or modernisation of a theatre, or the purchase of a work of art. The second condition means that the business purpose—generally advertising—must be the sole purpose for which the payment is made. The expenditure will not be admissible if it is incurred for a dual purpose—e.g. both promoting a business and promoting a charitable or benevolent object.

Apart from the general "wholly and exclusively" test for business expenses there is a special tax rule which disallows gifts in computing business profits. From 1980–81 a gift to charity which would otherwise be allowable will not be disallowed by the rule about business entertaining and gifts. This replaces in part the existing extra-statutory concession which continues to apply to gifts which are reasonably small in relation to the donor's business, satisfy the wholly and exclusively rule and are made to a local body established for educational, cultural, religious, recreational or benevolent purposes.

GIFTS

Capital transfer tax (CTT) and capital gains tax (CGT)

(a) *Outline of the taxes*

3. CTT is levied on a cumulative basis on all lifetime gifts and bequests on death. There is no charge until the cumulative total exceeds £50,000.

4. CGT is charged on lifetime gifts made other than to individuals to the extent that the market value of the gift exceeds the donor's acquisition costs. There is no CGT charge on death.

(b) *General exemptions for gifts*

5. The first £2,000 of gifts in each year is exempt from CTT as are all gifts not exceeding £250 in any one year to each of any number of donees. The first £3,000 of gains, including gains arising on gifts to persons other than individuals, in each year is exempt from CGT.

(c) *Detailed provision affecting gifts of works of art*

6. Gifts and bequests to charities and certain other bodies attract exemption from CTT and CGT as follows:

(i) *Gifts to charities*. Lifetime gifts to charities are exempt from CTT. But for gifts made within one year before death, and bequests on death, the exemption is limited to a total of £200,000.[4] There is no CGT charge on a lifetime gift to a charity.

(ii) *Gifts to Public Institutions*. All gifts and bequests to the bodies specified in paragraph 12 of Schedule 6 to the Finance Act 1975 (listed in the Annex hereto) are exempt from CTT and are not charged to CGT. In addition, where the gift or bequest is of a heritage object subject to conditional exemption from CTT and/or CGT in respect of a previous transfer (see paragraph 7 below), there is no clawback of the tax previously exempted.

(iii) *Other gifts for public benefit*. A gift of national heritage property to an appropriate non-profit making body may be exempted from CTT and CGT if the Treasury so direct. Eligible property is land of outstanding scenic, historic or scientific interest; buildings of outstanding historic or architectural, or aesthetic interest, together with land used as the grounds of such a building and chattels associated with the building; and any picture, print, book, manuscript, work of art or scientific collection of national, historic, scientific or artistic interest. The Treasury will have to be satisfied that the body concerned has the financial capacity to maintain the property. The body will have to have as one of its main aims the preservation of the property for public benefit, and undertakings will be required in respect of public access, maintenance and preservation. The donor can retain no interest for himself. In addition, when the property given or bequeathed has been conditionally exempt from CTT and/or CGT on a previous transfer (here again, see paragraph 7 below), there is no clawback of the tax previously exempted because the undertakings which the body is obliged to give are equivalent to those needed for conditional exemption.

---

[4] Increased as from March 9, 1982 to £250,000 by the Finance Act 1982, s.92(2) and abolished as from March 15, 1983 by the Finance (No. 2) Act 1983, s.9.

OTHER CAPITAL TAX RELIEFS FOR THE ARTS

7. Apart from reliefs for gifts described in paragraph 6 there are other CGT and CTT measures designed to encourage public enjoyment of works of art, and also outstanding buildings and land.

(i) *Conditional exemption.* Gifts, and bequests on death, of works of art and other national heritage objects, land of outstanding scenic, historic or scientific interest, buildings of outstanding historic or architectural interest (together with land which adjoins such a building and is essential for the protection of its character and amenities, and objects historically associated with such a building) can be exempted from CTT and CGT if certain conditions are met. The works of art and other objects eligible are "any pictures, prints, books, manuscripts, works of art, scientific collections or other things not yielding income which appear to the Treasury to be of national, scientific, historic or artistic interest". The Treasury is guided in this by expert advice from the national museums and galleries. An undertaking has to be given by an appropriate person broadly to the effect that reasonable steps will be taken to preserve the property and to secure reasonable public access to it. The CTT and CGT charges are reinstated if the undertaking is broken.

(ii) *Maintenance funds.* Conditionally exempt works of art are often displayed in historic houses which are themselves conditionally exempt. There is an exemption from CTT and CGT for transfers of property to a trust fund devoted to the maintenance of an outstanding historic house or its contents or adjoining amenity land, and such a fund is exempt from the CTT charge on capital distributions and the periodic charge on discretionary trusts.

(iii) *Acceptance in lieu and private treaty sales.* A sale by private treaty to a body specified in paragraph 12 of Schedule 6 to the Finance Act (see Annex 1) or the acceptance of a work of art (or outstanding building or land) in lieu of CTT payable, does not lead to the withdrawal of any previous exemption and there is no charge to CGT.

HERITAGE TAX RELIEFS

8. The capital taxation reliefs for national heritage property are explained in greater detail in the memorandum of guidance, *Capital Taxation and the National Heritage*, re-issued in December 1980,[5] copies of which have been circulated to the Committee.

HM TREASURY

13 January 1981

ANNEX I

BODIES LISTED[6] IN PARAGRAPH 12 OF SCHEDULE 6 TO THE FINANCE ACT 1975

The National Gallery
The British Museum
The Royal Scottish Museum
The National Museum of Wales
The Ulster Museum
Any other similar national institution which exists wholly or mainly for the purpose of preserving for the public benefit a collection of scientific, historic or artistic interest and which is approved for the purposes of this paragraph by the Treasury. (See Annex II).
Any museum or art gallery in the United Kingdom which exists wholly or mainly for that purpose and is maintained by a local authority or university in the United Kingdom.
Any library the main function of which is to serve the needs of teaching and research at a university in the United Kingdom.

---

[5] Further re-issued by HM Treasury July 1983, resulting from Recommendation 60 in the Education, Science and Arts Committee's report: (1982; H.C. 49–I).

[6] The statutory list of bodies specified in paragraph 12 of Schedule 6 to the Finance Act 1975 was not initiated by that Act. It began after the First World War with the appearance of the first two in the Finance Act 1921, s.44. Additions were made in subsequent fiscal statutes, and, even before the Memorandum dated January 13, 1981, the Finance Act 1980 in s.118(5) had added the National Heritage Memorial Fund. The list will inevitably be extended further, and an indication in that direction is the administrative restructuring of various approved bodies listed in Annex II by the National Heritage Act 1983.

The National Trust for Places of Historic Interest or Natural Beauty
The National Trust for Scotland for Places of Historic Interest or Natural Beauty
The National Art Collections Fund
The Trustees of the National Heritage Memorial Fund
The Friends of the National Libraries
The Historic Churches Preservation Trust
The Nature Conservancy Council
Any local authority (Note: this includes National Park Authorities)
Any Government Department (including the National Debt Commissioners)

ANNEX II

BODIES APPROVED AS SIMILAR NATIONAL INSTITUTIONS

British Museum
   (Natural History)
Science Museum
Victoria and Albert Museum
Imperial War Museum
London Museum
National Maritime Museum
National Portrait Gallery
Tate Gallery
The British Library
National Army Museum
Royal Marine Museum
Submarine Museum

Wallace Collection
Geological Museum
National Galleries of Scotland
National Museum of
   Antiquities of Scotland
National Library of Scotland
National Library of Wales
Ulster Museum
Ulster Folk Museum
Tower Armouries
RAF Museum
Fleet Air Arm Museum

Appendix IV: Income and Corporation Taxes Act 1970, s.130

Chapter IV

Trades, Professions and Vocations: Computational Provisions

General provisions

130. General rules as to deductions not allowable

Subject to the provisions of the Tax Acts, in computing the amount of the profits or gains to be charged under Case I or Case II of Schedule D, no sum shall be deducted in respect of—

(a) any disbursements or expenses, not being money wholly and exclusively laid out or expended for the purposes of the trade, profession or vocation,

(b) any disbursements or expenses of maintenance of the parties, their families or establishments, or any sums expended for any other domestic or private purposes distinct from the purposes of the trade, profession or vocation,

(c) the rent of any dwelling-house or domestic offices or any part thereof, except such part thereof as is used for the purposes of the trade or profession, and where any such part is so used, the sum so deducted shall not, unless in any particular case it appears that having regard to all the circumstances some greater sum ought to be deducted, exceed two-thirds of the rent bona fide paid for the said dwelling-house or offices,

(d) any sum expended for repairs of premises occupied, or for the supply, repairs or alterations of any implements, utensils or articles employed, for the purposes of the trade, profession or vocation, beyond the sum actually expended for those purposes, (*e*) any loss not connected with or arising out of the trade, profession or vocation,

(*f*) any capital withdrawn from, or any sum employed or intended to be employed as capital in, the trade, profession or vocation, but so that this paragraph shall not be treated as disallowing the deduction of any interest,

(*g*) any capital employed in improvements of premises occupied for the purposes of the trade, profession or vocation,

(*h*) any interest which might have been made if any such sums as aforesaid had been laid out at interest,

(*i*) any debts, except bad debts proved to be such, and doubtful debts to the extent that they are respectively estimated to be bad, and in the case of the bankruptcy or insolvency of a debtor the amount which may reasonably be expected to be received on any such debt shall be deemed to be the value thereof,

(*j*) any average loss beyond the actual amount of loss after adjustment,

(*k*) any sum recoverable under an insurance or contract of indemnity,

(*l*) any annuity or other annual payment (other than interest) payable out of the profits or gains,

(*m*) any interest paid to a person not resident in the United Kingdom if and so far as it is interest at more than a reasonable commercial rate,

(*n*) any royalty or other sum paid in respect of the user of a patent, or

(*o*) any rent, royalty or other payment which, by section 156 or 157 of this Act (mining etc. rents and royalties), is declared to be subject to deduction of tax under Part II of this Act as if it were a royalty or other sum paid in respect of the user of a patent.

Appendix V: Income and Corporation Taxes Act 1970, Sched. D

108. The Schedule referred to as Schedule D is as follows:—

1. Tax under this Schedule shall be charged in respect of—
   (a) the annual profits or gains arising or accruing—
      (i) to any person residing in the United Kingdom from any kind of property whatever, whether situated in the United Kingdom or elsewhere, and
      (ii) to any person residing in the United Kingdom from any trade, profession or vocation, whether carried on in the United Kingdom or elsewhere, and
      (iii) to any person, whether a British subject or not, although not resident in the United Kingdom, from any property whatever in the United Kingdom, or from any trade, profession or vocation exercised within the United Kingdom, and
   (b) all interest of money, annuities and other annual profits or gains not charged under Schedule A, B, C or E, and not specially exempted from tax.

2. There shall also be charged under this Schedule, to the extent provided in Chapter VIII of this Part of this Act, income tax (but not corporation tax) in respect of the gains accruing to any person resident and ordinarily resident in the United Kingdom from his acquisition and disposal of assets.

3. The provisions of paragraphs 1 and 2 above are without prejudice to any other provision of the Tax Acts directing tax to be charged under this Schedule, and the tax so directed to be charged shall be charged accordingly.

Tax to be charged under seven Cases

109.—(1) Tax under Schedule D shall be charged under the Cases set out in subsection (2) below, and subject to and in accordance with the provisions of the Tax Acts applicable to those Cases respectively.

(2) The Cases are—

Case I—tax in respect of any trade carried on in the United Kingdom or elsewhere;

Case II—tax in respect of any profession or vocation not contained in any other Schedule;

Case III—tax in respect of—

(a) any interest of money, whether yearly or otherwise, or any annuity or other annual payment, whether such payment is payable within or out of the United Kingdom, either as a charge on any property of the person paying the same by virtue of any deed or will or otherwise, or as a reservation out of it, or as a personal debt or obligation by virtue of any contract, or whether the same is received and payable half-yearly or at any shorter or more distant periods, but not including any payment chargeable under Schedule A, and

(b) all discounts, and

(c) income, except income charged under Schedule C, from securities bearing interest payable out of the public revenue;

Case IV—tax in respect of income arising from securities out of the United Kingdom, except such income as is charged under Schedule C;

Case V—tax in respect of income arising from possessions out of the United Kingdom, not being income consisting of emoluments of any office or employment;

Case VI—tax in respect of any annual profits or gains not falling under any other Case of Schedule D, and not charged by virtue of Schedule A, B, C or E; and

Case VII—income tax chargeable by virtue of Chapter VIII of this Part of this Act in respect of gains accruing from the acquisition and disposal of assets.

(3) The provisions of subsection (1) above are without prejudice to any other provision of the Tax Acts directing tax to be charged under one or other of the said Cases, and the tax so directed to be charged shall be charged accordingly.

Appendix VI: Extract from I.B.A. Television Programme Guidelines

Appendix IV: Coverage of Sponsored Events and Display Advertising on Independent Television[1]

Introduction

1. Many events in which Independent Television has a legitimate interest because of the intrinsic appeal to the audience are sponsored by commercial organisations. Indeed their continued existence depends on sponsorship. The number of events, particularly in sport but also in the arts and other entertainments, attracting sponsorship is increasing and is likely to continue to increase. The legal position of Independent Television is laid down in the Independent Broadcasting Authority Act 1973. One of its most important provisions is that a clear distinction must be maintained between programmes or advertisements. Nothing may be included in programmes and advertisements that could give viewers the impression that a programme, or part of a programme, has been suggested or provided by an advertiser. This obligation, coupled with the wish of TV company sales departments not to give 'free' on-site advertising during the coverage of sponsored events, leads to the considerations outlined below. There is inevitably a conflict between the priorities of Independent Television and the priorities of the sponsor. sponsor. We want the best and most complete coverage of the event, the sponsor wants maximum exposure for his sponsorship.

---

[1] This appendix is taken from a draft of raised guidelines obtained from the I.B.A. in November 1983. Readers are advised that the I.B.A. guidelines should be finalised and available on publication of this book.

2. Sponsored Sporting Events (including Beauty Contests and Talent Contests) – General Practice

Independent Television reserves the right to decide the acceptability on television of particular company or brand names as sponsors. Subject to acceptability the sponsor's name can normally appear in the main title of the event and in the title of the *TV Times* billing. During the programme the practice is as follows:–

(i) Two sponsors' signs may appear on the course or on the arena. The siting of such signs must not, in the opinion of the producer at the time of his survey, obtrude either on the television pictures or on the action of the event.

(ii) There may be two verbal credits relating the sponsor to the event during the transmission of the programme.

(iii) The name of the competition may appear on the scoreboard at the event.

(iv) The presentation of prizes at the end of the event is often made by someone connected with the sponsoring organisation. Coverage of this is permissable with no more than one mention of the sponsoring body.

(v) In *Athletics* the International Athletics rules allow the name of a sponsor to appear on a competitor's number card. This is anomalous but in practice ITV accepts it.

3. Horse Racing

Guidelines have been agreed jointly (1974) between the Race Course Association, ITV and the BBC. These are as follows:–

(i) The problem on each racecourse is different and a rigid official agreement would create as many difficulties as it would solve. The best solution is for each racecourse with a TV contract, and also for those confident of obtaining *ad hoc* TV coverage, to agree with the appropriate TV authorities on a particular solution applicable to their own course, to stick to it and to see that their sponsors stick to it. If the RCA recommendations are followed there should be no difficulty in obtaining such agreement.

(ii) It should be realised that an individual TV producer with several cameras in use can easily select a camera which will avoid an advertisement, in some cases to the detriment of the race coverage, which is undesirable from all points of view. If the advertising is kept within agreed limits the producer can get on with his presentation without any worry, which would be to the advantage of everyone, both viewers, racecourses and sponsors.

Static Hoardings

(iii) Most racecourses who stage meetings with TV cover now sell static advertising hoardings on an annual basis. They may or may not do so through an advertising agency. In general these static hoardings will only cause trouble if they:–
(a) are sited to obtain 'freeze frame' TV coverage near the finish;
(b) are sited to obtain prolonged single shot coverage near the start;
(c) are sited outside the view of the stands;
(d) advertise tobacco brand names rather than house names.
In these cases TV producers could be expected to avoid them deliberately or, in the case of tobacco brand names, insist on the signs being covered up or taken away.
(iv) The RCA recommendation is, therefore, that race courses should keep their TV associates informed on the size, site location, colour and subject matter of static hoarding advertisements, so that any TV objections can be considered well before the day of racing.

Sponsors' Banner

(v) Where one sponsor is concerned the following sites are acceptable to the TV authorities for spot advertising on the day of sponsorship and are recommended by the RCA:–
(a) A device at the winning post; or nearby where the winning post is not technically feasible. A horseshoe should be not more than 4ft in diameter.
(b) The race name on runners and riders boards.
(c) A banner near the start giving the name of the race.
(d) Two banners on or near the track.
(vi) The main problem is the positioning of any banners near the finish. Sponsors will wish them to be in the re-run but at the same time they must avoid the 'freeze frame' area within about 20 yards either side of the finishing post. Each track is different and it is most desirable that agreed positions be established so that they can be offered to sponsors with complete confidence.
(vii) Where there is more than one sponsor on one day, an

extra two banners are recommended and extra start banners giving the name of the race, so long as a separate start is in use for the other sponsors. It will be for the racecourse to allocate the banners and the device at the winning post between the sponsors.

4. Tobacco Sponsorship

Cigarette advertising is not permitted on ITV, though advertisements for pipe tobacco and cigars are acceptable. Special conditions have been agreed between the Department of the Environment, the Tobacco Advisory Committee, the tobacco manufacturers, Independent Television and the BBC. These provide for advertisements for cigarette brands to be covered up during the period of television transmission from a sporting event at which such advertisements may be present. House or brand names of tobacco firms are acceptable e.g. 'Benson and Hedges' or 'Marlboro' but qualifying words such as 'filter', 'king-size', 'No. 4', etc., which have individual cigarette brand connotations are not acceptable.

The most recent Code of Practice (1982) agreed between the Department of the Environment and the Tobacco Advisory Committee includes the following notes:–

(i) Fixed signs featuring advertisements for cigarette brands and which therefore carry tar group information as well as the Government Health Warning may, in accordance with current practice, be covered up by the television authorities.

(ii) The display of house or brand names or symbols on participants and their equipment, or on officials and their equipment actively involved and likely to come within range of the television cameras, is not permitted during the course of a televised activity in the U.K.

5. Visual Advertising at Outside Broadcast Events

At all public events at which large numbers of spectators are to be found there is also to be found a wide variety of display advertising. It is absent only if the organisers of the event have taken steps to prevent it; even then they can not always count on complete success. Much advertising would appear irrespective of television coverage as it does, for example, in Piccadilly Circus. But experience has not unexpectedly demonstrated that it is likely to increase substantially whenever there is a possibility that television cameras will be present. Attempts have been made, notably by the European Broadcasting Union, to control this tendency, specifically in relation to international sports events. The aim, embodied in a model contract drawn up by the EBU legal department, has been broadly speaking to limit the amount of display advertising on sports grounds to those signs, posters and hoardings that are more or less permanent features of the site, or at least to those that were recorded as present at the time the contract for coverage rights was negotiated. Even this procedure cannot be claimed to have achieved total success and discussions are still continuing within the EBU. It is still the case that at international matches display advertising can be seen that is manifestly addressed not to the public of the country where the match is being played but to the home public of one of the competing teams.

Within the U.K. the following are the agreed limits:—

(i) The location of any advertisement boards on site must be declared at the beginning of the season in the case of regular events e.g. football. The location should be checked on site by the producer or director before recording the transmission. No more than two posters or banners for any one product or brand name can be placed side by side on advertising boards in range of television cameras. There will be only one-tier advertising at ground level. Where a match is sponsored, two additional banners may be permitted for the sponsor but no other mobile (i.e. temporary) advertising is acceptable. Any departure from these arrangements is a breach of ITV's agreement with the Football League and the club concerned should be asked to remove any additional advertising.

(ii) No advertisement must in the judgement of the producer or director interfere with any television picture that may be selected to give proper coverage of the event.

(iii) No advertisement must interfere with the action of the event.

(iv) These conditions apply equally to events sponsored by or advertisements for charitable organisations. ITV's ultimate sanction, if faced with excessive display advertising, is to refuse to go ahead with the transmission if all attempts to get the offending advertisements removed have failed. Before a decision to withdraw is taken the producer should consult with his Head of Department who in turn should consult with his Programme Controller. Each company will have its own detailed system of referrals.

Advertising on players' dress and equipment (ranging from tennis racquets to racing cars), and on trailers and ball boys is a particular problem. On racing cars for example the name of a sponsor on the car is bound to be in vision, and clearly recognisable if the lettering is sufficiently large, because the car itself is the centre of the action. As a result of the recent agreement between the football authorities and the broadcasters sponsors' names are now permitted on players' jerseys in televised games subject to the lettering being no larger than sixteen square inches in all to a maximum height of two inches. Advertising materal may not be worn on both the front and back of shirts nor is it permitted on any other item of footballers' clothing or equipment. The same rule applies to other sponsored sports but in boxing contests advertising will only be permitted on ringposts (see 2(i)) above. It is impractical to set down hard and fast rules to cover every possible instance of this kind. The cardinal principle is to get such incidental advertising removed if at all possible or at least to minimise its appearance on screen.

6. Sponsored Cultural Events

The sponsorship of public events by commercial enterprises for publicity purposes has spread from sporting occasions to 'cultural' events such as symphony concerts, opera or ballet performances, exhibitions of painting and sculpture. The events are not always completely sponsored to the extent that they are initiated, planned and organised by the sponsor. Often he does no more than provide the substantial financial backing. Although the motives of this generosity are undoubtedly similar to those inspiring the sponsorship of sporting occasions, the publicity advantages sought are related to a different section of public opinion. The funds are therefore just as likely to be provided by relatively 'up-market' enterprises such as banks or insurance companies as by tobacco or soap or alcoholic drink manufacturers. The 'respectability' of these sources of subsidy to the arts does not in any way invalidate an obligation to avoid an undue element of advertising. The event will be televised – if at all – because of its own intrinsic interest to an audience. The name of the sponsor can normally be mentioned, as for example in the name of the event, at most twice. At such events advertising placards and the display of posters are not generally acceptable. End credits acknowledging the sponsors may be agreed.

Index